The GARDEN DIY EXPERT

Dr. D.G. Hessayon

1st Impression   250,000

pbi PUBLICATIONS · BRITANNICA HOUSE · WALTHAM CROSS · HERTS · ENGLAND

Contents

Printed and bound in Great Britain by Jarrold & Sons Ltd, Norwich

ISBN 0 903505 37 1   © D G HESSAYON 1992

CHAPTER 1

INTRODUCTION

Other Expert books are about the living things which are planted in the garden. Flowers and lawns, fruit and roses ... all the major groups have been covered to some degree. But a garden is not just a collection of these things — from earliest times there has always been a permanent skeleton provided by non-living objects. In the ancient gardens of Islam it was water, paving and tiles which dominated the scene, with plants playing little or no part. The opposite picture can be seen in some of the suburban front gardens and rural cottage gardens of today — a path and some fencing, but it is the plants which almost completely fill the site. Our average garden lies somewhere between these two extremes. Flowers, fruit, vegetables, trees and a lawn share the plot with a range of non-living things such as paths, walls, greenhouse, furniture, pots, patio, shed etc.

This wide collection of non-living items poses a problem for the author who wants to write about them as a whole. It is easy to group together flowers, fruit, vegetables and so on under a single and simple heading — **plants**. But what single and simple heading is there to encompass the pond and the patio, the path and the plastic cloche? There isn't one. However, even though there is no single satisfactory term for these items they are all sold in a single type of outlet — the large DIY superstore or the DIY section of a large garden centre. Many of these non-living items have to be erected at home, and so the all-encompassing term used here is **garden DIY**.

A simple term, but not fully satisfactory. The reason is that this book deals with items which can be bought in a DIY store, but is certainly not restricted to items requiring do-it-yourself activity. Some of the features in the following pages involve no construction work for anyone — shop-bought items include furniture, containers and portable barbecues. With some other items you have a choice — when you want a fence, pool lining or a garden seat it is necessary to decide whether to buy a ready-built version or to start from scratch in the garden. Finally there are the items where

there is no choice to make — there is no alternative to building or laying paths, patios and flights of steps on site.

Which brings us to two fundamental questions. Is it better to buy ready-made items or to buy the materials and make or have them made at home? Secondly, if there is building or erecting to do, is it better to do the work yourself or call in a professional?

The basic approach in this book is to recommend that most features, such as sheds, fences, gates and furniture are better bought than made from scratch, unless you are an experienced do-it-yourself fanatic. Some of these items come as easy-to-erect bits rather than in fully finished form, but they are designed for the ordinary garden owner and should not pose a problem if you have an able-bodied and willing helper or two.

The real problem arises when the work *has* to be done at home and it calls for both some skill and hard work — examples include laying a path with paving slabs, erecting a fence, putting up a shed or greenhouse and building a wall with reconstituted stone blocks. There are two obvious advantages in doing the work yourself — you can save money and you also get the satisfaction of having created something. Other advantages include the ability to do the work when the weather is just right, which is important for jobs like concreting and outdoor painting. You also have complete control of the quality of the materials used, which means that the nightmare of the 'cowboy' contractor is avoided.

But don't rush for the saw or the bag of cement just yet. First of all, you must be strong enough and fit enough for the job. Standard-sized paving slabs weigh about 35 lb each and pushing a barrowload of concrete is not for the infirm. Next, have you the necessary skill and the helpers? Obvious examples where skill and help are required include fence building and patio laying. If physical condition and/or lack of skill are a problem, do go to a professional contractor if you can afford it — but choose with care. The best method is to use someone who has done satisfactory work for you or others — failing that make sure that the company belongs to a relevant trade association. Get several quotes, if practical, and never give a job to a man who casually calls and "just has a load left on the lorry".

CHAPTER 2

GARDEN FEATURES

As a general rule the first feature you see on approaching the garden is a living hedge or more usually a non-living boundary fence or wall. The difference between a fence and a wall concerns the nature of the foundations and not the materials used for their construction. There is evidence that the fence and the wall were the first features in time — our word 'garden' is derived from the old Germanic 'gart' meaning an enclosure.

Within this boundary there has always been a selection of other non-living features ranging in size from tiny garden gnomes to mansion-like garden pavilions. In the average garden all of these features could be grouped until quite recently into just five types. The first type provides **protection**, and for this purpose we erect walls and fences and put in gates — in recent years there has been an increase in the use of lighting to safeguard the property.

The second type of feature improves **movement** around the garden, and here belong the paths (for people), drives (for vehicles) and steps. Of course our garden is much more than a place for protection and easy movement — it is a place for plants. So the third type of feature is extremely important — the ones designed to improve **plant growth**. There are plant support systems to keep stems upright, watering systems to ensure growth in dry weather and glasshouses to ensure out-of-season growth in cold weather.

These plant growth features tend to be thoroughly practical and do not add to the attractiveness of the garden, but there is an important group which does have this vital role — the fourth type of feature is designed to improve the **beauty** of the garden. Some of them can play a dual part by helping plant growth as well as improving the appearance of the plot. A good example is the arch or pergola clothed with climbing plants — others include rockeries which support alpine plants, ponds which support aquatic plants and containers filled with bedding plants. Not all of the decorative features have a practical use,

however, and they are grouped together as ornaments (pages 65–67).

The fifth and final type of garden feature found in the mid-20th century garden was the building or enclosure to provide **cover** for us or our equipment. Included here are the shed, summerhouse and tool store.

It was in the latter half of the 20th century that an additional type of feature rose dramatically in prominence. Slowly at first, but by the 1980s items designed for **outdoor living** were to be seen in ordinary gardens throughout the country. The centrepiece is the patio, and on this stands the furniture for lounging, sitting or eating in the open air. The barbecue stands here — in the garden itself there may be play areas for the children and wildlife areas for the birds. Decorative lighting and plant containers have become much more popular.

So nowadays there are six and not just five types of non-living features which enable you to derive maximum enjoyment from your garden, a place for living and not just for working in and admiring. Before World War II the nursery and the home garden were filled with plants, and there was only a small area devoted to non-living items — today the situation is quite different. The garden centre and DIY store devote large areas to all sorts of slabs, stones, pots, pool liners, ornaments, lights, furniture and so on.

The choice really is up to you, depending on the size of your garden and your pocket. But it is perhaps a good idea to remember the difference between fixtures and fittings when making a major purchase. A fitting is a 'removable chattel' — it can be moved without causing any material damage to the land or the house. This means that a tenant can take it when moving house, and so can the seller of a house if the fitting was not part of the contract. Examples include furniture, containers and buildings without sunken foundations. Fixtures, however, cannot be moved by the tenant as they are part of the structure, nor by the seller of a house except with the written agreement of the purchaser. Most of the features of the garden are included here — as well as the trees, shrubs and perennials there are the paths, pool, light fittings, built-in furniture and barbecue, fences, buildings on foundations, rockeries and pergolas.

WALLS

The fundamental difference between a wall and a fence has nothing to do with the construction material — you can find wooden walls (page 7) and concrete fencing (page 13). The essential feature of a wall is that there is a firm foundation along its entire length. This nearly always consists of a substantial concrete base — the footings. At the top of the wall is laid the coping — a protective layer of bricks, reconstituted stone, metal or concrete.

Walls serve a variety of purposes. Firstly there is the boundary wall, dividing you from your neighbours or from the road. A wall is chosen rather than a wooden fence for this task where maximum privacy, permanence and noise reduction are required. A high brick wall may seem a good idea, but do think of the problems. It will be costly, and piers (brick pillars) or buttresses (sloping supporting walls) will have to be built at intervals. As with fences, there may be a number of restrictions in the bye-laws and house deeds (see page 13) and you might create a number of gardening problems.

Shade is such a problem, of course, but also turbulence in windy weather and perhaps a frost pocket in wintry weather.

Internal walls are an important feature in many gardens. There are screen walls to enclose areas or hide unsightly views, and there are retaining walls as described below.

For both boundary and internal walls there is a choice of materials. Bricks have long been the traditional material for this purpose — the familiar clay brick which is easy to lift but both tricky and time-consuming to lay. Leave the building of walls over 4 ft high or on sloping sites to the professional or experienced DIY expert. Blocks have come to the rescue of the ordinary DIY person — send for a selection of catalogues. There are standard concrete blocks available, but the popular choice is reconstituted stone.

With these blocks any handyperson with little or no experience can build low walls or attractive garden features. Blocks with a highly textured face will hide minor laying imperfections, and large interlocking units make wall-building a relatively speedy job.

Wall Types

FREE-STANDING WALL

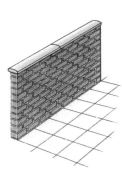

The basic example is the boundary wall. This must be soundly constructed for safety reasons — the maximum height of a brick wall without piers is 1½ ft (4 in. thick wall) or 4½ ft (8½ in. thick wall). Above these heights piers must be incorporated at 6–8 ft intervals.

Another type of free-standing wall is the screen wall built from pierced concrete blocks. Use with care — this modern feature can look out of place in an old-world garden.

LOAD-BEARING WALL

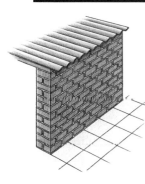

Not a common feature in the garden, but it may be required if you plan to build a carport, conservatory, or old-style greenhouse. The simple rule is that you should leave this work to the professional if you feel that you do not have the necessary experience nor have a helper who has built such walls. The weight of the roof exerts a great deal of pressure on the wall.

HEAVY-DUTY RETAINING WALL

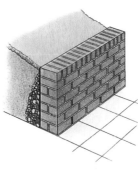

A wall built to hold back a bank of earth has to withstand a great deal of pressure — it should be at least 8½ in. thick. The wall should slope slightly backwards and it requires weep-holes near the base so that water can escape. The easiest plan is to leave mortar out of a vertical joint every 3 ft. Line the inside face with a plastic membrane and pile rubble against this membrane before replacing soil.

LIGHT-DUTY RETAINING WALL

This is the walling around a small or moderately-sized raised bed. The bricks or blocks are vertical, not sloping backwards as in the heavy-duty version. The wall can be just one block thick — not a minimum of 8½ in. as required for a bank-retaining wall. Leave weep-holes and treat the inside with bituminous paint before filling with earth.

WALLING MATERIALS

BRICKS

Clay bricks are available in a vast assortment of colours, textures, surfaces and weather-resisting properties. Picking the right one is complex, as they are grouped by basic name, quality, variety and texture. For garden walling choose Facings — go for Ordinary quality for standard conditions or Special quality if the site is subject to heavy frosts. With variety and quality fixed, choose a brick with the colour and texture which appeal to you.

Concrete bricks are much less popular than clay ones. There is a wide range of colours and textures, and of course they are lighter to lift than concrete or reconstituted stone blocks. This is a minor advantage — choose blocks instead of concrete bricks as they are easier to lay.

Always buy all the bricks you will require *before* you start work — order a few extra for accidental breakages, etc. Protect the stack of bricks from rain with a plastic or tarpaulin cover.

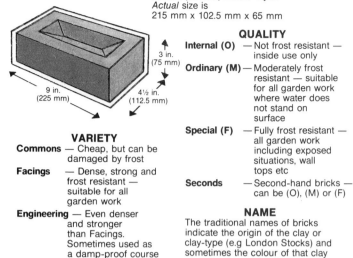

Nominal size allows for normal (10 mm) mortar layer. *Actual* size is 215 mm x 102.5 mm x 65 mm

3 in. (75 mm)
9 in. (225 mm)
4½ in. (112.5 mm)

QUALITY

Internal (O) — Not frost resistant — inside use only

Ordinary (M) — Moderately frost resistant — suitable for all garden work where water does not stand on surface

Special (F) — Fully frost resistant — all garden work including exposed situations, wall tops etc

Seconds — Second-hand bricks — can be (O), (M) or (F)

VARIETY

Commons — Cheap, but can be damaged by frost

Facings — Dense, strong and frost resistant — suitable for all garden work

Engineering — Even denser and stronger than Facings. Sometimes used as a damp-proof course

NAME

The traditional names of bricks indicate the origin of the clay or clay-type (e.g London Stocks) and sometimes the colour of that clay when fired (e.g Blue Staffs)

Bonding

Bricks must be bonded so that the vertical mortar joints of one row do not line up with either the row below or the row above.

RUNNING BOND
The running (or stretcher) bond is the simplest form of bonding

HONEYCOMB BOND
The honeycomb bond is the open form of bonding

ENGLISH BOND
The English bond is the strongest form of bonding

FLEMISH BOND
The Flemish bond is the most attractive form of bonding

STRETCHER
(A brick laid sideways)

QUEEN CLOSER
(A brick cut in half along its length)

HEADER
(A brick laid end on)

Anatomy of a Brick Wall

Coping
The covering layer may be engineering bricks set on end, bull-nosed (rounded) bricks, concrete bricks etc which are flush with the wall. It is better to use a slab which overhangs the wall — rainwater is kept away from the upper lines of bricks

Damp-proof course
A line of tiles is sometimes set under the coping to ensure that the cover is fully waterproof

Jointing
Smoothing the mortar between the bricks to a uniform appearance is known as *jointing*. As noted on page 8 it is called *pointing* when it is carried out at a later stage by removing old mortar and replacing with new material

Damp-proof course
Layer of engineering bricks or a strip of bituminous felt, tiles, copper sheet etc to stop water rising. Essential if wall is attached to house. Not recommended by all experts for free-standing walls — strip DPC can weaken wall. Not needed for retaining walls

Strip footing
Must be deep enough and wide enough to support the wall from being affected by movement of the earth below

Blocks made from natural stone, concrete and reconstituted stone are much larger than a brick. Laying time is reduced, and blocks with a 'natural' face mask minor imperfections. This does not mean you can save time when creating the footings — sound foundation and a final coping are as vital with a concrete or reconstituted stone wall as with a brick one.

STONE BLOCKS

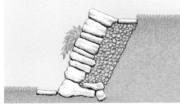

Many types of stone can be used for walling — limestone, granite, sandstone, slate etc. If you have one, you are lucky. If not, then the cost and work involved make it an impractical idea. The usual pattern is a random rubble wall — irregular blocks carefully sorted and placed on top of each other to form a tight-fitting wall. Such walls can be constructed without mortar (dry walling), and plants can be grown in the crevices.

OTHER BLOCKS

Wooden sleepers and peat blocks can be used to prepare dry retaining walls. They have no place in a small formal garden but are extremely effective in a woodland or semi-wild garden. Peat blocks can be used to make a raised bed which is filled with a soil/peat mixture for acid-loving plants. The crevices between the blocks are used for planting Ferns, Heathers etc. Algae and moss develop on the surface of the peat blocks, and no other walling material blends in quite so well with the natural environment.

BLOCKS

CONCRETE BLOCKS
The standard structural block

9 in. (225 mm)

18 in. (450 mm)

4 in. (100 mm)

Cheap and easy to lay, but with no charm at all. Choose a decorative concrete block instead

Nominal size allows for normal (10 mm) mortar layer.

QUALITY
A —Strong, durable but expensive

B — The standard grade for outdoor work

C —Lightweight — internal, non-loadbearing walls only

The decorative facing block

Facing blocks have a decorative face and so can be used for garden walling. They are cheaper than reconstituted stone blocks, but they look less natural. However, a wide range of colours, sizes and surface textures is available. A great boon for the DIY enthusiast — a head-high wall can be built without piers or buttresses.

The standard thickness is 4 in. Various heights are offered and a popular length is 18 in. The large ones are sometimes hollow, made of dense concrete with supporting ribs between the two faces.

The screen block

Square concrete blocks are available which are pierced with a variety of patterns, and are made in numerous colours. They are used to form screen walls, the blocks being stack bonded (each vertical mortar joint lining up with the one above and the one below).

Their use is a matter of personal taste, but some garden designers feel that screen blocks are better employed as occasional items in a solid wall rather than on their own to form a lace-like wall.

RECONSTITUTED STONE BLOCKS

Some purists argue that stone walls and brick houses don't go together, but the public doesn't agree. The reconstituted stone block has become the favourite DIY walling material, although perhaps it is not a good idea to have a look-alike stone wall attached to a brick-built structure.

Crushed stone is used in place of aggregate in the concrete mix and this 'reconstituted stone' is moulded into a wide variety of shapes. Surface textures range from the near-smooth to the deeply-hewn pitched face. Apart from individual blocks there are 'blocks-within-a-block' available. Each of these blocks appears to be made up of 4–10 small blocks. Obviously much less mortar and much less time are required to build the wall.

Apart from free-standing and retaining walls, reconstituted stone blocks can be used to make seats, barbecues, planters, pergolas, sundials etc. And the rules of good wall building have been changed. In the makers' catalogues you will find recommendations for building low walls on firm paving rather than on concrete footings, and 6 in. wide blocks are available for dry walling.

Building a Solid Wall

As noted on page 5, it is easier to build a block wall than a brick one. In both cases, however, you will need to have a firm foundation (see below) and a number of tools. The bricklayer's kit includes a laying trowel and a smaller pointing trowel. A bolster chisel and club hammer are needed for cutting bricks, and to ensure that the levels are right you will require a spirit level, twine, pegs, a builder's line and a long board to serve as a straightedge. You will also need a long board with lines 3 in. apart to serve as a gauge stick. Professionals use profile boards for marking out (see illustration on right) but for a simple wall it is more usual to use pegs and twine. You will also need 2 buckets, 2 spades, a wheelbarrow and watering can plus a mortar board and a builder's square for checking right angles.

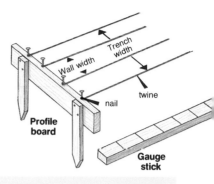

Profile board

Gauge stick

STEP 1:
MARK OUT THE SITE
Use profile boards or pegs with twine stretched tightly between them to mark out the width of the foundation trench.
See Step 2 for recommended width.
Use a spade to mark the edges of the trench

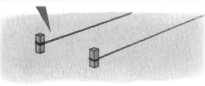

STEP 2:
DIG THE TRENCH
The recommended depth and width of the trench depend on the height and width of the wall to be built and also on the firmness of the soil. If the bottom of the trench is not firm, remove the soft earth and replace with tightly-packed hardcore

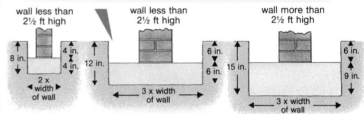

wall less than 2½ ft high — 8 in., 4 in., 4 in., 2 x width of wall

wall less than 2½ ft high — 12 in., 6 in., 6 in., 3 x width of wall

wall more than 2½ ft high — 15 in., 6 in., 9 in., 3 x width of wall

STEP 3:
POUR THE CONCRETE
Drive stakes into the ground at intervals. The tops of the stakes should be at the desired height of the foundations — check *very* carefully that all the stake tops are level. Pour a foundation mix of concrete (see page 107) into the trench — the stake tops should be level with the concrete surface after tamping down. Leave to set for at least 4 days

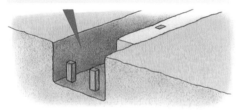

STEP 4:
LAY THE FIRST COURSE
Spread a ½ in. thick layer of mortar (see page 107) along the concrete between the string guidelines. Lay the first brick — check that it is perfectly horizontal. Lay a second brick 6 brick-lengths away — use a straightedge and spirit level between the 2 bricks to check the level. Repeat the process until the far end of the wall is reached. Fill the gaps between the widely-spaced bricks. Check both vertical and horizontal levels regularly — the quality of the first course largely determines the quality of the finished wall

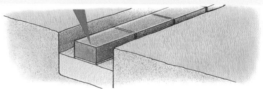

STEP 5:
BUILD UP THE ENDS
The corners or piers are built up as a series of steps ('leads') 4-6 bricks high. Check levels and heights with spirit level and gauge stick. Stretch a builder's line between these leads to serve as a guide when laying the courses to fill in the spaces between the corners

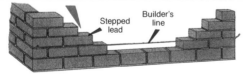

Stepped lead

Builder's line

STEP 6:
FINISH OFF THE WALL
The mortar between the bricks will need to be smoothed. Various finishes are used for these joints — the process is called *jointing* when building a wall and *pointing* when repairing a wall. See page 111 for details. Lay coping

Bricklaying Technique

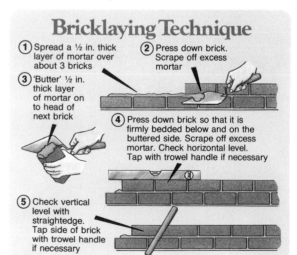

① Spread a ½ in. thick layer of mortar over about 3 bricks

② Press down brick. Scrape off excess mortar

③ 'Butter' ½ in. thick layer of mortar on to head of next brick

④ Press down brick so that it is firmly bedded below and on the buttered side. Scrape off excess mortar. Check horizontal level. Tap with trowel handle if necessary

⑤ Check vertical level with straightedge. Tap side of brick with trowel handle if necessary

Building a Screen Wall

There are a few important differences between the way a screen wall and a solid wall are built. Screen walls are stack bonded, which means that each joint runs vertically from the bottom of the wall to the top. This form of bonding is rather weak, so that pillar supports (pilasters) or brick piers at both ends are essential. If the span between the ends is more than 10 ft you will require intermediate supports. Another difference compared to solid bricks and blocks is the inability to cut perforated blocks, so very careful planning, measuring and levelling are essential. Always set out the first course of supports and blocks dry on the site before you begin.

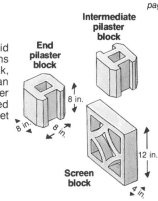

End pilaster block

Intermediate pilaster block

8 in.

8 in.

8 in.

Screen block

12 in.

4 in.

STEP 1:
PREPARE THE FOOTINGS
Follow Steps 1, 2 and 3 on page 8. The trench should be 16 in. wide and 8 in. deep. Pour in a 4 in. layer of a foundation mix of concrete (see page 107). Walls more than 2 ft high need extra support — this calls for embedding an iron rod into the concrete to reinforce the pilaster blocks. Measure carefully the required distance from this reinforcing rod to the position of the next rod at the other end — insert an iron bar into the concrete at this point. Support these rods with guyropes until the concrete is set (4–7 days)

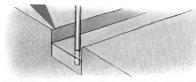

STEP 2:
START TO BUILD THE PILASTERS
Slide a pilaster block down the iron rod at one end of the proposed wall and bed into a ½ in. layer of mortar. Pour mortar inside the hole running through the block.
Check both vertical and horizontal levels. Build up a pilaster of 3 blocks — repeat the process at each reinforcing rod location. Leave the mortar to set for at least 1 day

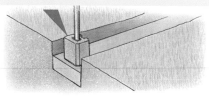

STEP 3:
FILL THE SPACE BETWEEN PILASTERS WITH SCREEN BLOCKS
Follow the standard bricklaying technique (see page 8) to fill the space between the pilasters with a course of solid concrete blocks. Lay the next course with screen blocks. With each course fit the first and last screen blocks within the grooves on the pilaster blocks. Use a builder's line when laying the first course. Make sure that you check both horizontal and vertical levels. If tapping down with the trowel handle is necessary, cover the surface with a piece of wood. Take care to keep mortar off the face of the screen blocks

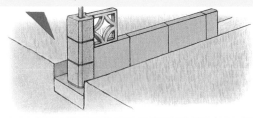

Planting Walls

Both dry stone walls and peat block walls can be planted along their faces, but a true planting wall is used for growing flowers in compost contained within the wall itself. There are 2 basic types — the traditional planting wall is a double brick or block wall with weep-holes at the base and a fill of soil or compost on gravel. A modern type consists of U-shaped concrete blocks which fit together to form a line of containers.

STEP 4:
CONTINUE THE PROCESS
Build further columns of pilaster blocks and fill the spaces between with screen blocks until the wall is complete. If the blocks are white you should have either worked with a mortar of white cement and silver sand or you should remove a little of the standard mortar used and then joint ('point') with a white mortar mix. The final step is to lay a row of coping slabs in mortar along the top course and to cover the pilasters with caps

Walls Illustrated

Most walls these days are built from reconstituted stone blocks rather than bricks. One of the advantages is that units of various sizes can be used, as in this Atlas Gloucester stone wall. ▷

◁ *A block wall need not be made of neat square or rectangular units. This Ryedale walling from Marshalls is bonded with a special adhesive to give a dry-stone wall effect.*

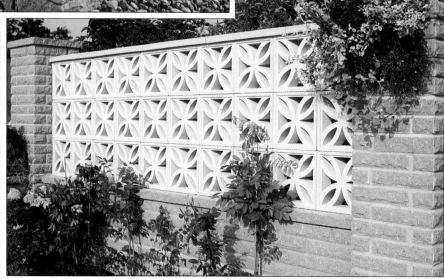

△ *Screen walls are an attractive feature, providing protection whilst allowing the garden to be seen from outside. The popular style is to incorporate the screen blocks in a solid brick or block wall.*

FENCES

Walls take experience and effort to erect — hedges take time to grow and become established. A fence provides the quickest and usually the easiest way to mark the boundary of your property. If privacy is an important factor, a solid fence is the answer. This nearly always calls for the use of wood, and you can either make a closeboard fence on site or buy ready-made panels for fixing between the posts. Whichever you choose, stout supports will be necessary and these will have to be fixed firmly. The distance can be at your discretion (for closeboard fences) or at standard 6 ft widths (for panel fences). The standard heights of ready-made panels are 2, 4, 5 and 6 ft. Choose carefully — a tall and solid fence may seem a good idea if you like your privacy but it will cast a lot of shade and can be quite claustrophobic in a small garden.

Fences are more than boundary markers. They can also be used to hide unsightly objects, separate sections of the garden, provide protection against the wind, act as supports for climbing plants and keep both children and pets in (or out!).

The range of materials for fencing is much greater than for walling. The basic choice is wood or concrete for the posts and wood or metal for the fence itself. In recent years plastics have moved into the low fencing market with designs ranging from the stylishly beautiful to the frankly awful.

The fencing you pick should be in keeping with the position and style of both house and garden. A ranch-style fence around a cottage garden would be as out of place as chestnut paling around a modern house. Money can also be an important consideration. Iron railings may appeal but they are very expensive. On the other hand chain link fences are cheap but are rarely right at the front of the house.

So you must ask many questions before you make your decision. Do I want complete privacy or will a partly open fence do? Must it be animal-proof? Do I want a low-maintenance fence, such as plastic or hardwood, or am I prepared to treat it every couple of years? The choice is up to you.

Anatomy of a Closeboard Fence

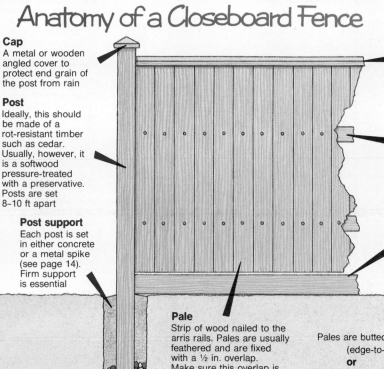

Cap
A metal or wooden angled cover to protect end grain of the post from rain

Post
Ideally, this should be made of a rot-resistant timber such as cedar. Usually, however, it is a softwood pressure-treated with a preservative. Posts are set 8–10 ft apart

Post support
Each post is set in either concrete or a metal spike (see page 14). Firm support is essential

Capping rail
Horizontal board to protect end grain of the pales from rain

Arris rail
Board, triangular in cross section, fixed between posts. Use 2 (4 ft high fence) or 3 (6 ft high fence). Attach to posts with metal arris brackets. Nail pales to each arris rail

Gravel board
Horizontal board to prevent the bottom of the pales from rotting. This board and not the pales should touch the ground

Pale
Strip of wood nailed to the arris rails. Pales are usually feathered and are fixed with a ½ in. overlap. Make sure this overlap is the correct width before nailing down

Pales are butted (edge-to-edge)

or

feathered (thinner at one edge and overlapped)

Fence Types

HORIZONTAL LAP PANEL

An alternative to the ever-popular interwoven panel — slightly more expensive but rather more durable. The pales are square-, feather- or waney-edged boards. Standard panel width is 6 ft but narrower panels can be ordered for finishing off the run. Make sure that the overlap is adequate (1 in. for waney-edged pales) and these pales should be nailed to the vertical stiffeners.

VERTICAL LAP PANEL

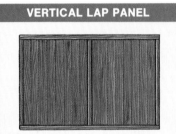

The most expensive of the peep-proof panel fences, and also the most durable. The pales are square- or feather-edged, and when erected it looks like a closeboard fence. Standard panel width is 6 ft but narrower panels can be ordered for finishing off the run. Make sure that the overlap is adequate (½ in.) and the pales should be nailed to the cross rails as well as to the frame.

INTERWOVEN PANEL

The most popular of the solid panel fences, made from thin strips of wood woven between a number of vertical stiffeners. The result is a closed but not completely peep-proof fence. Standard panel width is 6 ft but narrower panels can be ordered for finishing off the run. Make sure that the wood strips fit closely together and are attached to the stiffeners. Interwoven panels are made of softwood — preservative treatment is essential.

CLOSEBOARD FENCE

A peep-proof fence made on site using 4–6 in. wide pales which are nailed on to arris rails (see page 11). More expensive than panel fencing but it is also more durable — expect 20–25 years of active life. You will need more time and skill to erect a closeboard fence than would be required for a fence using ready-made panels, but this extra effort is worth it if your site has a distinct slope.

Panel Buyer's Checklist

If possible inspect both posts and panels before buying. Check the following points:

- The panels should have a frame on both sides to support the strips of wood

- The panels should have been treated with a wood preservative

- The pales should be neither bowed nor warped, and should be nailed to the frame. Look for a generous overlap with lap fencing

- All nails and staples should be rust-proof

- Post caps and panel capping rails are necessary — check whether they are included in the quoted price

- Posts should be made of hard-wood or pressure-impregnated softwood. Ask for a certificate of treatment and a 10–25 year guarantee. Reject split or cracked posts — avoid ones which have been sawn at an angle to the grain

- Knots should be few and far between, and should not measure more than 1 in. across

CHESTNUT PALING

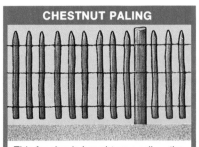

This fencing is bought as a roll — the pointed chestnut stakes are bound at the top and bottom by horizontal lengths of twisted wire. The fence has little inherent strength, but it provides an effective barrier if attached to 2 or 3 strong wires stretched between posts at 6 ft intervals. Not a thing of beauty, perhaps, but it is cheap and easy to erect. Camouflage, if necessary, by planting shrubs in front of it.

WATTLE PANEL

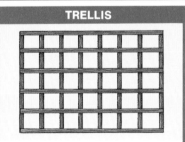

Strips of flexible branches woven horizontally around stout upright poles. The panels are usually 6 ft wide and are made in various heights. Each section is secured by pushing the vertical supports into the ground and then tying the panel with strong wire to its neighbours. A fence full of rustic charm to keep animals at bay and to serve as a windbreak, but quite out of place in the suburban garden.

TRELLIS

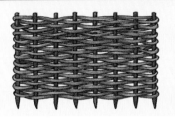

Trellis is made of thin strips of wood (laths) or larch poles (rustic work) arranged to form a square or diamond pattern. It is usually bought as an expanding panel although framed panels of trellis are available. Trellis requires a stout holding frame and is rarely used as a boundary fence — the main role is to support climbing plants. It is used for internal fencing or as a decorative top for solid boundary fencing.

RANCH-STYLE FENCE

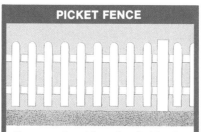

Strong broad boards are screwed (not nailed) on to evenly-spaced uprights to provide an attractive boundary fence. The cross pieces are usually softwood (occasionally plastic) and white paint is the favourite finish. The number of horizontal boards (2–9) is a matter of taste and a ranch-style fence offers little privacy — many children regard it as an ideal climbing frame! It is popular in the U.S., where it is called baffle fencing.

PICKET FENCE

For many the white-painted picket (or palisade) fence is a symbol of a cottage in the country, but this type of fencing is not out of place in an urban setting. The stout round-topped or pointed pales are rarely more than 4 ft high and are attached to horizontal rails. Leave about 3 in. between the pales. The bottom of these pales should be 2–3 in. above the ground to prevent rotting. A picket fence is child-but not cat-proof.

WIRE PICKET FENCE

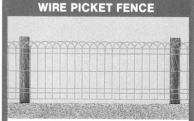

Nearly all of the fences described on these 2 pages are stout structures used to mark the boundaries of the property. Privacy and/or security are important features, but wire picket fencing is at the other end of the scale. A series of small hoops of plastic-coated wire are linked together to form a low and unobtrusive fence for beds, borders etc. Strong supports are necessary and the fence must be drawn taut between them.

POST & CHAIN FENCE

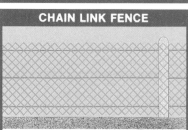

The post & chain fence is a purely decorative way of marking a boundary — it provides neither privacy nor protection. Metal or wooden posts and chains are the usual form, but plastic versions are available. The chain consists of oval steel links which alternate with diamond-shaped spikes — galvanized, white-painted or black-japanned for rust-protection and decoration. Low post & chain fences may be used as path markers within the garden.

Fences and the Law

The basic rule is that you must seek planning permission before building a boundary wall or fence which is more than 2 m high. If the wall or fence is to be erected adjacent to a highway, then you will require planning permission if it is to be more than 1 m high.

Unfortunately, it isn't always quite that simple. For example, seek permission irrespective of height if your house is on a corner site or if the fence you plan to erect could obstruct pedestrians.

In addition check the deeds of your house. These will tell you if walls or fences are banned or restricted — the construction material may be specified. The deeds will also tell you whether the fence line is yours or your neighbours. It is usually easier to tell this on site — the posts and rails nearly always face the owner's property.

A few councils have bye-laws which require householders to maintain their fences, but in nearly all areas there is no law which compels your neighbour to do so. If all else fails, your only answer to a neighbouring faulty fence will be to erect a new one on your side of the boundary line.

POST & WIRE FENCE

The post & wire fence is less decorative but more practical than the post & chain fence. Two or three strands of stout galvanized wire are drawn and fixed between concrete, wooden or steel posts. The end posts must be supported by struts, and the wires are kept taut by means of straining bolts on these posts — see page 15 for details. No privacy or security is provided, but a post & wire fence provides an excellent support for a hedge.

CHAIN LINK FENCE

A straightforward utilitarian form of fencing — strong, relatively inexpensive and capable of enclosing the garden at a fraction of the cost of a wooden fence. Squares of galvanized or plastic-coated wire are interlinked to form a net — choose a colour which merges with the surroundings. Firm wooden or concrete posts are needed. The usual height is 3 ft — not everybody's choice, but it's the one if you want maximum light transmission coupled with some security.

CONCRETE FENCE

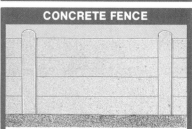

Slabs of concrete interlock when slid horizontally down the grooves in the concrete posts. Such a fence requires hardly any maintenance, and you are provided with the strength and privacy of a 'wall' without having to lay foundations. Useful in some situations, but most people find a concrete fence far too unattractive for the front of the house. It is also expensive — about twice the price of an interwoven panel fence. Maximum security and maximum durability, but little else.

Erecting a Panel Fence

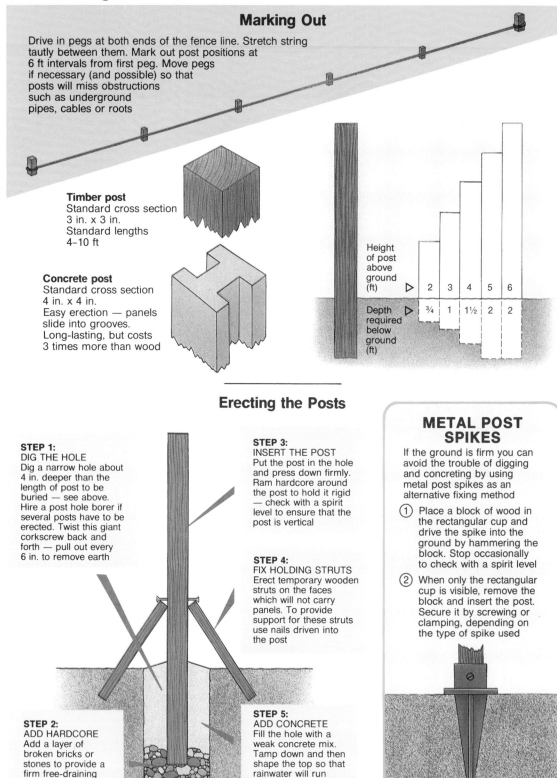

Marking Out

Drive in pegs at both ends of the fence line. Stretch string tautly between them. Mark out post positions at 6 ft intervals from first peg. Move pegs if necessary (and possible) so that posts will miss obstructions such as underground pipes, cables or roots

Timber post
Standard cross section 3 in. x 3 in.
Standard lengths 4–10 ft

Concrete post
Standard cross section 4 in. x 4 in.
Easy erection — panels slide into grooves.
Long-lasting, but costs 3 times more than wood

Height of post above ground (ft)	2	3	4	5	6
Depth required below ground (ft)	¾	1	1½	2	2

Erecting the Posts

STEP 1:
DIG THE HOLE
Dig a narrow hole about 4 in. deeper than the length of post to be buried — see above. Hire a post hole borer if several posts have to be erected. Twist this giant corkscrew back and forth — pull out every 6 in. to remove earth

STEP 2:
ADD HARDCORE
Add a layer of broken bricks or stones to provide a firm free-draining base for the bottom of the post

STEP 3:
INSERT THE POST
Put the post in the hole and press down firmly. Ram hardcore around the post to hold it rigid — check with a spirit level to ensure that the post is vertical

STEP 4:
FIX HOLDING STRUTS
Erect temporary wooden struts on the faces which will not carry panels. To provide support for these struts use nails driven into the post

STEP 5:
ADD CONCRETE
Fill the hole with a weak concrete mix. Tamp down and then shape the top so that rainwater will run away from the post. Remove struts after 2–4 weeks

METAL POST SPIKES

If the ground is firm you can avoid the trouble of digging and concreting by using metal post spikes as an alternative fixing method

(1) Place a block of wood in the rectangular cup and drive the spike into the ground by hammering the block. Stop occasionally to check with a spirit level

(2) When only the rectangular cup is visible, remove the block and insert the post. Secure it by screwing or clamping, depending on the type of spike used

Erecting the Panels

Erect a post ① and then attach a panel to it. Support this panel on bricks ② . Now erect the next post at the other end of the panel — again fix the panel to the post as shown ③ .

Attach the next panel to this post, supporting it with the bricks removed from the previous section ④ . Carry on with this post-panel-post-panel-post routine ⑤ until the fence is finished.

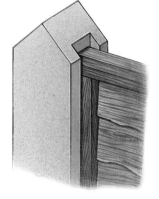

or

or

Panel clips avoid the problem of frame splitting which occurs when nailing is done badly

Nailing is the traditional method. Three 3 in. long galvanized nails are needed — drill holes in frame before nailing

No attachment is required when panels are used with concrete posts — simply slip the panel into the groove

Erecting a Chain link Fence

STEP 1:
INSERT BOLTS
Insert straining bolts (eye bolts) in the end post. Attach straining wires (line wires) to the bolts. Add central wire if fence is over 4 ft high

STEP 6:
ATTACH CHAIN LINK TO WIRES
Unroll the chain link, keeping it taut and using twisted wire to tie it to the straining wires at intervals of 1 ft

STEP 3:
TIGHTEN WIRES
Attach straining wires to the bolts inserted in the end post. Tighten the nuts with a spanner to make the wires taut

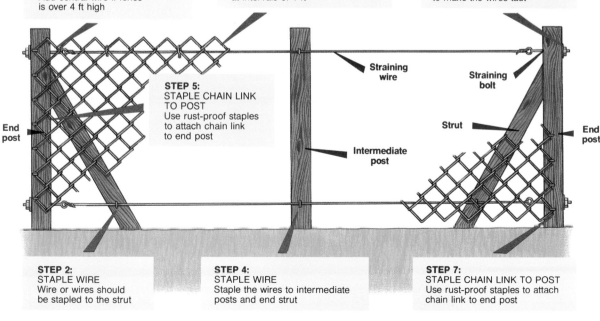

Straining wire

Straining bolt

End post

STEP 5:
STAPLE CHAIN LINK TO POST
Use rust-proof staples to attach chain link to end post

Strut

End post

Intermediate post

STEP 2:
STAPLE WIRE
Wire or wires should be stapled to the strut

STEP 4:
STAPLE WIRE
Staple the wires to intermediate posts and end strut

STEP 7:
STAPLE CHAIN LINK TO POST
Use rust-proof staples to attach chain link to end post

Fences Illustrated

Trellis fencing without climbing plants can seem rather plain. Decorative types include shaped wooden panels to give a wave effect, as illustrated by this Larch-Lap fence — a popular style which is now widely available. ▷

◁ Wattle panels are often useful where a purely practical fence or windbreak is required, but they are generally avoided where a pleasing appearance is desired. Within the right frame, however, they can be attractive.

△ The cast-iron fence was once seen everywhere, from terraced slum to royal palace. Their wholesale removal during World War II brought in the era of the wooden fence, and new cast ironwork became a rarity.

GATES

In some gardens it is essential rather than desirable to enclose the fence or wall with one or more gates. There may be toddlers to keep in or animals to keep out — in either case you will need a wooden or metal gate.

For the rest of us a gate is an optional extra. You may regard a garden as unfinished without its outer door — for others having to open and close a gate is just one more extra job. It is your decision, but think carefully about drive gates. Having to park on a busy road in order to open the gates can be both difficult and dangerous in some situations.

The choice is immense. There are wooden ones in all fencing styles — see pages 12–13. Choose a hardwood gate for staining or a pressure-impregnated softwood one for painting. Standard widths are 3, 3½, 4 and 5 ft.

Metal gates are extremely popular, and are usually called 'wrought iron'. True wrought iron gates are expensive — cheaper ones are really mild steel and must be properly primed and painted to prevent corrosion.

Metal or wood, large (over 4 ft tall for security) or short — don't go bargain-hunting for gates. They must be strong and the posts must be stout. Choose a style in keeping with the fence or wall, and make sure that both size and design are in keeping with the surroundings.

Gate Types

GARDEN GATES
A **garden gate** is a single gate in the boundary wall, fence or hedge. The maximum width for standard pedestrian gates should be 4 ft.

A **side gate** is a 6 ft high door of metal or wood designed to provide security.

| Ledged-and-braced gate | Wrought iron gate | Side gate |

DRIVE GATES
A **drive gate** closes the driveway used for a car. The usual style is a pair of wooden or metal gates which lock at the centre. Alternatively, a single wide gate such as a five-barred gate may be used. Drive gates should always open inwards.

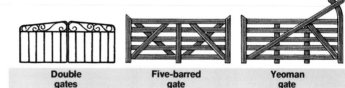

| Double gates | Five-barred gate | Yeoman gate |

Gate Posts

METAL
Metal posts are square, rectangular or circular in cross section. Fixings are usually attached. Unless they are plastic-coated it will be necessary to paint the below-ground section with bitumen paint.

WOOD
Pick oak, larch or Spanish chestnut. Buy pressure-impregnated softwood instead if you plan to paint the posts.

Gate width	Post size	Depth below ground
Up to 3 ft	4 in. x 4 in.	1½ ft
Over 3 ft	5 in. x 5 in.	2 ft
4–8 ft Five-barred gate	6 in. x 6 in.	3 ft

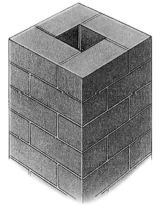

BRICK
The foundations should be 1½ ft deep and should extend at least 6 in. beyond the area occupied by the brick pier. Recommended size is 13 in. square as shown — larger size required for wide and heavy gates. Leave for 2 weeks before hanging gates.

CONCRETE
Concrete gate posts complete with fittings are available, but it is more usual to buy ordinary fence posts and then bolt on pieces of wood on which the hinges and catch have been screwed.

Erecting a Gate

The experts can't agree on the 'best' way to erect a wooden gate — below is one of the widely recommended methods but there are others. The essential features of all methods are firm foundations (concrete is essential), careful checks with a spirit level (both horizontal and vertical) and a check on the distance between posts if the batten method shown here is not used. Metal gate posts usually have the fittings attached. Follow the manufacturer's instructions exactly because these fittings must be lined up carefully.

STEP 1:
PREPARE POSTS
Set the gate on the ground. Lay the posts alongside, leaving enough space for the fittings. Nail down battens on posts to ensure correct spacing of the posts during installation. The bottom batten should line up with the bottom of the gate

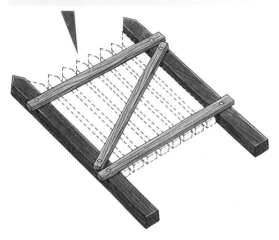

STEP 2:
FIX POSTS
Dig post holes and place broken bricks or stones at bottom. Place posts in holes, leaving a 3 in. gap between the bottom batten and the base of the path or drive. Fill the holes with concrete, using props to keep the structure upright. Check both horizontal and vertical levels before leaving to set

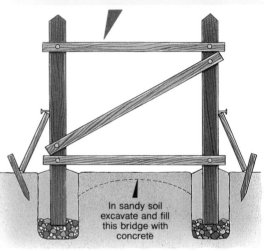

In sandy soil excavate and fill this bridge with concrete

STEP 3:
HANG GATE
After about 14 days remove the props and battens. Attach the gate, fixing the hardware in the following order: hinge pins (if required) → hinges → catch.
Hanging a heavy gate is a job for 2 people

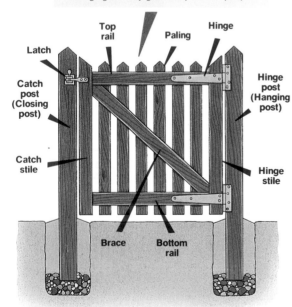

Latch

Top rail

Paling

Hinge

Catch post (Closing post)

Hinge post (Hanging post)

Catch stile

Hinge stile

Brace

Bottom rail

Gate Hardware

Automatic latch
Usual type for low wooden gates

Ring latch
Opens from inside only

Thumb latch
Opens from both sides

Loop-over catch
Usual type for double wooden gates

Drop bolt
Used for securing double gates

T hinge
Usual type for wooden garden gates — also called Strap hinge

Double strap hinge
Usual type for wooden drive gates

Gates Illustrated

A simple palisade gate which is meant to be strong and serviceable but is not designed to be an eye-catching feature. Always choose good quality, as a sagging gate is an annoying nuisance. ▷

◁ An ornate wrought metal gate is a decorative feature in any garden, and this J B Corrie model shows that white can highlight the tracery to more effect than the traditional black colour. Repaint regularly to prevent rust.

△ The yeoman gate provides an imposing driveway entrance in the right setting. This example from British Gates & Timber stands in front of a large house in rural surroundings. Not for the suburban side-street.

ARCHES & PERGOLAS

Both the arch and pergola are decorative features which add height and should also add beauty to the garden. An arch is a relatively narrow structure — a pergola is an extended archway or a series of linked arches.

The first rule is that an arch or pergola should have a definite purpose. It should never stand as an isolated feature in the middle of a lawn or at the side of a flower bed. The classical use of the arch and the pergola is to cover part or the whole of a pathway with flower-bedecked vertical and overhead supports, but there are many other uses. An arch can be set against a wall or hedge with a seat or statue below, or it can be used as an entrance to a particular part of the garden. A modern use for the pergola is to provide an outside room on the patio.

Wood is the traditional building material in the average-sized garden but there are many other types such as plastic, metal, brick and stone.

The second rule is to make sure that the material and design fit in with the house and garden style — rustic poles look attractive in a traditional setting but would look quite out of place in ultra-modern surroundings.

The third vital rule is that the structure must be strong enough and sufficiently well-anchored to withstand the force of a gale when it is clothed with the climbing plants and/or roofing material you intend to use.

Arch Types

THE POPULAR DIY MODEL

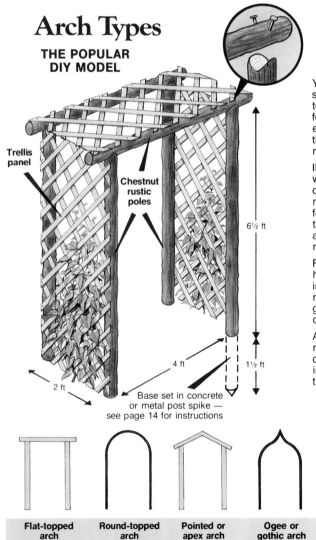

Trellis panel

Chestnut rustic poles

6½ ft

4 ft

2 ft

1½ ft

Base set in concrete or metal post spike — see page 14 for instructions

You can start from scratch using rustic poles or sawn timber, but it is much more usual these days to buy a kit or a ready-made arch. Whichever form you choose, remember that it must be large enough for comfort when clothed with plants — the height should be 6½–7 ft and the width 4 ft or more.

Illustrated on the left is the standard DIY model which may be flat- or apex-topped. The sides are clothed with wooden trellis or plastic-coated netting to support climbing plants. A simple job for the handyperson, but do make sure that all the timber is treated with a preservative and all joints are fixed securely with screws or nails which will not rust.

For most people it is better to buy a kit which will have ready-cut wooden pieces and clear instructions. Wood is, of course, not the only medium — round-topped and ogee arches are generally made from plastic-coated tubular steel or solid metal.

At the top end of the scale are elegant archways made out of brick or stone. These are usually part of a wall — free-standing ones are items to admire in Grand Gardens but are usually out of place on the average plot.

| Flat-topped arch | Round-topped arch | Pointed or apex arch | Ogee or gothic arch | Hedge archway | Moon gate |

Pergola Types

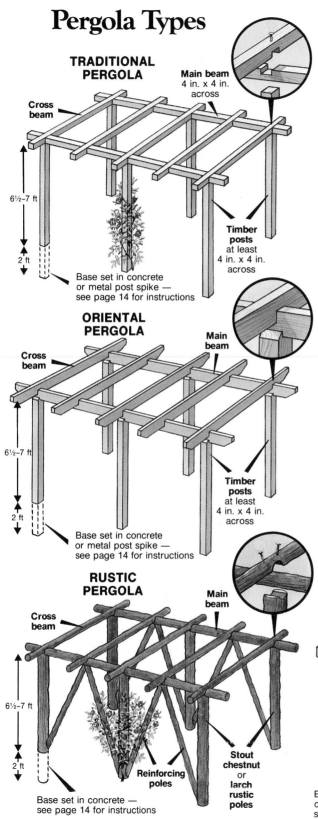

TRADITIONAL PERGOLA

Cross beam

Main beam
4 in. x 4 in. across

6½–7 ft

2 ft

Timber posts
at least 4 in. x 4 in. across

Base set in concrete or metal post spike — see page 14 for instructions

ORIENTAL PERGOLA

Cross beam

Main beam

6½–7 ft

2 ft

Timber posts
at least 4 in. x 4 in. across

Base set in concrete or metal post spike — see page 14 for instructions

RUSTIC PERGOLA

Cross beam

Main beam

6½–7 ft

2 ft

Reinforcing poles

Stout chestnut or larch rustic poles

Base set in concrete — see page 14 for instructions

Pergolas are one of our oldest garden features — they were used in Ancient Rome. In this country they have been a common sight in the great estates for generations, clothing long pathways with Roses or Wisteria, but only recently have they become popular in ordinary suburban gardens. The reason for this increase in popularity is two-fold. There is a wide variety of prefabricated kits available nowadays and the patio boom has stimulated the need for a semi-covered spot which links house and garden.

The traditional pergola in the Grand Garden is often a series of imposing brick or stone piers bearing stout wooden beams overhead or it is a series of iron hoops festooned with climbing plants. For the home garden wood is generally considered to be the best construction material, although metal pergolas can be extremely attractive in an ultra-modern setting.

Buy a kit from your garden centre or DIY store — these are sold in modular units so you can readily obtain the right length for your needs. Follow the instructions carefully, especially with regard to anchoring the main posts firmly, using a spirit level when positioning posts and beams, and fixing the beams securely to the posts.

Many people prefer the oriental pergola to the traditional type — here the cross beams have bevelled edges and fit into notches cut into the main beams. For a truly Eastern look the ends of the beams should curve upwards. The rustic pergola has long been a favourite for climbing Roses in old-world gardens, but there are one or two points to remember here. This structure is basically less robust than the other types, so you should use waterproof glue as well as galvanized nails when fixing the parts together, and it is wise to fix reinforcing poles between the uprights to increase the stability of the pergola.

The lean-to pergola can be used as an arbour (see page 97), but in recent years it has become a favourite way of enclosing part or all of a patio. Note that it is a stout structure, fixed to the wall by means of joist hangers or by attaching the cross beams to a horizontal wooden wall plate which has been bolted to the brickwork.

LEAN-TO PERGOLA

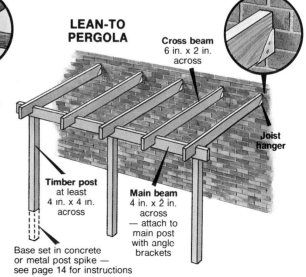

Cross beam
6 in. x 2 in. across

Joist hanger

Timber post
at least 4 in. x 4 in. across

Main beam
4 in. x 2 in. across — attach to main post with angle brackets

Base set in concrete or metal post spike — see page 14 for instructions

Arches &
Pergolas
Illustrated

Long pergolas in large gardens ▷
often have stone or brick pillars
rather than wooden posts.
Here the unusual spiral pillars
and stout wooden beams are
used to support climbing Roses.

◁ The arch with an Oriental-type pergola top has
become popular and is now found in garden centres
and DIY stores everywhere. This Forest Fencing arch
is a typical example — other styles are available.

△ A typical arch — apex-topped, trellis-sided and flanked by a simple
picket fence. Make sure that the posts are set firmly in the ground —
a flower-bedecked arch can be blown over by strong winds.

PATHS & DRIVES

A hard surface is required between A and B when regular traffic occurs between the two points. A **path** is designed for two-footed and two-wheeled traffic — a **drive** carries four-wheeled traffic. Nowadays there is a host of different paving materials and this makes selection difficult. There is rarely if ever a 'perfect' choice but there are a number of wrong choices for any particular situation. In order to avoid the pitfalls carefully study the questions below.

First of all, is the path purely functional with little or no decorative requirement? Examples are out-of-the-way walkways in the vegetable or fruit garden — here you can use an economical surface such as compacted earth, gravel, bark chippings or concrete. Grass paths are not suitable for heavy or regular traffic — they are not hard-wearing, require regular mowing and are unpleasant to walk on in wet weather.

In nearly all cases the path and drive have a decorative as well as a utilitarian purpose. The drive is the first part of the garden the visitor sees and paths often form a distinctly visible skeleton to the garden. The next question is one of price — how much can you afford to pay for a decorative surface? Natural stone slabs may be desirable, but they are expensive and difficult to handle. Concrete and gravel are much cheaper, but concrete can be dull and gravel is easily kicked on to the lawn or flower beds. The most popular choice these days are paving slabs made of reconstituted stone — they are medium priced and available in a wide range of colours, sizes, shapes and textures.

Path shape is another factor you must consider. In informal gardens curving paths are generally more attractive than straight ones, but bends should be gentle. Shape can affect your choice of paving material — a winding path offers no problems with gravel, bark chippings or crazy paving and only a little extra work with paving blocks, bricks and concrete. But with large slabs it can mean a stone-cutting nightmare.

A few rules. Make the path wide enough — 2 ft is the minimum for the average garden although 3 ft is better. The path should slope (minimum 1 in 100) to prevent standing water after rain. Small depressions must be avoided — frozen puddles in winter are a major hazard. If constructed next to the house, the surface must be at least 6 in. below the damp-proof course. Finally, remember to seek planning permission if you propose to create a drive which will make a new access on to the road.

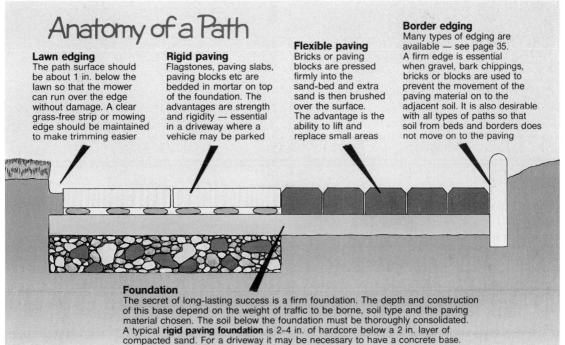

Anatomy of a Path

Lawn edging
The path surface should be about 1 in. below the lawn so that the mower can run over the edge without damage. A clear grass-free strip or mowing edge should be maintained to make trimming easier

Rigid paving
Flagstones, paving slabs, paving blocks etc are bedded in mortar on top of the foundation. The advantages are strength and rigidity — essential in a driveway where a vehicle may be parked

Flexible paving
Bricks or paving blocks are pressed firmly into the sand-bed and extra sand is then brushed over the surface. The advantage is the ability to lift and replace small areas

Border edging
Many types of edging are available — see page 35. A firm edge is essential when gravel, bark chippings, bricks or blocks are used to prevent the movement of the paving material on to the adjacent soil. It is also desirable with all types of paths so that soil from beds and borders does not move on to the paving

Foundation
The secret of long-lasting success is a firm foundation. The depth and construction of this base depend on the weight of traffic to be borne, soil type and the paving material chosen. The soil below the foundation must be thoroughly consolidated. A typical **rigid paving foundation** is 2–4 in. of hardcore below a 2 in. layer of compacted sand. For a driveway it may be necessary to have a concrete base. A typical **flexible paving foundation** is a 2 in. layer of compacted sand

BRICKS

Brick paths are an excellent choice where an old-world look is required. They can be laid on edge or on one face and you do not have to buy new ones — second-hand bricks provide an attractive weathered look. A word of caution — make sure you ask for 'Specials' — Ordinary bricks soon break up due to the action of rain and frost, and Engineering ones tend to be slippery when wet. Bricks, like paving blocks, are generally laid by the flexible paving method and although a firm base is required there is no need to use concrete or mortar. For laying instructions see page 27 — interesting patterns can be created and because each unit is relatively light this type of path-making is well-suited to the not-so-young and not-so-fit. There are some drawbacks — bricks are expensive and it takes a long time to cover a large area. Use an algicide to prevent moss and slime in winter.

STONE

Natural stone was once the near-automatic choice for the person who wanted a decorative rather than a utilitarian path. Flagstones of sandstone, slate and limestone were used, and the favourite was Yorkstone. But the age of stone has passed, as the cost is now very high and it is difficult to handle and lay. Flagstones have an irregular thickness and cutting such slabs to fit the path area requires special tools. For a few people natural stone remains the *only* material for a luxury path, but for the rest the use of slabs made of concrete or reconstituted stone is a satisfactory and much cheaper alternative. Lay flagstones in the same way as paving slabs (see page 30). Setts are small blocks of stone (usually granite) once widely used in road construction. Second-hand ones are available — treat like cobblestones (see below) to make a decorative insert in paving.

MACADAM

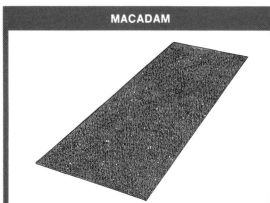

Macadam is the favourite material for drives. It is made of stone chippings coated with tar or bitumen and is referred to in a number of ways — asphalt, black-top, coated macadam, 'Tarmac' etc. This is not a job for the DIY enthusiast — such drives are laid using hot macadam and this should be left to the professional. Choose your contractor with care. For resurfacing an old drive or for making an asphalt path on a concrete base, brush on a coat of bitumen emulsion and allow it to stand for about 20 minutes. Then spread cold macadam which you can buy in bags from your local garden store. Choose from red, green or black. Rake out to form a 1 in. layer and press down with a heavy roller until firmly compacted. Keep the roller wet when working and scatter white chippings over the surface if you want a 'pepper-and-salt' effect.

COBBLESTONES

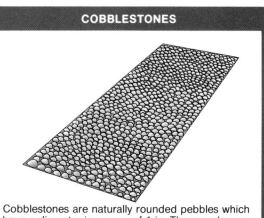

Cobblestones are naturally rounded pebbles which have a diameter in excess of 1 in. They can have a decorative appearance, but they are unsuitable for drives and have a strictly limited application in paving. The problems are that they are uncomfortable to walk on and can pose a hazard for the infirm and the very young. The best way to use them is as a geometrical insert (square, round or rectangular) in a large expanse of rather dull paving material. Prepare a rigid foundation as described on page 23 and place a layer of concrete on top of this base. Press the cobbles firmly into the concrete, packing the pebbles close together and pushing them down with a flat board so that the tops are level and the concrete surface is about ½–1 in. below the tops of the stones. There is no easy way to lay cobblestones — do not use the flexible paving method.

CRAZY PAVING

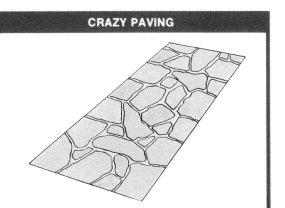

Laying paving slabs can be heavy work and you generally have to keep to neat straight lines — with crazy paving the pieces are smaller and the informal effect means that you don't have to aim for a perfect fit. Broken concrete slabs can be used, but pieces of natural stone about 1½-2 in. thick are much better. This latter approach need not be too pricey if you go along and collect the stones from the supplier. Follow the paving slab instructions (page 30) with a few variations. After preparing the base, place the larger pieces of stone in a random pattern to form the edges of the path. Now put the remaining large stones within the path area and fill the gaps with the smaller pieces. Make sure that each stone is bedded into the sand so that it is both firm and level with its neighbours. Finally, fill the gaps with a stiff mortar mix (1 part cement : 4 parts sand and very little water).

WOOD & BARK

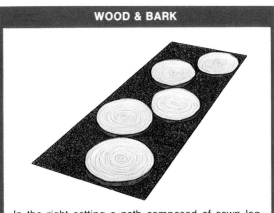

In the right setting a path composed of sawn log rounds can be extremely attractive — nothing could look better in a woodland garden, especially if the rounds are surrounded by shredded bark. Rot is a problem, so treat the wood with a preservative and set each piece on a bed of sand which has been spread on perforated polythene sheeting. Press down on each log round firmly and surround with bark or gravel. Railway sleepers are sometimes recommended as paving material, but in hot weather tar may ooze out and that will create a serious problem if tracked indoors. In recent years pulverized or shredded bark has become a popular material for paths in woodland gardens. It is soft underfoot and has a natural look, but it is expensive, needs a containing edge and requires topping up every few years.

Stepping Stones

A well-trodden route on the lawn, such as the walk from the patio to the vegetable plot, can pose a problem. The grass becomes worn, but to lay down a standard path would destroy the overall green carpet effect. Stepping stones are perhaps the best solution — stones or concrete slabs set in the turf at intervals convenient for walking. Place each stone on the grass and cut around it with a spade or trowel to remove the turf and some of the soil below. Put sand into the hole so as to form a compacted 1 in. layer and to support the stone at ½-1 in. below the surface of the lawn.

CONCRETE

Concrete is criticised by many for its austere look, but it remains a popular material for both paths and drives. It is durable, fairly inexpensive, suitable for curving or irregular pathways and it is maintenance-free if properly laid. It need not be dull — you can add a colouring agent during the mixing process and you can create a non-slip and more attractive surface by brushing with a stiff broom before it has set — see page 29. The major problems are that the preparation of the site does take time and the job itself is heavy and requires both care and practice. If the area is small you can mix concrete by hand, but for larger areas it is much better to hire a concrete mixer or to have ready-mixed concrete delivered to your home. Whichever method you choose, do remember to arrange to have people to help you as it is necessary to work quickly. Before doing any paving work with concrete, whether as the final surface or as a base for some other paving material, do read the section on the making and use of concrete (pages 106-107) and the instructions for laying a concrete path (pages 28-29).

Roll-up Paving

There are times when a temporary path is needed across bare ground or turf. It may be that building work is to be done on the other side of the lawn away from the house, and that calls for frequent use of a heavy wheelbarrow. Or there may be work to do in the vegetable garden in winter when the soil is extremely muddy. The age-old method is to use a series of wooden planks, but these are cumbersome and difficult to store. A better answer these days is to buy a roll of portable paving made of polypropylene. Simply stretch it out like a carpet and then hose down and roll up again after use.

GRAVEL

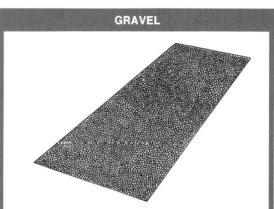

Gravel is by far the cheapest material for a drive and is very widely used where extensive areas have to be covered. Shingle (small stones smoothed by the action of water) or true gravel (stone chips obtained from a quarry) is used, and there are several advantages apart from low cost. Irregular and curved shapes offer no problem, and laying the path is quick and easy. Settlement hollows can be filled in and the crunching noise made by footsteps and car tyres is a satisfying sound to some people. There are, however, just as many drawbacks. Weeds can be a nuisance, and regular raking is necessary. Stones can be tracked on to lawns and carpets, and firm edging is needed. The best plan is to line the trench with perforated polythene sheeting and cover with 3 in. of firmly consolidated coarse gravel. Cover this with a 1–2 in. layer of pea gravel and roll to form a firm surface.

PAVING SLABS

By far the most popular decorative paving material for the garden path and patio these days is the pre-cast slab. These slabs come in a wide range of sizes — including the popular 1½ ft x 1½ ft squares and the 1½ ft x 9 in. or 1½ ft x 2 ft rectangles. There are also hexagons, circles and 'planters' to create circular flower beds. The basic material used is either reconstituted stone for maximum decorative effect or concrete for economy. The range of colours is extensive and there is also a variety of surfaces — see page 30. The list of advantages for paving slabs is impressive — there are grades to suit all pockets and there are shapes, colours and sizes to suit all gardens. But you must still choose with some care — for a driveway it is necessary to use hydraulically-pressed slabs which are no larger than 1½ ft x 1½ ft and a rigid foundation is essential. Paving slabs are quite straightforward to lay, but their weight can be a problem — don't lift stones larger than 1½ ft square unless you are strong and fit. You can hire a slab lifter to make the job easier. There are several ways to lay paving slabs — one of the standard methods is set out on page 30.

PAVING BLOCKS

These are tough units which are about the same size as a brick — 8 in. x 4 in. and 1½-2½ in. thick. Some of the blocks you can buy are distinctly brick-like although they are available in a wide range of colours and the edges are often bevelled. Other blocks are shaped — the zig-zag or curved patterns allow the blocks to be interlocked. You will find these units listed in the catalogues as blocks, pavers or paviors and they are made of clay or concrete. About 50 are required to cover a sq. metre and they are usually laid on a bed of sand by the flexible paving method (see page 27). Some form of firm edging is required, and a firmly compacted base is essential. The advantages and disadvantages are similar to those of bricks — simple to handle and lay but they are expensive and it takes a long time to cover a large area.

Laying a Brick or Block Path

Bricks and blocks can be laid as either rigid or flexible paving (see page 23) — shown here is the flexible paving method. It seems quite easy — no hardcore, no concrete base ... just set the blocks on sand. But think twice before using blocks instead of paving slabs. Creating permanent edges takes time and some skill, and both cutting blocks and tamping down are laborious. For these latter jobs it is a good idea to hire a hydraulic block cutter and a petrol-driven plate vibrator.

STEP 5:
LAY THE BLOCKS
Work to your chosen pattern from one end of the path to the other. Kneel on a board placed across the area you have already laid. Use whole blocks only — go back later and fill in with cut ones. Butt the blocks closely together

STEP 6:
TAMP DOWN THE BLOCKS
When laying is finished it is necessary to press the blocks down into the sand layer so. as to form a level surface. For a small area it is practical to use a piece of wood and a club hammer, but it is generally much more satisfactory to use a petrol-driven plate vibrator

STEP 2:
PUT IN A RETAINING EDGE
A permanent edge is essential in order to prevent the blocks and sand from moving outwards when the path or drive is in use. The simplest technique is to create an edging with timber boards which have been treated with a preservative — these boards must be held firmly with stakes to a depth below the sand layer. For a more attractive effect use either kerbstone blocks or long concrete edgings set in mortar, as illustrated here

STEP 7:
FINISH THE JOB
The final step is to brush fine silver sand over the surface. This fills the joints and will bind the blocks together

STEP 4:
ADD A LAYER OF SAND
A 2 in. layer of sharp (not building) sand is the next step. Level and press down this sand with a screeding board held horizontally

STEP 1:
DIG THE TRENCH
Remove earth to the depth and width required for the mortar base of the retaining edge, the foundations and the paving units. Consolidate the bottom of the trench firmly

STEP 3:
ADD A LAYER OF CONSOLIDATED EARTH
Replace some of the earth which has been removed and firm this down to form a solid base. If a drive is being created, this layer should be hardcore rather than soil — aim for a depth of 3–4 in.

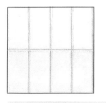

Simple bond

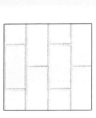

Running bond

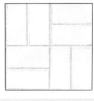

Basketweave bond

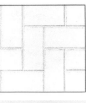

Herringbone bond

Caneweave bond

Laying a Concrete Path

Laying concrete is often regarded as a quick job — you have to be quick or the moist material will set before the task is completed. But the preparation of the site before you start does take time. This preliminary work must be tackled properly, so before you begin read all about the way to mix and buy concrete (pages 106–107) and how to create the formwork as set out in this section. You will certainly need someone to help you when you start but the work itself should be well within the ability of a reasonably strong person with some DIY experience. This applies to a moderately short and straight path — things are different for a wide driveway or an irregular-shaped area. Here you should seek assistance from someone who has successfully laid a large area of concrete before. Alternatively, have the work done by a professional. A few points about concreting. Avoid doing the job in frosty weather and with ready-mixed concrete it is a good idea to order about 10 per cent more than the calculated amount. If you are mixing your own, remember to prepare the concrete as close to the site as possible and wash all tools and equipment thoroughly as soon as you have finished.

STEP 6:
TIP THE CONCRETE INTO THE FORMWORK
You will need a 2 in. deep layer for a path or a 4 in. layer for a drive. Once the concrete is ready, pour a load into the formwork. The next step is to use a shovel to push the concrete into the sides and corners — it is essential to avoid air pockets. Do not spread the concrete too far at this stage — rake it approximately level so that it stands about ½ in. above the boards

STEP 7:
LEVEL THE CONCRETE
You will now need a tamping beam and a helper. The beam is a heavy board which should be about 2 in. thick. Holding the tamping beam at the ends you should both move steadily across the concrete — first compacting it with a chopping motion and then going over the area again with a sawing action to remove excess material. Fill any hollows and repeat the above procedure

STEP 5:
PUT IN EXPANSION JOINTS
Long paths need expansion joints every 8–10 ft to prevent cracking. The simplest type are ½ in. wooden planks cut to the width of the path and the planned depth of concrete. Attach these boards to the formwork

STEP 3:
CREATE THE FORMWORK
Wooden planks about ¾–1 in. thick ('formwork') must now be nailed to the stakes — old floorboards are ideal. If the path is to be a long one it will be necessary to use several planks which are joined together as shown in the illustration. The top of the formwork must be exactly level with the tops of the stakes

STEP 8:
CONTINUE UNTIL THE FORMWORK IS FILLED
Mix up more concrete and repeat Steps 6 and 7 until the whole of the formwork is filled with concrete

STEP 4:
ADD A LAYER OF HARDCORE
Put down a layer of hardcore to form a solid base within the formwork. For an ordinary path a 2 in. layer is enough, but for a driveway you should aim for a depth of 4 in. Level the surface and brush in sharp sand so that the crevices are filled. Firmly ram down this foundation layer

STEP 1:
DIG THE TRENCH
Remove earth to the depth required for the foundations and the layer of concrete. The width should be about 8 in. more than that planned for the finished path. Consolidate the bottom of the trench firmly

STEP 2:
PUT IN THE WOODEN STAKES
Prepare a number of 1 in. x 1 in. pointed wooden stakes — they should be about 1½ ft long. Using a taut string as a guide, drive these into the soil at 3–4 ft intervals so that the tops are level and at the desired height for the finished path. Put in another line of stakes at the other side of the path — these stakes must again form a level line but should be set about ½ in. lower than the first line so that the finished path will have a slight crossfall

STEP 9:
CREATE THE DESIRED SURFACE FINISH
The surface left after the use of the tamping beam is quite
acceptable for most purposes, but there are several other types of
finish from which you can make your choice. Do remember that
the surfaces created after tamping require an element of skill

Natural
The simplest surface, as it is
created by the tamping beam.
It is both slightly rough and anti-slip,
so that it is quite suitable for
a utility path. Created surfaces
carried out carelessly will make
the path look worse, not better

Brushed
A rippled surface, created
by brushing over the concrete in
parallel lines immediately after the
path has been laid. Hold the
broom at a shallow angle and do
not press down. Brush across
and not along the path

Smooth
A fine surface created by
smoothing over the concrete
with a float. Wait until the surface
has started to become stiff and
do not exert any downward pressure.
A steel float gives a fine finish

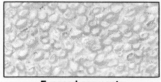

Exposed aggregate
Prepare a brushed surface — see
above. When the concrete has
started to stiffen, repeat the
brushing and spray to remove
the fine material on the surface —
the coarser aggregate is exposed

Mock crazy paving
Prepare a smooth surface with a
steel float — see above. When the
concrete is reasonably stiff, use a
pointed stick to mark the surface
into irregular-shaped slabs to
give a crazy paving effect

MAKING A CURVED PATH

Make a series of saw cuts in
the formwork, as shown below.
Place stakes at close intervals
(1 ft or even less) around the
curve. Bend the boards gently
and attach to the stakes

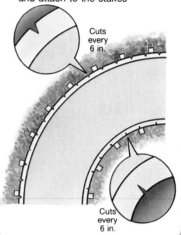

Cuts
every
6 in.

Cuts
every
6 in.

STEP 11:
FINISH THE JOB
You can now walk on
the path and finish the
job, but you will have
to wait at least another
week before driving
a car onto a new drive.
Remove the formwork
by tapping it downwards
to break the seal before
pulling out the boards.
Finally, fill the gap
alongside the concrete
with earth — ram
down firmly

STEP 10:
LEAVE THE CONCRETE TO CURE
It is necessary to ensure that the concrete does not lose moisture too
quickly during the setting ('curing') process. Lay polythene sheeting
over the surface once the path has been laid — place bricks around
the edge to keep it in place. Remove the polythene after 7 days

Laying a Paving Slab Path

For decorative paths and patios the first choice nowadays is paving slabs, as noted on page 26. Much time is spent poring over catalogues and looking around DIY stores — make sure you spend the same amount of time planning the path. If at all possible try to design an area which can be completed with whole slabs. Splitting them is arduous — this can be done with a bolster chisel and a club hammer, but it is much better to hire a slab splitter. Always wear protective goggles when cutting paving material.

STEP 5:
LAY THE REST OF THE SLABS
Finish the path using the technique outlined in Step 4. Use a spirit level to make sure that the desired slope is achieved. Pull out the spacers and leave the mortar to set

STEP 6:
FINISH THE JOB
After a couple of days the new path is ready for jointing (pointing). The usual recommendation is to brush a dry mortar mix (1 part cement : 3 parts sand) into the cracks, but this can disfigure the surface. It is much better to point with moist mortar and a trowel, using masking tape to protect the surface of the slabs

STEP 4:
LAY THE FIRST LINE OF PAVING SLABS
Place the first line of slabs along a string which marks the edge of the path. Lift the first slab and place 5 blobs of mortar on the sand below. Replace the slab and bed it down using a block of wood and club hammer. Check that it is level. Repeat with the rest of the slabs, inserting two wooden spacers (¼ in. thick) between the slabs

STEP 3:
ADD A LAYER OF SAND
A 2 in. layer of sharp (not building) sand is the next step. Level and press down this sand with a screeding board held horizontally

STEP 2:
ADD A LAYER OF HARDCORE
Put down a layer of hardcore to form a solid base. For an ordinary path or patio a 2 in. layer is enough, but for a driveway you should aim for a depth of 4 in. Mix the hardcore with some ballast so that all the spaces between the broken bricks and stones are filled with gravel and sand. Ram down this layer

STEP 1:
DIG THE TRENCH
Remove earth to the depth and width required for the foundations and the paving slabs. Consolidate the bottom of the trench firmly

Smooth
Plain surface — the cheapest type of paving slab. However, the marble-like Polished slab is expensive

Textured
Roughened surface — either brushed or with aggregate exposed. Good slip resistance is the main advantage

Riven
Split-stone surface — a good choice where a natural stone look is required. Very widely available

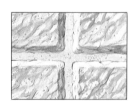

Patterned
Deeply-impressed surface — varieties available include simulated bricks, blocks, crazy paving and tiles

Paths & Drives Illustrated

An informal path in an informal setting. ▷
This line of sawn log rounds set in shredded
bark provides a pleasing walkway in a
woodland glade in the Beth Chatto garden.

◁ Combining different materials to make a path
or drive can reduce the danger of dullness, as
in this gravel and wooden tile (see page 43) path.
Take care not to mix too many paving materials.

△ An ordinary concrete path can be distinctly uninteresting, and this
is undesirable in many situations. However, it is this plainness which
makes it an ideal foil for the multicoloured beds in this garden.

STEPS

In millions of gardens there is at least one place where you have to move from one level to another. This may involve stepping up from a path to the patio or down from the lawn to the driveway. The obvious way to make this easy is to build a flight of steps, but you should consider whether a gently sloping concrete ramp would be a better idea. Not as attractive perhaps, but it would certainly make things easier if you have to move a heavy lawn mower from one level to another.

Still, the usual choice for nearly everyone is to build a series of steps. There are two basic types. **Cut-in steps** are the easier ones to make — here the steps are cut into the bank or slope and the earth below provides the basic foundation. With **free-standing steps** the structure is built against a vertical face and takes you from one flat level to another. Simple ones are within the scope of the DIY enthusiast, but complex brick steps of this type are best left to the professional.

There is a wide range of building materials available. Bricks and blocks make the most popular risers, but stone, sawn logs and railway sleepers are also used. The favourite treads these days are paving slabs, but you will also find gravel, bricks, natural stone, bark, paving blocks and wood. Whichever you choose there are three basic considerations to bear in mind — the steps must be safe, practical and attractive.

Safety is of prime importance — falling down steps is one of the most common of all garden accidents which require hospital treatment. Make sure that all the risers are the same height and all the treads the same depth — do not exceed the dimensions shown below. Also ensure that the treads have a non-slip surface — never choose smooth concrete or smooth paving slabs. Do not use bricks other than Special Quality ones and always remove slime and moss.

The steps must also be practical. Make sure that they are soundly constructed and also wide enough for easy passage of both people and equipment. Beauty is very much a matter of personal taste, but there are a few general rules. Curving steps are considered by many to be more attractive than straight up-and-down ones, and the materials chosen must fit in with the style of the garden and also the surfaces used for adjacent paths, patio and walls.

Treads need not be rectangular — circles and hexagons are attractive in the right setting. In an informal woodland garden a flight of steps made from logs and bark can provide a simple alternative to the popular brick and paving slab combination.

A final word of caution. Plan carefully before you begin and choose a step width which will allow you to use whole slabs or sleepers as cutting is laborious.

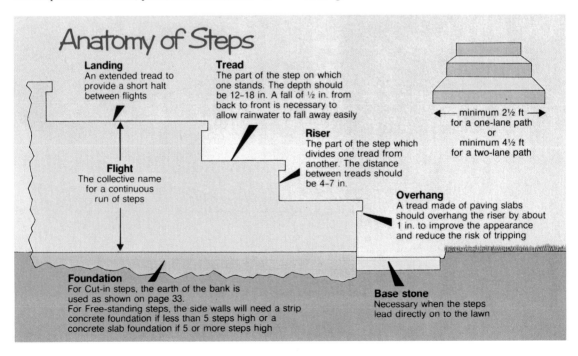

Anatomy of Steps

Landing
An extended tread to provide a short halt between flights

Tread
The part of the step on which one stands. The depth should be 12–18 in. A fall of ½ in. from back to front is necessary to allow rainwater to fall away easily

minimum 2½ ft for a one-lane path
or
minimum 4½ ft for a two-lane path

Riser
The part of the step which divides one tread from another. The distance between treads should be 4–7 in.

Flight
The collective name for a continuous run of steps

Overhang
A tread made of paving slabs should overhang the riser by about 1 in. to improve the appearance and reduce the risk of tripping

Foundation
For Cut-in steps, the earth of the bank is used as shown on page 33.
For Free-standing steps, the side walls will need a strip concrete foundation if less than 5 steps high or a concrete slab foundation if 5 or more steps high

Base stone
Necessary when the steps lead directly on to the lawn

Making Paving Slab Steps

STEP 1:
ROUGHLY CUT STEPS INTO THE BANK
Carefully measure the height from the top of the bank to the
bottom and then work out the number of steps you will need.
Study the diagram — remove the earth as shown. Note that
the base stones will require a foundation of a 3 in. deep
layer of hardcore and a 3 in. layer of concrete.
Firm the earth steps

STEP 4:
FINISH THE JOB
Continue building risers, infilling with hardcore and
bedding down treads in mortar until the final tread
is laid level with the upper surface of the bank.
Replace earth to fill the gaps at the sides and
foot of the steps. Cover the edges with plants
and/or large stones

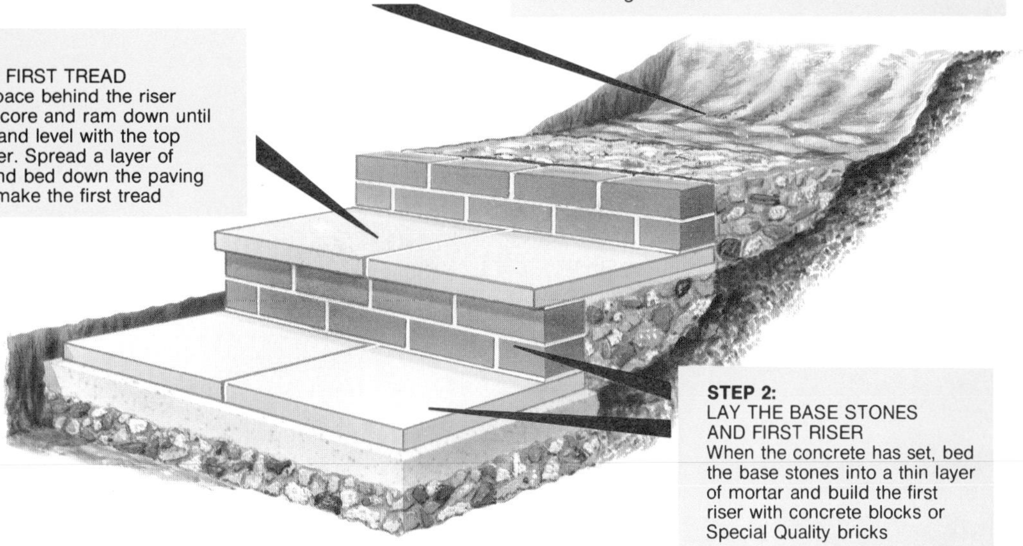

STEP 3:
LAY THE FIRST TREAD
Fill the space behind the riser
with hardcore and ram down until
it is firm and level with the top
of the riser. Spread a layer of
mortar and bed down the paving
slabs to make the first tread

STEP 2:
LAY THE BASE STONES
AND FIRST RISER
When the concrete has set, bed
the base stones into a thin layer
of mortar and build the first
riser with concrete blocks or
Special Quality bricks

Making Wooden Steps

STEP 1:
PREPARE THE BASE
Cut a shallow trench from the top of the bank to the bottom.
Consolidate the base of the trench by rolling or treading

STEP 5:
FINISH THE JOB
Add a layer of gravel or shredded bark on top of each
step to form the treads. Level and then consolidate
firmly. Replace earth to fill the gaps at the sides of
the steps. Cover the edges with plants and/or stones

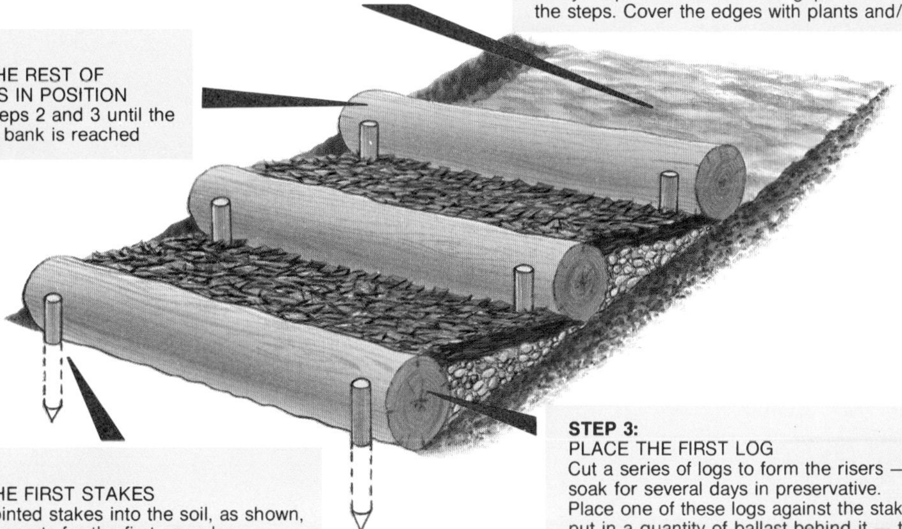

STEP 4:
PLACE THE REST OF
THE LOGS IN POSITION
Repeat Steps 2 and 3 until the
top of the bank is reached

STEP 2:
PUT IN THE FIRST STAKES
Drive 2 pointed stakes into the soil, as shown,
to form supports for the first sawn log

STEP 3:
PLACE THE FIRST LOG
Cut a series of logs to form the risers —
soak for several days in preservative.
Place one of these logs against the stakes and
put in a quantity of ballast behind it — tamp
down and level the surface. This ballast layer
should be about 2 in. below the top of the log

Steps Illustrated

A brick staircase linking wall, pathway
and house. Treads of natural or reconstituted
stone is the usual pattern, but here bricks
are used and Marshalls kerb blocks serve
as the fronts of the treads and risers. ▷

◁ A popular combination — risers of
reconstituted stone blocks and treads of
paving slabs with a riven surface (see page 30).
Less usual is the shape — the double curve
breaks up the regularity and adds interest.

△ Grand houses call for grand treatment. The free-standing flight of
steps leading from the pathway is flanked by Haddonstone balustrading.
A good example of keeping features and house in balance.

EDGINGS

In gardening DIY manuals the important subject of edgings for paths, drives, beds and borders is often omitted. This is a pity, as these lowly features nearly always have a practical as well as a decorative role to play.

This practical purpose is one of two types. The first job of an edging is to keep a path or drive from spreading — without a proper edging small-unit paving material (gravel, blocks laid on sand etc) would move sideways on to turf or soil. The other job edging can do is to keep the earth of a bed or border and the grass of a lawn from spreading — without a proper edging the soil from a bed could wash on to a path or patio, and keeping lawn edges neat would be extremely difficult.

There are many forms of edgings and they are available in all sorts of materials. Choose carefully — pick an edging which is right for the situation, the desired purpose and the money you have to spend.

BELOW-SURFACE EDGINGS

The purpose is to divide lawns from walls, paths or borders and to allow mowing right up to the edge

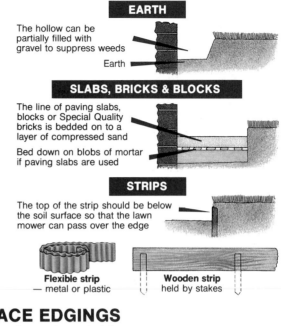

EARTH

The hollow can be partially filled with gravel to suppress weeds

Earth

SLABS, BRICKS & BLOCKS

The line of paving slabs, blocks or Special Quality bricks is bedded on to a layer of compressed sand

Bed down on blobs of mortar if paving slabs are used

STRIPS

The top of the strip should be below the soil surface so that the lawn mower can pass over the edge

Flexible strip — metal or plastic

Wooden strip held by stakes

ABOVE-SURFACE EDGINGS

The purpose is to keep soil or paving material from moving on to an adjoining area

BRICKS & BLOCKS

Standard paving blocks or Special Quality bricks can be used — kerbstone blocks with a chamfered edge are also available. Make sure that bricks or blocks are firmly bedded into the soil or foundation

| Upright brick edging | Dragon's-tooth brick edging | Peat block edging |

STRIPS

The quickest and most convenient way to create straight-line edging, but only Logg Roll is suitable for sharp curves. Many types are available — lengths are 1½–3 ft and heights 6–8 in. Make sure that strips are firmly bedded into the soil or foundation

Available as Round Top or Scalloped Top

Concrete or **Reconstituted stone strip**

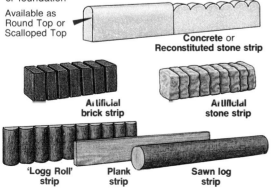

Artificial brick strip

Artificial stone strip

'Logg Roll' strip

Plank strip

Sawn log strip

TILES

Glazed or unglazed, edging tiles were an indispensible part of the Victorian garden. In today's garden they are useful for beds or a border in a formal setting, but tiles have no place in the informal, woodland or 'natural' plot. The usual size is about 9 in. x 6 in.

| Plain tile | Roll Top tile | Rope Top tile | Chelsea tile |

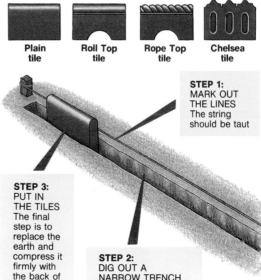

STEP 1: MARK OUT THE LINES The string should be taut

STEP 2: DIG OUT A NARROW TRENCH About ⅔ of the tile will need to be buried. Firm the bottom

STEP 3: PUT IN THE TILES The final step is to replace the earth and compress it firmly with the back of a trowel

PLANT SUPPORTS

Several garden features such as arches, pergolas and fences are often used to support climbing plants, but these structures all have other practical or decorative roles to play. The plant supports described here are used solely for their ability to allow climbing or weak-stemmed plants to grow successfully in the chosen spot.

Good plant supports of this type have two basic properties. They must be strong — a vigorous climber exerts a heavy pressure on its support, which is greatly heightened if the support is in the open garden and a strong wind is blowing. The support should also be as unnoticeable as practical — the idea is to see the plants and not the supports.

Plant supports are of two basic types. Firstly, there is the **free-standing support** which is used for either decorative plants (e.g a pillar or wigwam for Roses) or for food plants in the vegetable or fruit garden (e.g a frame for Runner Beans or a fence-type support for Cordon Apples). Secondly, there is the **wall support** which enables part or all of a vertical surface to be clothed by the plant and is generally used for decorative plants (e.g a house wall for Roses, Wisteria or Clematis).

FREE-STANDING SUPPORTS

The basic point to remember is that these supports do not have a wall behind them to give extra strength and to provide protection against strong winds. This means that a firm foundation is essential — this can range from pushing bamboo canes deeply into the soil to providing stout pillars with a concrete base. Wood should always be treated with a preservative.

CANES & STAKES

Wherever possible staking should be carried out at planting time — pushing in a cane or pole after planting can cause root damage. The single-stake method is suitable for herbaceous plants with a spire-like head, such as Delphiniums. In most cases, however, tying border plants to a single stake should be avoided as an ugly 'drumstick' effect is produced. It is better to insert 3 or 4 canes around the stems and enclose the shoots with twine tied round the canes at 9 in. intervals. Alternatively you can use a circular support as described below.

For trees you will need a stout stake rather than a cane. Put in the stake after the hole has been dug but before the tree has been planted. The support should be 1–2 ft below the surface but only about half way up the stem.

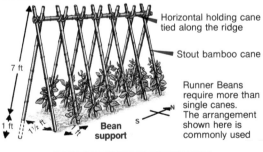

Horizontal holding cane tied along the ridge

Stout bamboo cane

7 ft

1 ft

Bean support

Runner Beans require more than single canes. The arrangement shown here is commonly used

CIRCULAR SUPPORTS

A range of circular supports is now available for the flower garden. They are 1–4 ft tall to suit Chrysanthemums, Lilies, Carnations, Paeonies etc.

PILLARS & WIGWAMS

Stout poles or pillars are not often seen in the garden, but they can be an attractive feature when densely clothed with a climbing Rose or Wisteria. Remember to train the stems in an ascending spiral rather than attaching the stems to one side of the support.

Wigwams are made in various ways. Rustic poles and trellis are used for Roses and other flowering climbers — canes are the usual material for Peas and Beans in the vegetable garden.

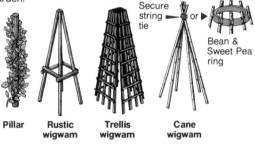

Secure string tie

or ▶

Bean & Sweet Pea ring

Pillar **Rustic wigwam** **Trellis wigwam** **Cane wigwam**

GROWING BAG SUPPORTS

Several proprietary types are available — buy a stout one for Tomatoes or Cucumbers.

NETTING SUPPORTS

Can be used for flowers (Sweet Peas, Nasturtiums etc) or for vegetables (Peas, Beans etc).

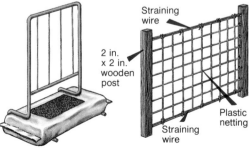

2 in. x 2 in. wooden post

Straining wire

Plastic netting

Straining wire

WALL SUPPORTS

WIRES

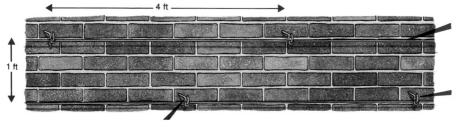

← 4 ft →

1 ft

Plastic-covered straining wire pulled taut between the wall fixings. Make sure the wire is strong enough to hold the plants in full leaf and bloom

Leave a 1–2 in. gap between the wire and the wall

Wall fixings. Rust-proof masonry nails or vine eyes can be used, but for heavy and vigorous plants it is better to use eye bolts which are set in plastic or fibre wall-plugs

TRELLIS

Wood

  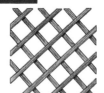 

Square mesh	**Diamond mesh**	**Expanding diamond mesh**	**Fan**
Popular — mesh size 4–8 in. Panel size — 1 ft x 6 ft to 6 ft x 6 ft	Much less popular than square mesh. Usual panel size — 3 ft x 2 ft	Very popular — expands to 6 ft. Available in hardwood	Attach to wall for a single plant or use as a wigwam (see page 36). Panel 6 ft high

Other materials

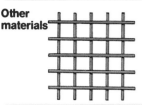 

Square mesh: rigid plastic or steel	**Mesh: flexible plastic**	**Expanding diamond mesh: rigid plastic**	**Fan: rigid plastic or steel**
Popular — mesh size 5–8 in. Panel 5–6 ft high	Inexpensive, but needs good support and not suitable for heavy plants	Similar to wooden version — expands to 6 ft	Same use as the wooden fan — see above. Not good for wide-spreading plants

Fixing Trellis to the Wall

STEP 2:
ATTACH THE TRELLIS TO THE BATTENS
Drill the trellis slats and then fasten with galvanized nails. With square mesh trellis fix the panel with horizontal slats facing outwards

STEP 1:
PLACE SPACERS BETWEEN THE WALL AND TRELLIS
Do not attach trellis directly to the wall — a space here will allow plants to spread inside. In addition taking down the trellis will be much easier if pointing or decorating is required. One method of attachment is to fix a 1½ in. x 1½ in. batten to the wall with fibre-plugged brass screws — drill the battens before screwing. Place this first batten above the damp-proof course — place other battens above at 3 ft intervals. Instead of battens you can use cotton reels or plastic tubes as spacers

Tying Tips

- Many types of proprietary ties are available but soft string is as successful as any
- Tying properly involves attaching the stem to the support before the plant has started to flop. It is also necessary to attach the stem quite loosely
- When training climbers on to trellis, wires etc you should not tie the stems vertically — spreading them at first horizontally to form an espalier or at an angle to form a fan can dramatically increase the display
- Tying trees to stakes is more complex than dealing with flower and vegetable stems. You should wrap a short band of sacking around the trunk before tying with tarred string. Alternatively you can use an expanding tie. Tighten after a few weeks
- When a tree has outgrown its stake it may still need support. This can be provided by fixing a collar to the middle of the trunk and then securing it with 3 strong wires which are secured to the ground

Plant Supports Illustrated

Bamboo canes are the simplest form of ▷
plant support, but you must do the job
properly. Note that several canes are
used here rather than a single post, and
staking is done well before flowering.

◁ The cane wigwam is a popular support for
Peas and Runner Beans in the vegetable garden,
but it can be an attractive feature in the
flower garden when clothed with Sweet Peas.

△ Poking canes through growing bags is not a good idea.
Several types of tailor-made supports are available for Tomatoes or
Cucumbers growing in bags — choose the sturdiest one on offer.

PATIOS

Until quite recently our idea of relaxing in the garden was to sit in a deckchair with a book or a drink. Today our concept of using the garden for enjoyment has drastically changed — now we have the patio.

A patio is basically a hard-surfaced area which is usually but not always attached to the house and is used for relaxation, enjoyment and perhaps entertaining. There may be just a small area of paving slabs with a plastic table and a couple of chairs, or the patio may be a multi-tiered structure with beds, ponds, pergolas and permanent furniture. In both cases, however, it is an 'outdoor room' — mean or magnificent depending on taste, space and the wealth of the owner.

The words 'patio' and 'terrace' are now used interchangeably to describe any paved area designed for sitting and relaxing. To the purist a patio is a wall-enclosed flagged area in Spain or parts of the U.S — the equivalent of the courtyard in this country. Again for the purist a terrace is a raised paved portion of a garden which is bordered by a wall or raised beds. But for the rest of us a patio or terrace is the brick-, block- or slab-covered area where we sunbathe,

eat outdoors in summer and sit on chairs to admire the view.

Building a patio takes a good deal of time and money, and this section stresses the need to plan carefully. You have to think about position, shape and paving material as well as several other factors — a mistake here can mean that the result will be too small, too shady or just plain dull. You will also have to think about features for this outdoor room — too few will make it look as bare as an empty house and too many may give a hopelessly cluttered appearance. You will find rules and suggestions on every page, but in the final analysis the key point is that the finished patio must appeal to you.

If you have an existing patio which you wish to improve, consider some of the features described in this section. A dull stretch of paving can be enlivened by lifting one or more slabs or groups of blocks and filling the space with another material or with plants. If you are creating a patio then a major problem will be to decide on the space you are willing to devote to this feature. If the back garden is very small it is worth considering the concept of turning the whole area into a patio with pots and planting pockets. After all, that would be a *true* patio and you would please the purists!

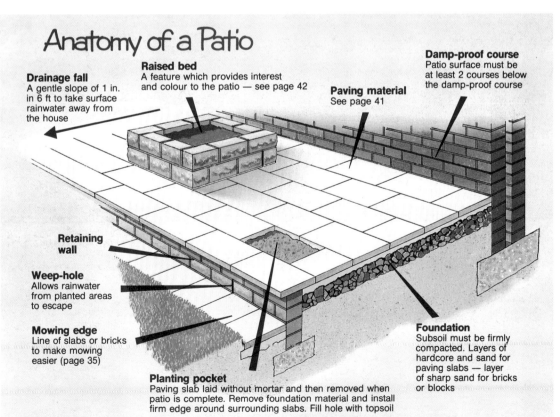

Anatomy of a Patio

Drainage fall
A gentle slope of 1 in. in 6 ft to take surface rainwater away from the house

Raised bed
A feature which provides interest and colour to the patio — see page 42

Paving material
See page 41

Damp-proof course
Patio surface must be at least 2 courses below the damp-proof course

Retaining wall

Weep-hole
Allows rainwater from planted areas to escape

Mowing edge
Line of slabs or bricks to make mowing easier (page 35)

Foundation
Subsoil must be firmly compacted. Layers of hardcore and sand for paving slabs — layer of sharp sand for bricks or blocks

Planting pocket
Paving slab laid without mortar and then removed when patio is complete. Remove foundation material and install firm edge around surrounding slabs. Fill hole with topsoil

Planning a Patio

The first job is to consider carefully the 6 key points — purpose, position, size, shape, paving materials and features. The next task is to prepare a plan on graph paper in which your various decisions are included. Make sure that you have not made one of the 2 cardinal errors. All the experts will warn you that a large expanse of a single paving material with no other features can look deadly dull, but the second error is less often discussed but equally serious. A patio, especially a small one, can look unpleasantly fussy if crowded with too many features on too many types of paving materials. The third step is to mark out the area with canes and string. Sit in the area, walk about, put in the table and chairs ... is it *really* the right size? Now it is time to get down to work. If you don't have the necessary skill or time then you should seek a local landscaping company — pick several with a good reputation and obtain quotes before making your choice. If the patio is to be a DIY job then order materials and do try to enrol a willing helper or two.

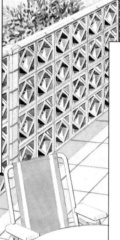

PURPOSE

What is the patio for? If it is merely to be a sitting-out spot for a couple then a small and simple area will do — a patch of slab or block paving to bear a table, chairs and perhaps a sunshade. At the other end of the scale you may want a true outdoor room where you can cook and entertain your friends and sun-bathe in the summertime. Here you must make it large enough for the comfort of the visitors and you must consider some of the optional extra features described later.

SIZE

The limiting factor is the area of the garden — a small patio can look out of place in a large property, but no more odd than an extensive, multi-featured patio in a tiny plot. The size of the patio should generally be in keeping with the size of the garden, but there is a minimum. Of course, experts differ on just how small a patio can be, but 40 sq. ft is about the smallest it should be. For comfort, eating outdoors and sunbathing it is better to aim at about 35 sq. ft for each person who will use the patio. After you have read the paragraphs on Shape and Paving Materials use these guidelines to create an approximate size for your proposed patio. Then modify the dimensions slightly so that the need to cut slabs, blocks, bricks etc is kept to a minimum.

POSITION

The best place is adjoining the back of the house, especially if there are French doors or patio doors — the task of taking out food and drink and bringing in cushions is greatly simplified. But it is not the only place for a patio — the prime considerations are sunshine, especially in the afternoon hours, and some shelter from the prevailing wind. You won't be able to change the position of the house and other buildings, of course, but you can consider pruning trees if they reduce the sunlight which falls on the chosen area. You can also create screens on an exposed site if wind or lack of privacy is a problem — see page 42. Existing trees or shrubs can be incorporated in the patio to give a feeling of maturity, but avoid Poplars, Willows, Limes and large deciduous specimens. So look for adequate sun, some shelter and privacy, and build your patio there.

SHAPE

The usual shape of the patio attached to a house is a rectangle. You can consider alternatives, but many writers go too far in claiming that the rectangle or square is uninteresting and you should be more adventurous. Straight lines are usually in keeping with the lines of the house and make the laying of paving slabs a straightforward job. Extra interest is easily created by using more than one paving material, adding extra features or by building the patio on more than one level. The situation is different when the patio is separated from the house — here curves and an irregular outline may well improve the appearance, especially in an informal garden. Be careful not to get too fanciful if you intend to use large-size paving material — slab-cutting to fit curves and bends is a laborious job.

PAVING MATERIALS

Most of the paving materials used for paths and drives (pages 24–26) can be used to create a patio, but there are two restrictions. Loose material such as gravel and bark should be avoided for overall surfacing and so should items like cobblestones and granite setts which feel uncomfortable underfoot. A single paving material should dominate the patio, and this should be in keeping with the nearby paths and walls. There is a general feeling that most patios can be improved by introducing a second paving material — a popular example is the use of a line of blocks around or across a large expanse of paving slabs. Another example is a patch of gravel or cobblestones set within a brick, stone or paving slab patio.

PAVING SLABS

If in doubt, choose paving slabs if the patio is to be square or rectangular. A mixture of square and rectangular slabs tends to give a more interesting surface than an all-square patio, and unnatural colours are best avoided. Colour and arrangement are a matter of personal taste, but multi-coloured and chess-board schemes are frowned upon by most garden designers. A selection of surfaces is shown on page 30 — three examples of patterned slabs are shown on the right. The cheapest slabs are 1½ in. thick concrete ones, but it really is worth investing in reconstituted stone slabs.

Crazy paving **Cobbled** **Parquet**

BRICKS & BLOCKS

Bricks (Special Quality grade) are a good choice in old-world and informal settings — their great advantage is the way they can be used for irregular or curving patios without the need for cutting. Blocks, both concrete and clay-based, have similar advantages and are available in several colours and shapes. Bricks and blocks need a firm edge when laid by the flexible paving method — see page 23. 'Classico' blocks can be used to produce circular paved areas.

CRAZY PAVING

A favourite surface until concrete and reconstituted stone slabs came along. Crazy paving is worth considering if you want an informal look — York stone is the popular type but there are others. Broken concrete slabs are an inexpensive alternative — some paving suppliers have them available at a very low price.

STONE

Natural stone is the surface you will find on the terraces of the Grand Garden, and is still the only choice for many traditionalists. Expensive, difficult to lay and not easy to find, Yorkstone still has a special and unique charm which you may feel outweighs the disadvantages.

TILES

Square tiles which are 1 in. thick have long been popular on the Continent and are now gaining favour in this country as a paving material for patios. The concrete ones are available in several sizes and numerous colours — some too bright for the average garden. Even brighter are the colourful ceramic tiles which give the patio a distinctly Mediterranean look.

DECKING

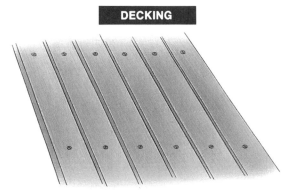

The wooden patio ('deck') is a common sight in Scandinavia and the U.S but it is only slowly gaining popularity in Britain. This is perhaps surprising — it blends in so well when surrounded by shrubs and trees. Use western red cedar or an ordinary softwood which has been pressure-impregnated with a preservative. For DIY decking the planks are fixed to stout wooden joists which in turn are stood on brick supports. The planks are attached to the joists with brass screws or galvanized nails. A ¼–½ in. gap must be left between the planks. DIY decking is a laborious job — it is generally a better idea to buy timber tiles. These are 2 ft square panels of strong slats on a timber frame. They should last for at least 20 years. No other paving material is easier to lay — see page 43 for details.

PATIO FEATURES

A patio without added features is like a room without furniture — an area in which you can stand but not a place where you would wish to stay. Many patio features are available — some are virtually essential whereas others are optional extras. Some are easy to make and cost virtually nothing but others are expensive and space-consuming. The choice is large and so it is worth repeating the warning that having too many features can be as wrong as having too few.

RAISED BED

An excellent way to add both height and colour to the patio. Obviously you don't want to take up too much valuable floor space, but there is a minimum size (1½ ft x 1½ ft x 1½ ft) if the soil is not to dry out too quickly. Weep-holes at the base may be necessary. See page 72 for more details.

PLANTING POCKET

One or more planting pockets help to blend garden and patio — all you have to do is plant up an unpaved spot or an area exposed by lifting one or more slabs. Annuals or bulbs are the usual choice, but do consider at least some evergreens such as a dwarf conifer to give year-round colour.

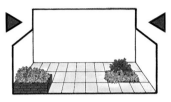

CONTAINER

Tubs and pots are the usual way to grow plants on the patio. Choose containers which are in keeping with the size and style of the paved area and keep them out of the line of traffic. Do remember that frequent watering will be necessary in dry weather. See pages 71–75 for more details.

BARBECUE

Cooking outdoors is one of the most outstanding features of the outside living revolution which has taken place in recent years. A built-in barbecue is always admired but it does have its drawbacks. It is more difficult to clean than a portable one, and it can't be wheeled away when cooking is over. See pages 62–64 for more details.

FURNITURE

The basic need is a table and sufficient chairs for the family — optional extras are a sun lounger and a large umbrella. The standard construction materials are plastic, resin and coated metal these days — lightweight structures which can be put away when summer is gone. However, a built-in seat is a good idea.

CLIMBING PLANTS

It is a pity to leave a bare and uninteresting brick wall at the back of a patio which adjoins the house. This is a place for one or more climbing annuals or perennials — create planting pockets in the patio and erect trellis or horizontal wires along the wall — see page 37 for more details.

PERGOLA

A lean-to pergola (see page 21) at one side of the patio can have a number of advantages. If it is high enough, wide enough and strong enough it could be a dining-out area, a place for climbers and hanging baskets, and a source of shade during the hot days of summer. Well worth considering.

LIGHTING

Entertaining and dining out on the patio at night have a special magic, and effective lighting is the key. You can have free-standing standard lamps or spotlights and lanterns on the wall — see pages 57–60 for details. Where wiring is a problem, choose garden flares which are stuck in the ground — but do take care.

WATER

A pool on the patio sounds such a good idea, but there are special require-ments. The site must be sunny, the volume of water must be large enough to reach a balanced state (see page 53) and toddlers must be kept well away. A simpler alternative is a self-contained fountain which you can buy as a ready-to-install unit.

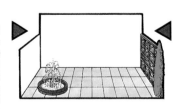

SCREENING

Screening is usually necessary for one or more reasons — privacy, protection from the prevailing wind and/or protection from the hot sun in midsummer. The solution depends on the situation — choose from an awning, a large umbrella, a line of leafy trees or shrubs, a fence covered with climbing plants or a wall of screen blocks.

Making a Patio

Making a patio is a big job — especially if walls, steps and raising the soil level are involved. Do not try to do this job yourself if you have never laid slabs or blocks before and if you are not used to strenuous exercise. Still, it is a DIY job for many, and so a few tips for the patio builder. Planning permission is unlikely to be required, but may be necessary if the property is a listed building or if you are a tenant. Never cover an air brick on the house wall — build a pit around it if necessary. Manhole covers can be an eyesore — you can buy shallow drain planters these days which fit over them and are used for growing bedding plants or bulbs.

Laying the Foundations

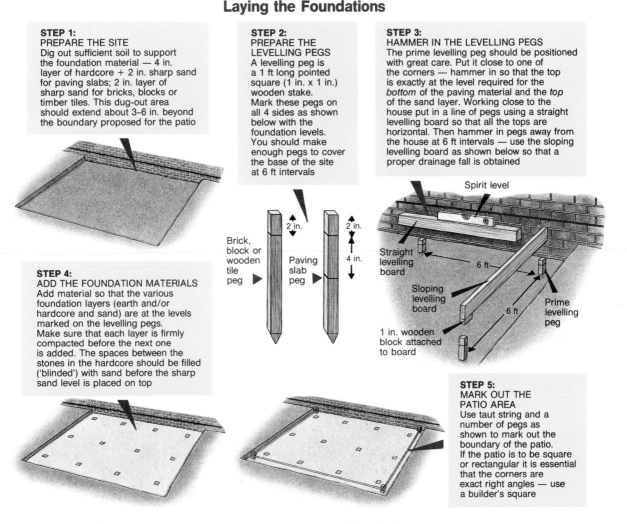

STEP 1:
PREPARE THE SITE
Dig out sufficient soil to support the foundation material — 4 in. layer of hardcore + 2 in. sharp sand for paving slabs; 2 in. layer of sharp sand for bricks, blocks or timber tiles. This dug-out area should extend about 3–6 in. beyond the boundary proposed for the patio

STEP 2:
PREPARE THE LEVELLING PEGS
A levelling peg is a 1 ft long pointed square (1 in. x 1 in.) wooden stake. Mark these pegs on all 4 sides as shown below with the foundation levels. You should make enough pegs to cover the base of the site at 6 ft intervals

STEP 3:
HAMMER IN THE LEVELLING PEGS
The prime levelling peg should be positioned with great care. Put it close to one of the corners — hammer in so that the top is exactly at the level required for the *bottom* of the paving material and the *top* of the sand layer. Working close to the house put in a line of pegs using a straight levelling board so that all the tops are horizontal. Then hammer in pegs away from the house at 6 ft intervals — use the sloping levelling board as shown below so that a proper drainage fall is obtained

Brick, block or wooden tile peg

Paving slab peg

2 in.   2 in.

4 in.

Spirit level

Straight levelling board

Sloping levelling board

1 in. wooden block attached to board

6 ft

6 ft

Prime levelling peg

STEP 4:
ADD THE FOUNDATION MATERIALS
Add material so that the various foundation layers (earth and/or hardcore and sand) are at the levels marked on the levelling pegs. Make sure that each layer is firmly compacted before the next one is added. The spaces between the stones in the hardcore should be filled ('blinded') with sand before the sharp sand level is placed on top

STEP 5:
MARK OUT THE PATIO AREA
Use taut string and a number of pegs as shown to mark out the boundary of the patio. If the patio is to be square or rectangular it is essential that the corners are exact right angles — use a builder's square

Laying the Paving Material

Wherever possible work *towards* the pile of paving material — in this way you will not have to walk on newly-laid paving.

PAVING SLABS
See page 30 for details. Begin with a line of slabs next to the house — then a line at right angles to form the left hand boundary. Between these 2 lines lay the rest of the slabs, fanning outwards until the patio is finished.

BRICKS & BLOCKS
See page 27 for details. Begin by laying the firm edges of wood, brick, block or concrete — then fill in with the chosen paving material.

CRAZY PAVING
Lay a line of large broken stones around all of the boundaries — then fill in with other stones. Try to keep the gap between the stones at 1 in. or less.

WOODEN TILES
Prepare a sand foundation as for bricks or blocks — see page 27. Lay the squares in a criss-cross fashion, as shown below. The timber can be stained after laying. Algal growth can make the wood slippery during the winter months — brush on an algicide if slime develops.

Patios Illustrated

The simplest style of all — just an area of paving slabs, a table and a few chairs. Nothing elegant nor impressive, but nevertheless a place for outdoor living during the summer months. ▷

◁ *The opposite extreme to the example above — a series of terraced paved areas with lights, raised beds, a pond and plants everywhere. Perhaps rather too much for some.*

△ *An outdoor living area which lies between the two designs illustrated above. There is plenty of open space for sitting out, but there are plants and a barbecue to remove the plainness.*

Many people feel that wooden patios have a much more natural look than stone or brick ones, but they have not become popular in Britain. Wooden tile ones as illustrated here are easy to create. ▷

◁ In most gardens the patio takes up only a small part of the total area, but where space is strictly limited it is often a good idea to devote the whole area to paving and pots.

△ Two highly desirable features are illustrated here. The formal pool with a variety of plants adds interest, and the planting pockets with evergreens provide year-round colour.

PONDS & FOUNTAINS

The sight of water has a fascination which is not easy to explain. Visitors may walk past your flower beds or shrubs, but they will stop by the well-maintained pond. Maybe it is the charm of a half-hidden world below the smooth surface — fish suddenly appearing and then disappearing certainly add to the attraction of the stillwater pond.

Moving water provides another dimension — the sight and sound of a fountain or waterfall provide extra interest, and so it is not surprising that the number of pools and other water features in British gardens has increased dramatically in recent years. This increase in popularity was made possible by the introduction of the flexible liner in the 1960s — no longer was it necessary to use concrete to make a pond which was large enough to house fish and a range of plants. A wide array of inexpensive water features has also appeared — submersible pumps, floating lights, pre-formed cascades and so on. All this has meant that water gardening is now a fairly simple DIY job for everyone and no longer an aspect of gardening for the wealthy gardener and the specialist contractor.

There is more to a pond than water, fish and aquatic plants — quite an assortment of wildlife such as frogs, newts, toads and dragonflies can be attracted to your garden. A thing of beauty, then, to provide so much interest during the summer months ... but *only* if the pond is constructed and stocked in the right way. All too often we see murky green water, overrun by weeds and infested with midges and mosquitoes. The cause is generally a combination of doing the wrong things at the start and then failing to do the few necessary tasks once the pond has become established.

You can avoid most problems by following a few basic rules. On the next page you will see that the pond must be large enough to support the plants and deep enough to support the fish. It's not just a matter of size — the pond must be put in the right position. When stocking the pond you must aim for the correct balance between the various components — that's the secret of clear water. Page 53 tells you how.

Chemicals and careful management cannot be relied upon to keep the water clear if the pond is too small, but this does not mean that you cannot have the charm of moving water if your plot is tiny — these days there are all sorts of self-contained fountains and other water features in kit form which are suitable for the patio or small garden.

Water should be a source of pleasure and not tragedy, so read the Safety paragraph on page 47 if small children use the garden. Remember that this also means occasional visitors, such as grandchildren and the toddlers of friends. In addition, remember that water and electricity can make dangerous partners — do not undertake outdoor wiring as a DIY job unless you *really* know what you are doing.

Anatomy of a Flexible liner Pond

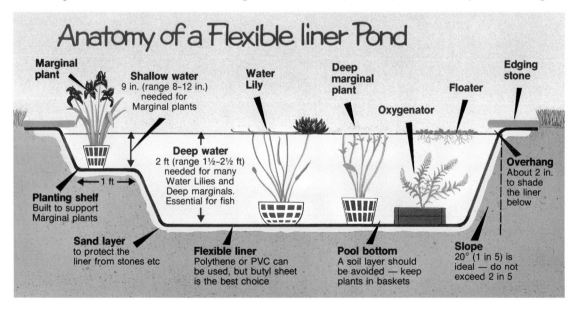

Marginal plant

Shallow water 9 in. (range 8–12 in.) needed for Marginal plants

Water Lily

Deep marginal plant

Oxygenator

Floater

Edging stone

Deep water 2 ft (range 1½–2½ ft) needed for many Water Lilies and Deep marginals. Essential for fish

← 1 ft →

Planting shelf Built to support Marginal plants

Overhang About 2 in. to shade the liner below

Sand layer to protect the liner from stones etc

Flexible liner Polythene or PVC can be used, but butyl sheet is the best choice

Pool bottom A soil layer should be avoided — keep plants in baskets

Slope 20° (1 in 5) is ideal — do not exceed 2 in 5

Planning a Pond

Plan your pond carefully before you dig the first spadeful of soil. The first step is to study each of the guide paragraphs on this page. You should then have a fairly clear idea of size, construction material and where the pond will go. The next thing to do is to mark out the outline with either rope or a hose pipe — then look at it from the house and other parts of the garden. Will it really be eye-catching? Will you be able to hear the proposed fountain when you sit on the patio? Do shadows fall across the proposed site during the morning or evening? Changes can be made at this stage — after construction these may be very difficult or impossible. Think about moving water features and lighting. A suitable electric cable will have to be laid, but it is usually quite acceptable to wait until the pond has been constructed before putting in a fountain. The situation is quite different with a waterfall or cascade — this may have to be incorporated whilst the pond is being built. Once you are happy with the plan the construction material can be ordered and work can begin.

SIZE

Small receptacles such as sinks and half-barrels can be used to house aquatic plants, but for a proper pool which can be expected to stay clear you should aim for a water surface of at least 40 sq. ft. The minimum depth of water should be 1½ ft, but 2 ft is better if you plan to have several types of fish in the pond. Large ponds should be 2½ ft deep.

SHAPE

Squares and rectangles can be made with concrete, and are also available as rigid liners. A wide variety of rigid liner shapes can be bought — circles, ovals, oblongs, triangles and L-shaped ponds as well as irregular shapes. With a flexible liner it is better to stick to a simple shape with gentle curves — avoid fussy shapes and sharp corners which are not easy to produce with polythene, PVC or butyl sheeting.

SITE

Choose a sunny spot which if possible is shaded from the east wind. It is essential to keep away from trees. Dead leaves decompose to produce salts and gases which are harmful to fish and encourage green algae — tree leaves which are toxic include Willow, Horse Chestnut, Holly and Laburnum. Tree roots can break a concrete pool wall. Garden designers try to place Informal ponds at the lowest part of the garden.

SAFETY

Ponds are attractive to visitors, wildlife ... and children. Crawling babies must be watched or a pond cover should be used — it is surprising that active toddlers can drown in a few inches of water. Some people prefer to have a fountain surrounded by pebbles rather than water whilst the children are small. Electricity is another danger area, especially if mains voltage is used. A safer approach is to have a transformer indoors and work with an outdoor supply of 24 V — there are many pumps which are powered by this low and safe voltage.

STYLE

There are 2 basic styles. One is no better than the other — the correct choice depends entirely on the situation. With the **Formal pond** the outline is clearly defined and the shape is either geometrical (square, oblong etc) or gently curved. It is separated from other garden features and is often used as a centrepiece. Floaters, Water Lilies and Oxygenators are essential for maintaining the correct balance. Marginals, however, are not really essential.

With the **Informal pond** the outline is not clearly defined — it merges into the adjoining feature or features such as a rockery or bog garden. The outline is irregular — the object is to make the pond look like a natural stretch of water. Because of this Marginals are essential as they obscure the edges of the pond.

The recommended choice for a formal garden or a small plot is the Formal pond. Provided the surface is at the laid-down minimum of 40 sq. ft, there is no reason why the pond should not carry fish and Water Lilies to make it an eye-catching feature for the compact garden of today. In such a situation and using such a size the Informal pond can look like a large puddle. This type of pond needs both space and informal surroundings, and in this environment it can be by far the better choice.

CONSTRUCTION MATERIALS

There are 3 basic materials. **Concrete** was used to make the great and not-so-great pools and ponds of yester-year. But its time has passed — making a satisfactory concrete pond takes a good deal of skill and even more back-breaking labour.

The **Rigid liner** (also known as the ready-formed, pre-cast or moulded pool) makes pond-making a much easier task — although not *quite* as easy as set out in the sales literature. The cheapest types are made from vacuum-formed plastic, and low price is the only advantage. They are fairly short-lived, available in not many sizes and are only semi-rigid — it is much better to choose a fibreglass one. Twice the price of a plastic one, but they are extremely durable.

The problem with the Rigid liner is that you are limited to the designs offered by the manufacturer and the size is restricted. To make a larger pond and/or one of your own design then you must use a **Flexible liner**, which is waterproof sheeting which moulds itself exactly to the shape of the excavation. Price is not a problem — the cost of the best sheeting is still less than that of a plastic Rigid liner. The major drawback is that Flexible liners are not suitable for sharp-cornered pools. **Polythene** sheeting was the first Flexible liner and is no longer a good choice. It is inexpensive, but it is also fragile, short-lived and has poor stretching properties. A **PVC** liner is a better choice, especially if it is laminated and reinforced with nylon. You can expect a life of about 10 years — for life-long reliability you should choose the synthetic rubber sheeting known as **Butyl**. Buy material with a guarantee of at least 20 years.

Making a Concrete Pond

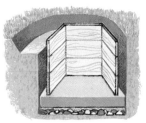

The traditional type of pool. It has lost favour in recent years, but still has one role to play. Concrete is used where a large square or oblong pool is to be built, but it is a professional and not a DIY job. If you still wish to try the following notes may help. The deep-water section should be square or rectangular. Aim for a wall 6 in. thick — build a wooden frame and install with a 6 in. gap between wood and soil (see illustration). Fill with concrete, pressing down to fill the corners, and remove wood when set. When dry, paint the surface with a proprietary sealing compound before filling and stocking — raw concrete is harmful to fish.

Making a Rigid liner Pond

Resin-bonded fibreglass is the usual and most satisfactory construction material. Unfortunately, nearly all ready-formed pools are too small to house more than one or two Deep marginals and the shallow depth makes winter freezing a serious threat to fish. Still, pool heaters are available and a Rigid liner can be a good way of making a formal pond where space is limited. But do choose carefully — there are so many different types and grades these days.

STEP 1:
MARK OUT
THE POND
Mark out the perimeter of the liner — make a second line about 1 ft out to mark the area of excavation

STEP 2:
DIG OUT THE HOLE
Cut along the excavation edge with a spade and remove soil. The bottom of the pit should be about 2 in. lower than the liner — measure the depth using a ruler and straightedge. Then make sure that the ledges and base are horizontal

STEP 3:
INSTALL THE LINER
Compact the base — add a 2 in. layer of sand. Lower the liner into the pit and bed down firmly into the sand. Check that it is level. If not, take out the liner and add or remove sand and/or soil as necessary

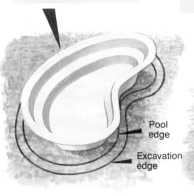

Pool edge

Excavation edge

STEP 4:
INFILL AROUND
THE LEVEL
Once the liner is level, insert battens to hold it in place. Start to fill with tap water — at the same time add sand or sifted soil to fill the space. Make sure that no gaps are left under the shelves or around the sides

STEP 5:
FINISH THE POND
Lay paving stones (crazy paving, slabs, natural stone etc) around the edge, so that they project about 2 in. over the water. These stones should be set on mortar and a board and spirit level used to ensure that the surround is level

STEP 6:
STOCK THE POND
Be very careful not to drop any mortar into the pool — if you do then emptying and refilling will be necessary as lime is harmful to fish. You are now ready to stock the pond, first with plants and then with fish. Read pages 50–52 if you are new to water gardening

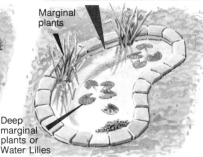

Marginal plants

Deep marginal plants or Water Lilies

Making a Flexible liner Pond

The pond made from a Flexible liner is by far the most satisfactory. It is reasonably easy to construct if you are used to digging — but is strenuous if you are not. For reasons outlined on page 47 it is foolhardy to economise when buying the sheeting. Choose butyl sheeting — it is the dearest but also the longest-lasting.

STEP 1:
MARK OUT THE POND
Mark out the shape on the ground, using a garden hose or thick rope for curves and string with pegs for straight lines.
Measure the size of the butyl sheeting required — note the extra requirement for the planned depth of the pond.
Order the sheeting

STEP 2:
DIG OUT THE HOLE
Cut along the marked pond line with a spade and remove soil to a depth of 8–12 in. — the level of the planting shelf. Next, mark and dig out the central area to leave a 1 ft wide shelf. Check with a board and spirit level to ensure that the top is not sloping — add or remove earth as necessary. Remove stones and roots from the hole and line the sides and base with a 1 in. layer of wet sand

STEP 3:
INSTALL THE LINER
Place the sheet across (not inside) the hole. Leave for a couple of hours — warmth makes it more flexible. Make sure the sheet is centred and then weigh down the edges with stones. Start to fill the pond slowly with tap water — the liner will stretch to the contours of the hole. As the water level rises, remove some of the stones to allow the liner to move gradually into the pond space

Shelf for Marginal plants

Planned maximum depth of the pond

STEP 4:
TRIM THE LINER
Make neat folds as necessary to cope with corners — turn off the water when the level is about 2 in. below the soil surface. Remove the stones. Trim the edge with scissors, leaving a 6 in. overlap all round. Pleat the liner to form a neat edge. Stretch and peg down this liner edge

STEP 5:
FINISH THE POND
Lay paving stones (crazy paving, slabs, natural stone etc) around the edge, so that they project about 2 in. over the water. These stones should be set on mortar and a board and spirit level used to ensure that the surround is level. Break or cut stones to fill any gaps between the paving — make sure that all the surface sheeting is covered

STEP 6:
STOCK THE POND
Be very careful not to drop any mortar into the pool — if you do then emptying and refilling will be necessary as lime is harmful to fish. You are now ready to stock the pond, first with plants and then with fish.
Read pages 50–52 for guidance if you are new to water gardening

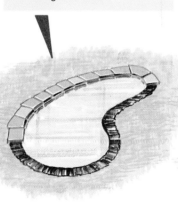

Marginal plants

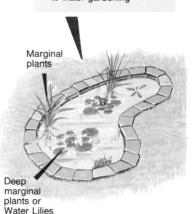

Deep marginal plants or Water Lilies

Stocking the Pond

A new pond filled with clear tapwater seems to invite immediate stocking with plants and fish, but it would be a mistake. The water should be left to stand for about a week, and then the golden rule is to put in plants before fish. The reason is that fish tug at submerged plants and nibble the leaves, so the Water Lilies, Marginals, Oxygenators and so on should be allowed to establish themselves in the pond for several weeks before introducing the Goldfish, Shubunkins etc. Another couple of rules. The ideal planting time is May to September and most plants should be introduced to the water gradually by standing each basket on one or more bricks before introducing it to its permanent base in deeper water. You cannot pick just the pretty ones — some of the plainest may be vital to ensure that the water remains clear and the fish stay happy.

PLANTS

The modern approach is to plant pond specimens in baskets rather than in soil at the bottom of the pool. In this way growth is controlled and plants can be easily lifted for dividing and re-potting when the soil is exhausted.

Latin name	Common name	Height above surface	Distance between crown and surface	Flowering period	Notes
WATER LILIES					Roots submerged — leaves and flowers on the surface. The Queen of pond plants, of course, but also important for keeping the water clear — the leaves provide surface shade and this discourages algae. Plant in Water Lily baskets filled with heavy loam — do not use peat-based compost. Cover the surface with gravel after planting. Place bricks at the bottom of the pond so that the crown of the plant is close to the surface. When new growth starts remove one or more bricks so that the plant is at the recommended depth
NYMPHAEA	Water Lily	Surface	6 in.–3 ft depending on the variety — usual depth 1–2 ft	June–September	Many varieties available in a wide range of sizes. The smallest are the Dwarfs (surface spread 1 sq. ft, crown 6–12 in. below surface) and the largest are the Very Vigorous varieties (surface spread up to 25 sq. ft, crown 3 ft below surface). Many colours available — white, yellow, pink, red, mauve etc — also the 'Changeables' (e.g N. Paul Hariot) which deepen in colour with age. Check the size group before buying

Water Lily type	Distance between crown and surface	Surface spread	Flower size
Very Vigorous	2½–3 ft	10–25 sq. ft	8–10 in.
Vigorous	1½–2 ft	5–10 sq. ft	6–8 in.
Moderately Vigorous	1–1½ ft	2–5 sq. ft	4–6 in.
Dwarf	6–12 in.	1–2 sq. ft	2–4 in.

Very Vigorous
N. Gladstoniana

Vigorous
N. Sunrise

Moderately Vigorous
N. Fire Crest

Dwarf
N. Paul Hariot

Latin name	Common name	Height above surface	Distance between crown and surface	Flowering period	Notes
DEEP MARGINAL PLANTS					Roots submerged — leaves and flowers on or just above the surface. Very few types available. In the absence of Water Lilies these plants are important for keeping the water clear — the leaves provide surface shade and this discourages algae. Plant in Water Lily baskets filled with heavy loam — do not use peat-based compost. Cover the surface with gravel after planting. Place bricks at the bottom of the pond so that the crown of each plant is close to the surface. When new growth starts remove one or more bricks so that the plant is at the recommended depth
APONOGETON DISTACHYUS	Water Hawthorn	Surface	1–2 ft	Spring and autumn	White petals, black anthers. Fragrant. Oval, glossy leaves. Not fully hardy in the North
NYMPHOIDES PELTATA	Water Fringe	2–3 in.	1 ft	July–September	Deep yellow flowers. Spreads quickly. Miniature Water Lily-like leaves 1½ in. across
ORONTIUM AQUATICUM	Golden Club	1–2 ft	1 ft	April–May	White poker-like stem tipped with yellow flowers. Leaves are blue-green. Hardy

Latin name	Common name	Height above surface	Distance between crown and surface	Flowering period	Notes
OXYGENATORS		Leaves, stems and roots submerged — flowers may be above the surface. Important for keeping the water clear. The leaves absorb minerals and carbon dioxide, and this discourages algae. Plant in the sunnier part of the pond — 1 bunch per 2 sq. ft. Some are temperamental — plant a mixture. Traditional method of planting is to tie a piece of metal to the base of a bunch of stems, and drop into the water. It is better to plant the bunch in a tray filled with a sand/fine gravel mix and then place the tray at the bottom of the pond			
ELODEA CRISPA	Goldfish Weed	Below surface	Not critical	—	Upright brittle stems — narrow curled leaves. Very effective. Do not plant E. canadensis
FONTINALIS ANTIPYRETICA	Willow Moss	Below surface	Not critical	—	Tangled masses of stems covered with dark green, mossy leaves. Grows in shade
HOTTONIA PALUSTRIS	Water Violet	6 in.	Not critical	June	Ferny leaves — whorls of pale lavender flowers on emerged stems
MYRIOPHYLLUM SPICATUM	Water Milfoil	Below surface	Not critical	—	Bronzy-green feathery leaves on long reddish stems
RANUNCULUS AQUATILIS	Water Buttercup	1 in.	Not critical	June	Surface leaves Clover-like, submerged leaves finely divided. White flowers just above surface
TILLAEA RECURVA	Tillaea	Below surface	Not critical	June–August	Dense green mat — used by fish as food. Insignificant white flowers
FLOATERS		Leaves, stems and flowers on, just below or just above the surface. Important for providing shade if Water Lilies or Deep marginal plants are sparse or absent. Planting could not be simpler — just drop the plants in the water			
AZOLLA CAROLINIANA	Fairy Moss	Surface	Floating	—	Dense green mat of ferny leaves — turns red in autumn
EICHHORNIA CRASSIPES	Water Hyacinth	6 in.	Floating	August–September	Very attractive, but not hardy. Glossy leaves, feathery roots and spikes of lavender flowers
HYDROCHARIS MORSUS-RANAE	Frog-bit	Surface	Floating	May	Good choice — small Water Lily-like pads and small white flowers
LEMNA TRISULCA	Ivy-leaved Duckweed	Surface	Floating	—	Small translucent leaves — the only Duckweed which will not take over the pond
STRATIOTES ALOIDES	Water Soldier	Surface	Floating	July–August	Rosettes of spiny leaves rise to the surface at flowering time
TRAPA NATANS	Water Chestnut	Surface	Floating	July–August	Large rosette of hairy, olive-green leaves. Flowers are small and white. Not hardy
MARGINAL PLANTS		Roots submerged — leaves and flowers clearly above the surface. Purely ornamental. Not required to maintain balance (see page 53). Traditional method of planting is to set in the soil on the shelf at the edge of the pool, but it is a better idea to plant in sacking-lined baskets. Use a sand/soil mixture and cover surface with gravel. Sink the basket gradually on to the shelf. Many types available. Plant in groups to soften the boundary between the pool and the paved edge			
ACORUS CALAMUS VARIEGATUS	Sweet Rush	2½ ft	3–5 in.	—	Erect, sword-like leaves — rich green with bold cream stripes
ALISMA PLANTAGO	Water Plantain	2 ft	0–6 in.	April–June	Oval leaves — spikes of small pink and white flowers. Remove seed heads
BUTOMUS UMBELLATUS	Flowering Rush	2½ ft	3–5 in.	July–August	Rush-like leaves — purplish when young. Heads of rose-pink flowers
CALLA PALUSTRIS	Bog Arum	9 in.	2–4 in.	May–June	Small, white Arum-like flowers in late spring are followed by red berries in autumn
CALTHA PALUSTRIS	Marsh Marigold	1 ft	0–3 in.	April–May	Cup-shaped yellow flowers borne above clumps of heart-shaped leaves on fleshy stems
IRIS LAEVIGATA	Blue Water Iris	2 ft	2–4 in.	June–September	Excellent choice — typical Iris flowers in white, blue, purple and pink
MYOSOTIS PALUSTRIS	Water Forget-me-not	9 in.	0–3 in.	May–July	Pale green leaves — bright blue flowers are yellow-eyed
PONTEDERIA CORDATA	Pickerel	1½ ft	3–5 in.	June–October	Spear-shaped leaves — blue flowers borne on spikes
RANUNCULUS LINGUA GRANDIFLORA	Spearwort	2 ft	2–4 in.	June–August	Dark green, narrow leaves — large Buttercup-like flowers
SAGITTARIA JAPONICA PLENA	Arrowhead	1 ft	3–5 in.	July–August	Arrow-shaped leaves — whorls of white Stock-like double flowers
SCIRPUS ZEBRINUS	Bulrush	3 ft	3–5 in.	June–July	An attractive Bulrush with stout stems which are striped green and white
TYPHA MINIMA	Dwarf Reedmace	1½ ft	1–4 in.	May–September	Brown heads on Reed-like stems. Good for small pools

FISH

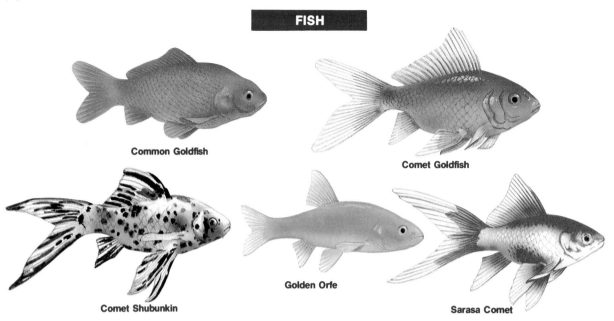

Common Goldfish

Comet Goldfish

Comet Shubunkin

Golden Orfe

Sarasa Comet

Fish add greatly to the interest and charm of a pond and they work for their living by keeping down the mosquito and midge populations. But they do not play a part in maintaining the balance in the pond which keeps the water clear — fish are desirable but not essential.

The main factor which should govern your choice is the size of your pond. If money is no object then you might want to pick the expensive and beautiful Koi Carp. Unfortunately these fish disturb and damage the oxygenating plants. Like all Carps they do not belong in a pool which is less than 80 sq. ft. At the other end of the scale are the hardy and accommodating Goldfish and Shubunkin which are at home in a pocket-sized pond if they are protected from a prolonged ice cover in winter. Between the Koi and the Goldfish is the Golden Orfe, which needs a minimum surface area of about 40 sq. ft.

Another factor to consider is visibility. Here the Goldfish and the more active Golden Orfe are an excellent choice as they stay close to the surface. Tench in black, green or gold are a poor choice as they live at the bottom and are therefore rarely seen.

Always buy from a reputable supplier — the fish should be at the 4 in. stage. They should be in a polythene bag which has been inflated with oxygen. Don't overstock — a good rule is 1 in. of fish body length for every sq. ft of water surface when first stocking your pond. This will give them the space and air supply to grow and you can add a few more fish at a later stage. Keep the bag cool and dark during the journey home, and then float it (covered with newspaper) in the water. Open after an hour or two and slip the fish into their new home.

Don't overfeed — fish will get most of their food from their environment. Supplementary feeding is desirable in spring and summer when the fish are active, but feed only once a day and use floating fish food. Remove any which remains after 10 minutes. Don't worry about holidays — the fish will happily fend for themselves while you are away.

You may want more than fish in your pond — you may want to attract wildlife such as newts, toads, frogs and dragonflies. The most important provision here is a gently sloping section which leads from the pond edge into the water. This will allow birds, hedgehogs and amphibians safe and easy access. Other needs include a pile of stones and logs for hibernation, a boggy area for wild flowers such as Water Avens and Marsh Marigold, and some long grass in which young frogs can hide.

GOLDFISH The **Common Goldfish** has short fins and the usual colour is deep gold. Rather more exotic is the **Comet Goldfish** which has larger fins and a long, flowing tail. Both are hardy — maximum length 1 ft. You will find even more exotic Goldfish in the textbooks and some garden centres — Fantails, Veiltails etc, but they are not hardy and are better suited to the aquarium.

SHUBUNKIN The **Common Shubunkin** is similar in shape to the Goldfish, but its scales are almost transparent and its body is a mixture of black, orange, yellow, red and white. The **Comet Shubunkin** has large fins and a long tail. Maximum length 9 in.

SARASA The **Sarasa Comet** is similar in shape to the Comet type of Goldfish, but it is a white fish with red markings. Very showy — easy to see in the pond. Maximum length 1 ft.

GOLDEN ORFE Pale salmon coloured — more slender and more active than Goldfish. A good choice for the larger-than-average pond. Maximum length 1½ ft.

GOLDEN RUDD Rather similar to the Golden Orfe but with duller colouring. Less visible in the pond than the Golden Orfe but it is a tough fish which can put up with less oxygen and higher temperatures than most other types.

Enemies

Cats and/or birds are usually regarded as the reason for the disappearance of fish, but their role is exaggerated. The hidden causes of most fish deaths are overstocking, disease and attack by insects such as Water Boatmen, Dragonfly nymphs and the Great Diving Beetle. The main bird enemy is the Heron and there is only one way of keeping this predator away from the fish. Wire stretched around the pond at a height of 1½ ft will stop this wading bird from entering the water, but the cure may be regarded as worse than the problem!

Pond Maintenance

SPRING

Fish will become active in April. It is time to start feeding when you see them swimming about — remember not to use too much fish food. April is also the month when you should check that the electrical circuitry is in good order. The pool heater is removed, cleaned and stored away, and the submersible pump for the fountain or waterfall is reconnected. May is the start of the planting season — restocking now will ensure a summer or autumn display. Overcrowded Water Lilies and other aquatics will need to be lifted and divided. This usually happens after 3–4 years, and it is a simple job if the plants are grown in baskets rather than in soil at the bottom or on the shelf of the pond. Pull or cut the plant into 2–3 pieces and re-plant in soil-filled baskets. Fertilizing established aquatics takes place in May and needs some care. Never sprinkle plant food in the water or on top of the baskets — it will feed the algae more than the plants. Use sachets of special aquatic plant fertilizer — push into each basket.

SUMMER

The main job in summer is to enjoy your pond — standing and staring is just as important as the jobs you have to do in spring and autumn. Continue feeding the fish — remove uneaten food after about 10 minutes. In hot and dry weather the water level can drop ½–1 in. in a week. Replace the loss regularly — don't wait until the level is low enough to lead to damage to the liner, fish and plants. Thundery weather poses its own problems for fish — you will see them gulping for air at the surface. To increase the oxygen turn on the fountain or spray the surface with droplets from a garden hose. Continue planting, and remove blanketweed from the surface by raking or winding on to a stick. A job which is often forgotten is the removal of faded flower heads before they set seed. Failure to do this task results in dead organic matter dropping to the bottom of the pond, weakening the strength of the plant, and unwanted seedlings appearing in the pond.

AUTUMN

Autumn is the busiest time of the year for the pond owner. Continue feeding as long as the fish are active and you can continue planting new specimens or dividing overcrowded ones until the cooler weather arrives in September. The big job is the annual clean-up before the onset of winter. As plants fade the foliage and flower stems should be cut down and removed — do not cut the stems of Marginal plants below the water level. Leave Water Lilies and plants with decorative flower heads to the last. Remove as much debris as you can from the pond and make sure that leaves are kept out. The best answer is to stretch small-mesh plastic netting over the surface until nearby trees are bare. A number of tasks must be carried out before the onset of frosty weather. Remove tender aquatic plants (e.g Water Hyacinth and Water Chestnut) and leave them to overwinter in water-filled buckets in a cool but frost-free place. Remove, clean and store the submersible pump and replace with a pool heater.

WINTER

Provided you have carried out the tasks set out for autumn, there is little or nothing to do during the winter months. The fish are now dormant and don't need feeding — the established plants have been cut down and the season is quite unsuitable for new planting. However, a really cold snap does call for attention. Obviously a very small and shallow pool can be turned into a block of ice, which means death to the fish and most plants. For this reason tiny ponds should be covered with boards and sacking if arctic weather is forecast. In a larger pool neither plants nor fish are directly killed by the ice, but there is still a problem. If a sheet of ice covers the surface for more than a couple of days, the gases which are produced by decaying organic matter build up to toxic levels which can kill the fish. Obviously an air-hole is necessary to let the vapours escape. Never forcibly break the ice or the fish will be concussed — you can stand a pan of hot water on the ice until it melts through. But in prolonged cold weather the hole soon freezes over again — the real answer is a small floating pool heater.

A Question of Balance

Each of the components of the pond — water, plant life, soil and dead organic matter must be so balanced as to keep the water free from the dreaded enemy — algae. Algae are either tiny microscopic organisms or long thread-like strands. They will turn the water cloudy and then green if left to develop unimpeded. The secret of successful balance is to create conditions which are suitable for plants and fish but not for algae.

The first need is to keep down the amount of unwanted organic matter in the pond. Remove fallen leaves — as rotting occurs they produce minerals and other products which harm fish, discolour the water and encourage the algae. Do not incorporate peat, compost or manure when potting aquatic plants and do not give more fish food than necessary.

Next, provide some shade — algae are sun lovers. This is achieved by growing Water Lilies and Deep marginals so that their floating leaves cover about a half of the surface. Introduce Floaters if there is insufficient surface cover. Oxygenators are also essential — they emit oxygen which is utilised by the fish and they absorb both harmful minerals and carbon dioxide.

Proper balance is not achieved immediately. The water in a new pool will turn murky and green for several weeks, but it will clear if you have introduced the right plants in the right quantity. Your pond will also turn slightly green and cloudy each spring, but this will soon clear once active growth starts. Pond size is a critical problem — it is difficult or impossible to achieve balance in a small pool — see page 47. Where algae remain a problem filters are available (see page 54) or you can try an algicide.

Moving Water

Moving water adds an extra touch to the pond and most (but not all) water gardeners have or would like to have one or both of the features which produce moving water. The **Fountain** is the easier one to install and is best suited to the formal pool. The **Waterfall** or cascade is much less comfortable in such surroundings — it is more at home in an informal pool which has been created to have a natural look.

At the heart of both features is the pump, and this is driven by electricity. This means that you will need a buried cable — never have electric cables on the soil surface. The basic requirement is for a cable and a waterproof connector to join the electricity supply to the lead from the pump. This connector should be kept wrapped in plastic sheeting. A residual current device (RCD) should be fitted either at the socket or in the consumer unit in the house.

Moving water has an advantage and a disadvantage for the pond population. There is a definite benefit for the fish as splashing water helps to increase the oxygen supply. Water Lilies are not so lucky — the plants suffer and the blooms may refuse to open in rapidly moving water. Moving water does not remove algae, but a filter can be installed at the inlet end of the pump. Such filters must be cleaned regularly.

PUMPS

Electric pumps are available in a wide range of sizes and prices depending on their output, but all of them belong to just 2 basic groups. For the average garden pond a **Submersible pump** is the one to choose — it is cheaper and easier to install. All you have to do is place it in the pond so that it is totally submerged but kept off the bottom by being stood on one or more bricks. Water is drawn in through a strainer and pumped out through a fountain head or along a hose to the top of a waterfall. A filter can be attached to the input end if algae are a problem. Wherever possible the pump should be removed and cleaned in autumn and then stored indoors until spring. If this is not possible then switch on for about an hour each week during the winter when the pond is not frozen. For safety's sake use a 24 V submersible pump with the transformer kept inside the house, but for maximum output you will have to buy a model which uses mains electricity. If you need an appreciably greater flow in order to operate both a powerful fountain and a large waterfall it will be necessary to install a **Surface pump**. This will have to be housed in a dry and well-ventilated chamber situated close to the pond.

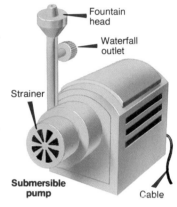

Fountain head

Waterfall outlet

Strainer

Submersible pump

Cable

FOUNTAINS

For many people a formal pond is not complete without a fountain at the centre. The simplest way to introduce one is to buy a kit containing a submersible pump fitted with flow adjuster, fountain head and jet. The traditional jet produces an arching column of droplets — these droplets should not be too fine or drifting will take place in breezy weather. You can, of course, be more adventurous. An off-centre fountain can sometimes be more interesting and will allow you to grow Water Lilies successfully at the other side of the pool. Jets can be supported above the surface at the top of tubes or decorative ornaments and you can buy types to produce solid water columns, water umbrellas or water bells. The main point is that the fountain should not dominate the pond. As a general rule the head of water (the height of the water column above the surface) should be no more than 1/3 of the width of the pond.

WATERFALLS

Waterfalls have a more restricted use than fountains in the average home garden. You do need a sizeable informal pool with a raised area to support both the waterfall and surrounding rockery if this feature is to be effective, and it should be incorporated when the pond is being built. Three construction materials are available — the same three used for ponds and the same advantages and disadvantages apply. Concrete is just too much work, and the rigid liner type is limited in design and quite tricky to install. A further drawback with this latter type is that the surface can look distinctly artificial, especially when the water isn't running. The best course is to make a waterfall out of a flexible liner. Choose butyl sheeting and the usual form is a series of pools emptying into each other. Choose a pump which will produce a flow of 50 gallons per hour per 1 in. width of water across the cascade.

Minipools

There are two reasons for having a miniature-sized pool rather than a regular-sized one. Space can be the problem or there may be young children about and an expanse of water could pose a risk. The minipool is suitable for patio or garden and can be either stillwater or moving water. The stillwater minipool can be made in any container which will hold at least 5 gallons of water, provided it is waterproof, non-corrosive and non-toxic. A flexible liner can be used to create a DIY minipool — a raised miniature pond is both eye-catching and safer for toddlers. Miniature stillwater ponds should be sited in a sunny spot and planted with one or more compact Marginal plants and/or a dwarf Water Lily or two. These ponds are not really suitable for fish, but can house a few Goldfish from late spring to autumn. Moving water minipools are self-contained units which can be placed in the sun or shade. Miniature fountains with one or more decorative basins are available — so are bubble fountains which fall on to pebbles and there are wall plaques which pour into small reservoirs.

Ponds &
Fountains
Illustrated

The small informal pond at its best. ▷
Climbing plants and a small rock garden
provide an attractive backcloth to
this pool, and both Water Lilies and
Marginals brighten up the surface.

◁ *The large informal pond at its best.*
The key feature here is the attractive
setting — much of the charm of a long
stretch of water lies in the reflection of
the trees and shrubs which grow above.

△ *An interesting patio feature at Stapeley Water Gardens.*
Here the small formal ponds are linked by narrow channels, with
a small fountain in one of the ponds to add extra interest.

Most fountains are of the traditional type — one or more jets produce a column of droplets. There are all sorts of alternative types these days — shown here is the bell fountain. ▷

◁ Always aim for a natural look when creating a waterfall. One of the ways to achieve this is to cover the edges and sides with densely leaved plants, as with this Lotus cascade.

△ You need space for a standard pond, but even the smallest garden can accommodate a minipool. Here a lion-head wall plaque spouts water into a pebble-filled reservoir.

LIGHTING

Nothing quite matches the drama of well-planned garden lighting. You have seen how a building which looks drab in daylight can be transformed by floodlighting, and how a thoroughfare may look much more exciting at night when the lights and signs are switched on.

The secret of good lighting design is to highlight certain areas and features, and to leave duller and unused places in the shadows. The lights should not all be set at the same height and you should use more than one type of lighting. As described and illustrated on page 59, spotlighting is used to illuminate a specific feature whereas floodlighting is used to light up an area. Downlighting illuminates paths, steps and low-growing plants — uplighting produces dramatic shadows and backlighting forms spectacular silhouettes.

There are a number of cardinal rules. First of all, don't overdo it — too much light means that shadows and mystery are lost — too much use of coloured rather than plain lights (see page 58) can produce bizarre and unnatural effects. Correct placing is also vital — wherever possible ensure that the lights shine on the objects to be illuminated and not in the eyes of the viewer. And remember your neighbour — spotlights shining into next door's windows have caused many an argument!

The popularity of garden lighting has grown in recent years as more DIY kits have appeared and the garden has been increasingly used as an outdoor living area. But there is a long way to go — for a million or more people, outdoor lighting remains a string of coloured bulbs around an evergreen close to the house at Christmas time. There are non-electrical systems (see page 60) but for nearly all purposes you will need an electric cable. This, of course, deters many people and a mains electric cable will certainly have to be buried deep in the ground. But low-voltage systems are now widely available, and cable laying here is a simple task.

The Uses of Lighting

There is more to garden lighting than impressing friends and neighbours with the sight of your trees and flowers lit up at night. This extension of viewing time is purely decorative and is of course important but so are the other benefits of outdoor lighting — improved safety, increased security and the extension of outdoor living time.

● EXTENSION OF VIEWING TIME

Installing lights within the garden means that the plants and features can be seen at night time. Obviously this is interesting for visitors and passers-by, but the great boon is that you can sit on the patio in warm weather at night or look out the window in winter and see your garden in a way that is quite different from its daytime appearance. To bring out this magic you should aim for separated areas of light, some of which illuminate an attractive living or non-living feature. The winter scene, with plants covered with frost or snow, can be especially attractive, but each season has its own charm. And yet, as stated earlier, the effect is lost if you try to light up the whole garden. The favourite spot for decorative garden lighting is the pond, and that is not surprising. Spotlights give the water of a fountain or waterfall a jewel-like quality, and submerged floodlights transform the rather plain daytime surface into a sparkling sheet. Perhaps the pond is the one area where you can break the rule by overdoing it!

● IMPROVED SAFETY

It is a sad fact of gardening that about 150,000 people are injured each year on garden steps and paths. Some of these mishaps are due to poor illumination, and so it is a good idea to provide lighting at any hazardous point in the garden where people pass by at night. A word of caution. An intense spotlight at the bottom of a flight of stairs or at a sharp turn in a path can do more harm than good. The person on the steps or path suddenly moves out of a cone of bright light and into total darkness, and that can increase the risk of a fall. You should aim for more general illumination with floodlighting which has a wide transition area between light and darkness. For the front steps and driveway you will need strong lighting and this calls for mains electricity — see page 58. For garden paths and steps, however, low-voltage (12 V or 24 V) lighting can be used.

● INCREASED SECURITY

It has been clearly shown that strong illumination around the home at night is an effective deterrent to intruders. In recent years the mains-operated floodlamp with a built-in PIR (Passive Infra-red) detector has become very popular. These lights work during the hours of darkness and respond immediately to body heat, switching on when anyone on foot or by car comes within range. This range of activation can be adjusted, and many types of these security lights are available from DIY shops, garden centres and mail order companies. The usual type is bracket-held and screwed on to the wall above or close to the garage door, but you can also buy post-type PIR detector lights for placing elsewhere in the garden. Do be careful not to put one in a position where it will be activated by every passer-by, and do choose a style which is in keeping with the house.

● EXTENSION OF OUTDOOR LIVING TIME

We have grown accustomed these days to eating, drinking and cooking on the patio when the weather is warm, and it is a pity to have to call a halt to all this when night arrives at quite an early hour in spring and autumn. The answer is patio lighting, which enables us to carry on with these activities long after the sun has set. There is no 'right' type of lighting for this purpose — it's all a matter of compromise. A 200 W floodlight attached to the wall of the house will illuminate an area of about 30 ft x 10 ft — extremely effective for outdoor living but of no decorative value. You can instead use spotlights to pick out features such as the pergola, containers or climber-clothed trellis — much more decorative but less effective if you are trying to cook and serve food. The third alternative is to have several low-powered lamps which provide soft pools of light on the patio — perhaps the most decorative but certainly the least practical.

Mains or Low~voltage?

If you require indoor-type brightness then you will have to use mains electricity at 240 volts. This will provide strong welcoming and security lights at the front of the house, dramatic uplighters and will give you globes which can produce a circle of light 20 ft wide. But all of this is at a price. The work of installation must be left to a qualified electrician and both the cost and disruption will be high. Cables in protective plastic conduits must be laid at least 1½ ft below the surface until the point is reached where you wish to fix either the light or a waterproof plug. Note that the plug must be attached to a wall or firmly-fixed stake — never to a wooden fence which can blow over and sever the cable. The time to think about a mains system is when the garden is being made — for the established garden a low-voltage system is a much better idea. It is cheap to buy and easy to install — you simply draw 12 V or 24 V current from the transformer which is plugged into an indoor socket. Cables can run along the soil surface, but you must be careful not to cut through them when cultivating.

A standard transformer will supply current for up to 6 lights although there are models which will support 12 lamps. The cable is simply pressed on to contact spikes at the base of each lamp. So simple, but you cannot expect dazzling illumination — a globe lamp will light up a circle no larger than 7 ft.

Plain or Coloured?

It is sad that so many people create a perfectly good garden lighting system and then spoil it by having a kaleidoscope of colour. Coloured lights do have a place in the garden. Yellow is less attractive to flying insects on the patio than white light — multi-coloured lights are often used by garden designers in the pond area. But in the general garden the purpose of lighting is to show us the natural colours of the plants and features and perhaps enhance them. So white is the most reliable colour and blue sometimes the most effective. Use other colours with care.

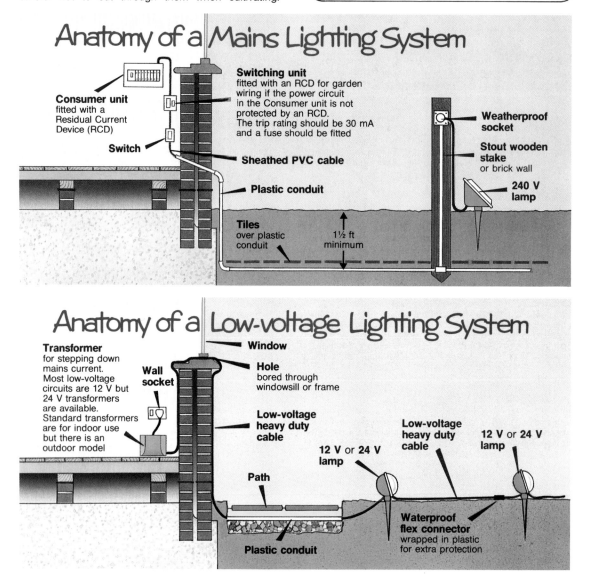

Anatomy of a Mains Lighting System

Consumer unit
fitted with a Residual Current Device (RCD)

Switch

Switching unit
fitted with an RCD for garden wiring if the power circuit in the Consumer unit is not protected by an RCD. The trip rating should be 30 mA and a fuse should be fitted

Sheathed PVC cable

Plastic conduit

Tiles
over plastic conduit

1½ ft minimum

Weatherproof socket

Stout wooden stake
or brick wall

240 V lamp

Anatomy of a Low-voltage Lighting System

Transformer
for stepping down mains current. Most low-voltage circuits are 12 V but 24 V transformers are available. Standard transformers are for indoor use but there is an outdoor model

Wall socket

Window

Hole
bored through windowsill or frame

Low-voltage heavy duty cable

Path

Plastic conduit

12 V or 24 V lamp

Low-voltage heavy duty cable

12 V or 24 V lamp

Waterproof flex connector
wrapped in plastic for extra protection

The Types of Lighting

There are 2 basic types of lighting — floodlighting and spotlighting. Unfortunately both these terms seem to indicate powerful illumination, but the fundamental difference between them is a matter of the spread and not the strength of the beam. The light may be brilliant or quite subdued with either basic type. With floodlighting it spreads out widely and declines gradually at the edges. With spotlighting the beam is confined to a limited area and the edges are quite sharp so that there is only a narrow band between the lit and unlit area. Spotlighting and occasionally floodlighting can be used in 3 special ways — downlighting, uplighting and backlighting.

FLOODLIGHTING

Floodlighting or general lighting is used to produce a diffuse pool of light covering an area rather than an individual plant or feature. Low-voltage types are generally used for decorative purposes rather than for illumination to work by — the halogen type is the strongest.

SPOTLIGHTING

Spotlighting is used to produce a beam which lights up a specific plant, group of plants or an attractive feature. This spotlight effect is due to the nature of the bulb or the use of a holder or shade which constricts the beam into a cone. For bright spotlighting you will need to use a mains-powered 100–120 W spot bulb.

UPLIGHTING

Uplighting is created by having a light which is fixed at ground level and is directed upwards at the plant group or feature. Try to conceal the fixture if possible and for standard uplighting the distance from the feature should be the same as the height of the feature. For an even more dramatic effect place the light at half this distance.

BACKLIGHTING

Backlighting is created by placing the source of illumination behind a tree, arch or other feature. The result is that the object is thrown into relief, standing out starkly as a silhouette against an illuminated background. A good deal of trial and error is necessary to achieve the desired effect — a slight displacement and the light will shine in your eyes.

DOWNLIGHTING

Downlighting is created by having a floodlight or spotlight which is fixed directly or obliquely above the area or feature to be illuminated. Examples include a wall-mounted mains light which is directed on to the patio, a spotlight suspended above a conifer or a small mushroom fixture (see page 60) shining on to the path.

Light Fixtures & Fittings

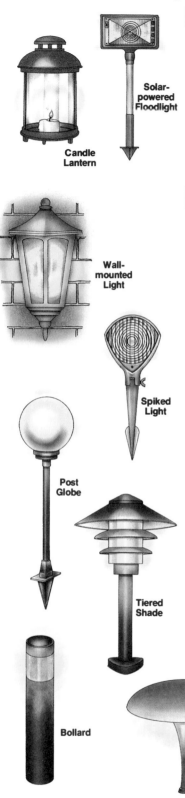

Solar-powered Floodlight

Candle Lantern

NON-CABLE LIGHTING

Garden lighting is not always linked to the mains supply of the house. Candle- or nightlight-filled jam jars suspended from branches or stood on tables have long been used, and these days you can buy fragrant or insect-repelling candles. In larger garden centres and DIY stores there are lanterns fuelled by lamp oil and also bright-burning flares borne on long spikes. A word of warning — all may pose a fire risk and can be hazardous where there are children present. For safety's sake you can use a battery-operated or rechargeable lantern on the patio table. A popular item in some mail order catalogues is the solar-powered garden floodlight — it costs nothing to run but do not expect illumination to work or eat by. The light is a soft diffuse glow which is best used for downlighting a group of low-growing plants.

CABLE LIGHTING

There are several types of **BASIC FIXTURES or FITTINGS**. For illuminating the front of the house or the whole of the patio the usual choice is a **Wall-mounted Light**. This type of fixture is more popular in a mains rather than a low-voltage circuit and the usual types of shade are the bulkhead, lantern, globe or rectangular floodlight — see below. A Wall-mounted unit is screwed on to the wood, brick or stone — the lamp holder may be fixed or mounted on a movable bracket. At the other end of the scale is the **Spiked Light** which is quite easily moved from one spot in the garden to another. The robust metal spike at the base of the fixed or movable lamp holder is pushed into the soil or lawn. The **Post Light** is a feature of many gardens — the solid and permanent Lamp-post type with a lantern shade or the slender Post Globe variety which can be moved from one spot to another. Bollards have the cylindrical shade as an integral part of the post. The **String Light** is a familiar sight at Christmas time — a long mains or LV cable bearing coloured lights at regular intervals. Don't leave it in its box until next Christmas — String lights fitted with plain bulbs give a festive touch to an evening patio party. The **Water Light** can be operated on a mains or low-voltage circuit — floating lamps are available and so are submerged floodlights. Fountains fitted with underwater lights which shine through the spray are quite spectacular.

Some light fixtures only require the right type of bulb to be screwed into the holder and the lamp is complete. With other fixtures some form of **SHADE** is required. A **Bulkhead** shade is made of glass or plastic and fits right against the wall — a **Globe** shade may be frosted or clear, coloured or plain. The **Rectangular Floodlight** has a textured glass face and is available in both mains and low-voltage form, and the **Lantern** in metal or plastic is based on the carriage lamp of old and is top-, side- or bottom-mounted, depending on the fixture. **Tiered** shades are used on Post Lights, and bear a series of narrow metal diffusers which direct the light downwards. **Shaded** shades have a single diffuser at the top but there is some side-lighting — with the metal- or opaque plastic-topped **Mushroom** all the light is directed downwards and this type of shade is useful for illuminating steps and pathways.

Fitting the right **BULB** may be as important as choosing the right fixture and shade. With mains fixtures which do not have a shade the right choice is a PAR (Parabolic Aluminised Reflector) 38 bulb — there are plain and coloured spots and floodlights available. For maximum illumination the best choice is usually a halogen bulb for a mains or low-voltage lamp — the golden rule is that you should use only the type of bulb recommended in the instruction leaflet which came with the fixture.

Wall-mounted Light

Spiked Light

Post Globe

Tiered Shade

Bollard

Mushroom Shade

Water Lights

Lighting Illustrated

The decorative effect of well-placed ▷ lighting is clearly shown here. Three post globes illuminate the finely-divided leaves whilst the rest of the garden is in near-total darkness.

◁ Non-electric lighting has only a small part to play in garden illumination, but this flower-ringed candle in a hurricane lamp provides a charming touch in an old-world garden.

△ For really dramatic effects put lighting and water together. This rather plain pool with two simple fountains and small statue is brought to life by submerged pond lights.

BARBECUES

Until quite recently the idea of cooking outdoors did not occur to the average gardener in this country. Sandwiches, tea and drinks on the lawn had been part of the domestic scene for generations, but outdoor cooking was something for Boy Scouts and Americans.

Things are different today — barbecues became one of the fastest-growing sectors of the garden market in the 1980s and this has continued into the 1990s. There are now more than 5 million in Britain and annual sales are at the 1 million mark. So no longer is it strange to be invited to lunch in summer and find that it is the man of the house who is slaving over the (outdoor) stove. There is no simple or single explanation for this barbecue craze — contributory factors include the rapid increase in the number of patios, the increase in the popularity of barbecue-type food such as hamburgers and hot dogs, and a succession of dry summers.

The range of barbecues now on offer is extensive in both price and variety. You can pay as little as £10 or more than £600 and sizes range from a tiny disposable barbecue to a large wagon with gas-fired grills and warming cupboards. The right choice depends on your personal taste, space available and the depth of your pocket, but there are two basic points you must consider. Firstly, do you want it to be a permanent feature or something you can put away after use? This is not a matter of price — a simple brick barbecue on the patio can be built for about £50 but you can pay ten times that amount for a portable trolley. The second point to consider is the fuel — charcoal for "real" barbecuing or easy-to-use but less romantic bottled gas or electricity?

Permanent or portable, charcoal or gas, you should think where to put your barbecue before you start. The patio is the favoured spot with easy access to the kitchen. Try to keep it some distance away from the neighbours who may be bothered by the smoke and away from over-hanging trees and woodwork which could pose a fire hazard. Use a windshield to protect the heat source from the wind.

And finally a warning which does not appear in the barbecue leaflet. Learn the art by practising on the family first rather than trying out new techniques at a party, and do not cater for more people than your skill and temper will allow. Barbecuing with people all around and with glowing charcoal *is* more difficult than cooking the same food in the kitchen!

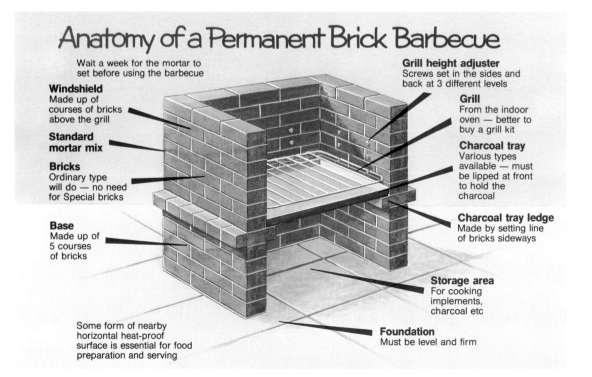

Anatomy of a Permanent Brick Barbecue

Wait a week for the mortar to set before using the barbecue

Windshield
Made up of courses of bricks above the grill

Standard mortar mix

Bricks
Ordinary type will do — no need for Special bricks

Base
Made up of 5 courses of bricks

Some form of nearby horizontal heat-proof surface is essential for food preparation and serving

Grill height adjuster
Screws set in the sides and back at 3 different levels

Grill
From the indoor oven — better to buy a grill kit

Charcoal tray
Various types available — must be lipped at front to hold the charcoal

Charcoal tray ledge
Made by setting line of bricks sideways

Storage area
For cooking implements, charcoal etc

Foundation
Must be level and firm

Barbecue Types

Hibachi

Brazier Barbecue

Kettle Barbecue

The heart of any barbecue is a firebox with a grill (other name — cooking grid) above. With a few types that is all there is. With popular store-bought sorts you will find a couple of refinements — a windshield and legs. In the most complex ones the simple heart of the barbecue is almost lost in a collection of cupboards, warming cabinets, griddle plates, motor-driven rotisserie for spit roasting, kettle cover, tool rack and so on.

The simplest barbecues are designed for use on a flat, fire-resistant surface. There is the **Disposable** or **Once-only Barbecue** — nothing more than a wire-topped shallow tray filled with charcoal. One of the simple re-usables is the **Packaway** or **Brief-case Barbecue** — a simple firebox with a rectangular grill which can be placed in 2 positions, and a plastic case plus handle to make it the ideal picnic barbecue. The other simple re-usable is the **Hibachi** — a cast iron firebox with a long-handled adjustable grill.

The popular type which you will see at the garden centre and DIY store is the portable **Brazier Barbecue**. The sheet metal firebox is round or rectangular and is raised to working level on sturdy legs. The essentials to look for are a windshield (a strong breeze blowing over the surface can double the cooking time) and robust construction. Desirable optional extras include an undershelf below the firebox and a wire warming rack above the grill. A hand- or motor-driven spit is sometimes available, fine for kebabs but there is always the danger of undercooking large pieces of meat or poultry. Wheels can also be a mixed blessing — there is always the temptation of moving the barbecue when it is lit, and that can be dangerous.

A more sophisticated type which has come to us from America is the **Kettle Barbecue**. The essential feature is a large dome-shaped lid which when closed turns the barbecue into an oven so that heat is retained and larger joints of meat and poultry can be cooked. Another sophisticated form is the **Wagon Barbecue** — this is a wheeled trolley bearing folding or fixed work surfaces.

Charcoal is the most popular but not the only fuel. Both **Electric** and **Gas Barbecues** are available — here re-usable lava rock is the material in the firebox and there are several advantages — finger-tip control, no dirt, short heating-up time etc. Gas barbecues tend to be heavy, so buy a wheeled model. For more information see the Fuel section on page 64.

There seems something so appealing in summer about having a **Permanent Brick** or **Stone Barbecue** built on the patio, but it often seems a bad idea in winter when it is a useless feature. Do try a portable barbecue first — if you are still keen then buy a firebox/grill kit and follow the plan on page 62. The bricklaying part really is simple.

Even easier to build is a **Dry Brick Barbecue** — all you have to do is buy a firebox/grill kit and create a tower of 'dry' bricks (without mortar) as shown in the diagram.

Wagon Barbecue

Gas Barbecue

Dry Brick Barbecue

Fuel

Charcoal is the favourite fuel. Use lumpwood charcoal for easy lighting but charcoal briquettes last longer and provide greater heat. Line the tray with aluminium foil to reflect the heat and make cleaning easier. You can buy instant-lighting charcoal but it is more usual to buy ordinary charcoal and use barbecue firelighters or lighting fluid. Remember to use a layer and not a heap of charcoal and light it in several places. The interval between lighting and cooking is about 45 minutes.

One of the no-fuss ways of barbecuing is to use **LPG** (liquefied petroleum gas). There are a number of models available using bottled propane or butane, and these range from simple brazier types to elegant wagons. There is push-button ignition and the barbecue is ready for use in 10–15 minutes. A **Mains Gas** barbecue in heavy cast aluminium is also available.

Electric models using a 2-2.5 kW element are often very sophisticated. Features which are available include automatic timing, vertical grilling, variable heat control and motor-driven spits. The barbecue is ready for use in 10–15 minutes.

Safety

Compared with cooking the evening meal, a barbecue can pose a number of hazards. With charcoal you can have a naked and somewhat unpredictable flame at start-up and occasionally during cooking. There is usually a shortage of work surfaces but no shortage of people clustered around and sometimes trying to help. In addition it is often the man of the house who acts as the barbecue chef ... even though his experience of cooking indoors may be extremely limited. The golden rules are to prepare properly before you begin to barbecue, have just one person in charge of the cooking and keep children and animals well away from the hot surfaces

!

Start early before your guests arrive. The site should be away from inflammable materials such as fences etc and the base must be firm. With charcoal you must use a lighting aid which is recommended for the purpose — see the Fuel section above for details. Never use petrol or cigarette lighter fuel. Heed the warnings in the gas barbecue instruction leaflet about the storage of canisters

!

Wear sensible clothing. The main things to avoid are ties, scarves and loose flowing garments which can so easily touch the firebox when bending over to tend to the food

!

Do not move a barbecue once it is alight. Never pour lighting fluid on to hot charcoal to liven up the fire. Use long-handled utensils — never make do with ordinary kitchen ones and never leave the barbecue unattended

!

Don't be in too much of a hurry. Wait until the charcoal is hot enough (see above) and make sure that food is cooked all the way through — especially important with chicken and sausages

Using your Barbecue

The unique flavour of barbecued meat, fish and poultry is derived in 2 or 3 ways. With charcoal some of the taste comes from wood smoke — for maximum smoky flavour soak hickory or mesquite chips in water and sprinkle a thin layer on to the hot charcoal. With all barbecues much of the flavour is due to the smoke arising from hot fat dripping on to the charcoal or lava rock. Finally there is the taste of the barbecue sauce which is basted on to the food during the cooking process. Many barbecue enthusiasts have their own special (and secret) recipe for this sauce, but for most others the shop-bought bottled variety is quite satisfactory.

To light your charcoal fire use firelighter blocks with small pieces of charcoal on top, or soak lumps in lighting fluid for about ½ hour before lighting. Do not begin cooking before the flames have died down and the charcoal pieces have a cover of grey ash.

Soaking meat in a marinade overnight will both tenderise and give more flavour to the food. The base of a marinade is usually beer, wine or lemon juice.

There are 4 basic long-handled utensils — tongs, fork, basting brush and turner. You will also need a poker for a charcoal barbecue. For the really keen there are all sorts of other items — broilers, skewers, thermometers and so on.

When cooking is finished leave charcoal to burn out and cool down — with gas models the lid should be closed and the gas turned on for about 5–10 minutes to burn off the grease. Clean the grill and tray as soon as they are cool and store indoors. Keep portable barbecues in a shed or garage to protect them from the rain.

Soak wooden skewers in water over-night before using for kebabs. This will reduce the risk of the wood scorching or igniting.

ORNAMENTS

The dividing lines between ornaments, containers and furniture are blurred. Is a stone urn filled with Geraniums an ornament or a container? The definition of an ornament in this book is simple — perhaps too simple. Objects are classed as ornaments if they are distinctly ornamental when not in use. So a large and decorated urn filled with Geraniums is indeed an ornament, whereas a tub or plastic pot filled with Geraniums is a container.

The range of ornaments is vast. Six basic groups are described here, but there are others — Victorian lamp-posts, bird baths, iron weather-vanes and so on. The proper home for large ornaments such as life-sized statues is the Grand Garden, and some styles (French, Italianate etc) demand the presence of such objects. But there is a place for ornaments in the ordinary home garden provided that the basic rule is followed — not too big and not too many.

The two main sites are in and around the pond for added interest and at the end of vistas to serve as focal points. Finding suitable ornaments is part of their charm — the easiest way is to study the catalogues of garden centres which specialise in water gardening. You will also find them listed in the catalogues of specialist suppliers who advertise in gardening and countryside magazines. Garden ornaments can sometimes be found tucked away in junk shops, car boot sales, antique shops and fairs and even in scrap yards.

Remember the effect of weathering. Cast iron becomes more brittle with age and rust can occasionally be a problem. Lead does not rust but it is easily damaged. Rough stone becomes crusted with lichens much more quickly than the smooth type, and soft limestone is soon damaged by rain and frost.

There has been an increase in interest in ornaments, but millions of people continue to dislike the idea of having such things in their garden. Ornaments are not essential unless you are trying to build a Japanese garden, but many plots can be improved by careful choice with regard to style and size of a suitable ornament.

STATUES

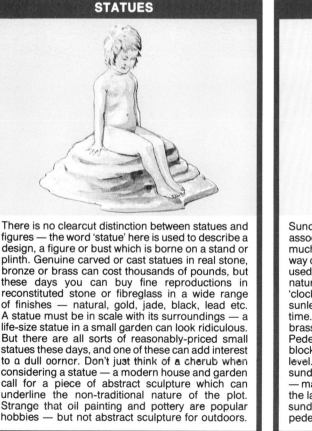

There is no clearcut distinction between statues and figures — the word 'statue' here is used to describe a design, a figure or bust which is borne on a stand or plinth. Genuine carved or cast statues in real stone, bronze or brass can cost thousands of pounds, but these days you can buy fine reproductions in reconstituted stone or fibreglass in a wide range of finishes — natural, gold, jade, black, lead etc. A statue must be in scale with its surroundings — a life-size statue in a small garden can look ridiculous. But there are all sorts of reasonably-priced small statues these days, and one of these can add interest to a dull corner. Don't just think of a cherub when considering a statue — a modern house and garden call for a piece of abstract sculpture which can underline the non-traditional nature of the plot. Strange that oil painting and pottery are popular hobbies — but not abstract sculpture for outdoors.

SUNDIALS

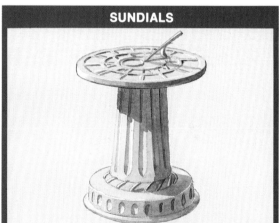

Sundials on walls or pedestals have long been associated with gardens — 400 years ago they were much more common than clocks and were the basic way of telling the time. These days, however, they are used for their ornamental rather than practical nature. 'Apparent solar time' is slightly different to 'clock time' and there is the added complication of sunless days and the introduction of daylight saving time. Sundial plates are generally made of bronze or brass and are sold with or without a pedestal. Pedestals are easily made with bricks or stone blocks, but do make sure that the top slab is perfectly level. Before beginning construction decide how the sundial will have to be positioned. This is simple to do — mark out a N–S line using a compass and note that the large part of the gnomon (the upright part of the sundial) must point due North. Plan and construct the pedestal accordingly.

URNS

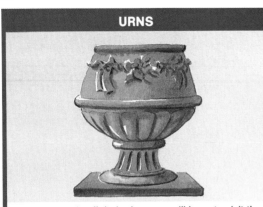

To see urns in all their glory you will have to visit the gardens surrounding stately homes. Starting in the 16th century there has been a vogue to decorate balustrades with these wide-mouthed vases of stone or metal. Designs have long been based on the funerary urns of Ancient Greece and Rome. Some people have found them depressing — Dr Johnson said "Sir, I hate urns. They are nothing, they do nothing, they mean nothing, convey no ideas but ideas of horror". It was the Victorians who found a use for them — the novel idea of using them as plant containers. That is how they are used in gardens today and you can buy reasonably-priced ones in terracotta or reconstituted stone. In addition to urns you can buy lead or simulated lead cisterns which are highly decorated — once used for collecting rainwater but now more generally used as plant containers.

JAPANESE FEATURES

At the beginning of the century there was a Japanese Gardening craze which disappeared before World War 1. In the past few years there has been some renewed interest, and Japanese ornaments are offered in the water garden catalogues and at some larger garden centres. Quite simply, ornaments are essential if you wish to give a Japanese feel to your garden. First come the lanterns — the squat, broad-topped Snow-viewing Lantern *(yukimi-gata)*, the ornate Pedestal Lantern *(tachi-gata)* and the simple Buried Lantern *(ikekomi-gata)*. The Water Basin *(tsukubai)* gives an authentic feel and so do small stone pagodas and carved stepping stones. But don't overdo it — Oriental Maidens, Buddhas and Mandarins are quite out of place. To improve the Japanese feel you will need bamboo fencing, some rocks, an area of water and 'Japanese' plants such as Azalea and Flowering Cherry.

WATER FEATURES

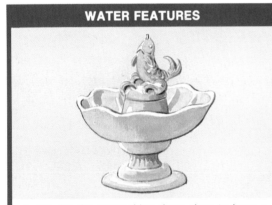

It may be the smart thing these days to have a fountain which emerges from the pool surface and which is illuminated from below at night, but for many people a fountain is a stone figure or statue from which a spray or jet of water emerges. For fountains of real stone and impressive size go and admire them at a Grand Garden — for your own plot look through the catalogues or visit a garden centre and choose a reconstituted stone one. Do make sure that it is in keeping with the pond — it should be stylish enough to enhance it but not big enough to overwhelm it. Some are self-contained (see page 54) and are suitable as ornaments for the patio. All sorts of finishes are available with these reconstituted stone minipools — silver, jade, Oriental red and so on. The designs range from cherubs to abstract modern sculpture.

FIGURES

Apart from water features, figures in reconstituted stone or other materials are the most popular ornaments in the home garden. Unfortunately one immediately thinks of the Garden Gnome — colourful, beloved by children and with its own Protection Society, but a thing of horror for most gardeners. The painted Garden Donkey with a small planter on its back has a similar group of admirers and haters, but we really should look elsewhere. In the garden centre and catalogues you will find a range of attractive animal figures which can be housed close to the pool or in a rockery — not to everyone's taste but certainly not offensive. However, don't overdo it — one or two provide an amusing touch but a stone zoo is not part of good garden design. Human figures are a little more difficult to place, but they can sometimes be used effectively.

Ornaments Illustrated

The sundial is a traditional feature of the ▷ stately home garden — this example serves as a focal point on the lawn at Burford House Gardens. Inexpensive modern-day models are available.

◁ All sorts of figures are sold these days at garden centres and DIY stores. Most designs are quite ordinary but you can find unusual subjects — here a terracotta cat chases a butterfly down the wall.

△ Stone lanterns are an indispensable part of the Japanese Tea Garden. There are several types — in this garden an ikekomi-gata (buried lantern) lights up the pathway and the bamboo fence.

WATERING SYSTEMS

The problem is depressingly simple. Soil bearing an average cover of plants loses about 4½ gallons of water per sq. yd each week in summer and 2 gallons per week in spring and autumn. This requires 1 in. of rain or applied water in summer and ½ in. in spring or autumn. If there is no rain and you have not watered the ground, this water comes from the soil reserve and drying out occurs.

A point is reached when there is not enough water left in the soil to support healthy plant growth. The effect is dramatic with newly-planted shrubs and shallow-rooted types such as bedding plants. Foliage turns dull, leaves roll and wilt, and the final stage is death. Deep-rooted established plants like Roses can also suffer — the visual effect on the foliage is less

obvious but the length of the flowering season is seriously reduced.

The answer, of course, is to water — but to do this properly is not as easy as it sounds. Timing, quantity and method all have to be considered. There are, however, a few general principles:

● **Don't wait too long**. Wilting means you have started too late — begin when the soil a few inches down is dry and plant foliage is dull

● **Don't apply small amounts of water every few days**. This constant soaking of the surface encourages harmful surface rooting and the germination of weeds

● **Choose between point watering and overall watering** — see below and page 69

● **Water thoroughly once you decide to start and repeat if rain does not fall** — see below for details

POINT WATERING

Point watering is used where there is a limited number of large plants to deal with — the methods are designed to restrict the water to the immediate zone covered by the roots of each plant.

It is essential to use enough water to get down to the lower roots and not merely to drench the top inch or two of soil. This calls for 1–4 gallons of water per plant, depending on the size of the shrub or tree. Hold the hose or spout of the watering can close to the base of the plant and apply water slowly.

There is no easy way during a period of drought to determine the right time to repeat this watering. Dig down with a trowel and examine the soil at 3–4 in. below the surface. If it is dry, then water. As a general rule you should water about every 7 days if rain does not fall.

The main problem with using a hose or watering can is that the water tends to spread beyond the root zone and may run off on a sloping site. The pot and basin watering techniques described on the right are designed to stop this happening.

GARDEN HOSE

The most practical method for point watering — use the hose without a nozzle or on the jet setting if one is present. The basic type of hose is the round type. Always buy a reinforced double-walled brand — the single-walled ones tend to kink and may leak. Lay-flat tubing is easy to use and lightweight — worth considering. Neither type should be left as a heap on the garage or shed floor — contain them on a suitable holder as noted on page 69. There are 2 types of fittings — screw-on and quick-release. Both are satisfactory, but make sure you buy compatible attachments and connectors.

WATERING CAN

Vital for point watering a few plants or containers but quite impractical for large areas. Choose your can with care — it can be metal or plastic and it should have a capacity of 1½–2 gallons. Look for a long spout with a narrow end and do not use it for applying weedkillers.

Pot watering is a useful method where a limited number of large plants (e.g Tomatoes, Dahlias) are grown. Bury a large flower pot near the base at planting time — *don't* delay this task until later or the roots will be disturbed. Fill the pot slowly with the required amount of water.

Basin watering is a useful method for large shrubs or Roses growing in free-draining ground which dries out quickly. Build a ridge of soil around each bush and fill this basin using a hose pipe or watering can each time you water.

OVERALL WATERING

Overall watering must be your choice if you have a large area to cover and many plants of various sizes. This technique involves drenching the whole of the planted-up site rather than restricting the water to the root zone of each plant. Some people use a watering can with a rose, but you really need a hose pipe if watering is not to be a prolonged chore. The usual procedure is to walk slowly along borders and around beds with a hand-held hose fitted with a suitable nozzle. A sprinkler makes the job easier and is essential for all but the tiniest lawn. Perhaps the best method of watering vegetables and shrubs is the sprinkler hose but it is expensive.

Watering must be thorough or you may do more harm than good. With overall watering apply 2–4 gallons per sq. yd, using the higher amount in midsummer, in sandy soils and with high-risk plants. If rain does not fall it will be necessary to repeat the operation — see 'point watering' on page 68 for details.

The commonly-used methods of overall watering are shown on this page — less common are the sophisticated techniques such as buried hoses fitted with pop-up sprinklers, and travelling sprinklers which move slowly over the area to be watered. There are also metering units which turn the water on and off at set times.

GARDEN HOSE WITH NOZZLE

The most practical method of overall watering plants, but not suitable for lawns. For large plants, water around the base of the stems and not over the leaves. Use a fine spray setting for small plants — be careful not to disturb soil and dislodge plants.

Hoses should always have a holder. Round hoses are wound on a reel which may be static, wheeled or mounted on the wall. A simple version is shown below — it is a better idea to buy a 'through-feed' type as the hose can be used without the reel having to be unwound. Lay-flat tubing is bought in a cassette — choose the type which is fitted with built-in rollers which squeeze out the water.

Round hose reel

Lay-flat tubing cassette

SPRINKLER HOSE

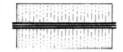

Basically a flattened hose pipe bearing a series of fine holes on the upper surface. A long rectangular spray pattern is obtained — excellent for vegetables and shrub border. Check if local authority allows this type of hose.

WATERING CAN WITH ROSE

Quite impractical for overall watering in anything larger than a tiny garden. Choose the 1½–2 gallon size. You will need 2 roses — a fine one for seedlings and a coarse one for older plants. Use the rose pointing upwards to avoid damaging plants.

STATIC SPRINKLER

The simplest type of sprinkler. Water output is high and pattern is quite even, but area covered (25–30 sq. yd) is relatively small. Buy stalked model for beds and borders — use a ground-level one for lawns.

ROTARY SPRINKLER

Two or three rotating arms produce a circle of fine droplets over 60–80 sq. yd. Some types are adjustable for fineness of spray and area covered — stalked models are available. Very popular.

PULSE-JET SPRINKLER

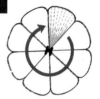

Expensive, but a larger area (approximately 300 sq. yd) is covered than with the other types of sprinkler. A single jet produces a narrow arc of droplets, the jet rotating as a series of pulses. Choose a stalked model for borders.

OSCILLATING SPRINKLER

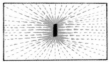

A horizontal tube bearing a series of small holes slowly oscillates from side to side. A rectangular spray pattern is obtained, so gaps and overlaps on the lawn can be avoided. All are adjustable for area covered.

BIRD FEATURES

The proper construction and siting of bird features are extremely important. Our aim is to attract robins, finches, nuthatches, starlings, blackbirds, sparrows, thrushes, tits, goldcrests and others to the garden — poor siting and the lack of protective elements in the features can make the birds easy prey for predators. The Royal Society for the Protection of Birds offers both advisory leaflets and a range of well-designed feeders and nest boxes. If you want to make your own, carefully follow the requirements set out below.

Winter is the time when feeders and bird baths come into their own. At this time of the year food and unfrozen water may be in short supply, and many birds lose their natural shyness. Set out the tit-bits in the morning and you must supply food regularly once you start. The birds will come to rely on you and can die if the supply is suddenly cut off. Clear away uneaten scraps before adding more food and provide a supply of water. The feeding season extends from October to April. During spring and summer the birds should hunt for their own food — your well-meaning provisions may be quite unsuitable for rearing young chicks.

These chicks are raised in the nest, and as a general rule nest building should be left to the birds as they instinctively pick safe and suitable sites close to a natural food supply. Many wildlife-minded gardeners like to help by providing nest boxes — hole-fronted ones for tits, nuthatches and tree sparrows, and open-fronted boxes for robins and blackbirds. Putting up these boxes is recommended, but only if they are the right size and in the right site. The time to put one up is between September and November.

Anatomy of a Bird-friendly Garden

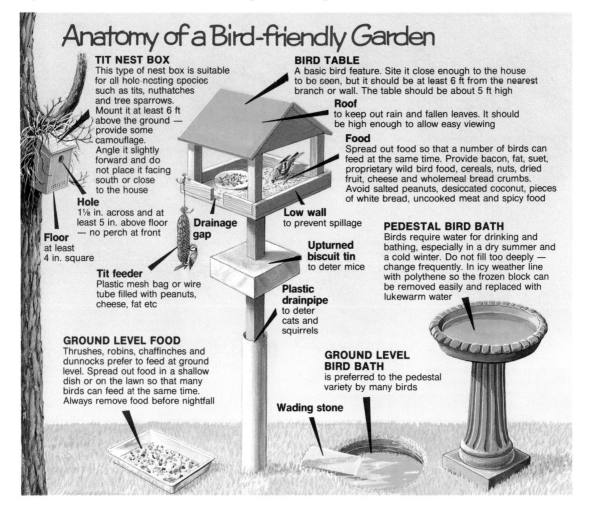

TIT NEST BOX
This type of nest box is suitable for all hole-nesting species such as tits, nuthatches and tree sparrows. Mount it at least 6 ft above the ground — provide some camouflage. Angle it slightly forward and do not place it facing south or close to the house

Hole
1⅛ in. across and at least 5 in. above floor — no perch at front

Floor
at least 4 in. square

Tit feeder
Plastic mesh bag or wire tube filled with peanuts, cheese, fat etc

Drainage gap

BIRD TABLE
A basic bird feature. Site it close enough to the house to be seen, but it should be at least 6 ft from the nearest branch or wall. The table should be about 5 ft high

Roof
to keep out rain and fallen leaves. It should be high enough to allow easy viewing

Food
Spread out food so that a number of birds can feed at the same time. Provide bacon, fat, suet, proprietary wild bird food, cereals, nuts, dried fruit, cheese and wholemeal bread crumbs. Avoid salted peanuts, desiccated coconut, pieces of white bread, uncooked meat and spicy food

Low wall
to prevent spillage

Upturned biscuit tin
to deter mice

Plastic drainpipe
to deter cats and squirrels

PEDESTAL BIRD BATH
Birds require water for drinking and bathing, especially in a dry summer and a cold winter. Do not fill too deeply — change frequently. In icy weather line with polythene so the frozen block can be removed easily and replaced with lukewarm water

GROUND LEVEL FOOD
Thrushes, robins, chaffinches and dunnocks prefer to feed at ground level. Spread out food in a shallow dish or on the lawn so that many birds can feed at the same time. Always remove food before nightfall

GROUND LEVEL BIRD BATH
is preferred to the pedestal variety by many birds

Wading stone

CONTAINERS

Flower-bedecked tubs and troughs now stand at the fronts and backs of houses down every suburban street. These items were not commonplace half a century ago when gardening was all digging, hoeing and mowing, but the use of containers is as old as gardening itself. Just think of the Hanging Gardens of Babylon, the large tree-filled tubs of Ancient Greece and the terracotta pots packed with Gillyflowers in Elizabethan gardens.

The reason for the heightened interest in recent years is easy to understand. The increase in the number of apartment blocks has meant that there are balconies to fill, and the dramatic growth in the number of patios has meant that there are bare paved areas to clothe.

Containers everywhere — but it is not easy to agree upon an exact definition. Perhaps the simplest approach is to regard a container as a receptacle for growing plants which is not open to the garden soil below. This means that a raised bed created on open ground is a *bed* — when built on paving it is a *container*.

Containers are usually bought as such from garden centres, hardware stores or mail order companies, but they are a DIY feature for some gardeners. This involves buying a non-garden object (old sink, chimney pot etc) and turning it into a container or buying a DIY kit to make a wooden or other type of container. Alternatively some begin from scratch and make a large container out of brick, wood or reconstituted stone. Shop-bought or home-made, containers range in size from small pots to man-sized urns, which means that making the right choice is not easy. Obviously you will be guided by your own personal taste and the depth of your pocket, but general guidelines are set out on page 75.

In a tiny garden the display from containers may be more important than the open ground features, but in most cases the pots and troughs are restricted to just a few well-defined areas. These containers can be used singly or grouped with others. When grouping it is usually wise to have a limited range of *types* (wood, plastic etc) but a distinct range of *sizes* — wide and tall ones with smaller pots or troughs around them. The experts tell us that an odd number is better than 2, 4 etc.

Container gardening is set fair to increase in popularity, which is not surprising when you consider the advantages set out on page 75. There is, however, one distinct disadvantage — frequent watering is essential in summer and this may mean using a watering can or hose daily during a dry spell. Regular feeding every 2–4 weeks is also required. Another drawback you must avoid is the likelihood of a container blowing over if it is small and the planted-up specimen is tall. On an exposed site use a heavy tub which is at least 1½ ft across and 1 ft high if leafy and reasonably tall plants are grown.

Anatomy of a Container Garden

Front door & Porch
An excellent place for containers — either singly or as a pair of matched pots. Careful selection and maintenance are essential as the display must always be in first-class condition

Path or Steps liner
A line of identical pots or troughs can enhance the appearance of a plain walkway or flight of steps

Focal point
A large container or a group of smaller containers can be used to provide a focal point. Attractive trees and shrubs have an important role to play here — pot and plants must be in scale with the surroundings

Patio
The favourite place these days for free-standing containers. The starkness of bare walls and paving slabs is relieved by the presence of plants. Bedding plants and bulbs are the usual planting material

Balcony
Trailing plants to grow over the container and climbers to clothe the railings are widely grown. Use a lightweight container and a peat-based compost. Exposure to strong winds can be a problem

Hanging basket
A popular feature these days — about a third of gardens have one. The best site is partly sunny during the day and is protected from strong winds. Remember daily watering may be necessary in summer

Window sill
Window boxes add colour and interest to dull walls and windows. The construction material and its colour should not detract from the plants — make sure that the box is firmly attached

Greenhouse
Planting vegetables in the border soil can create all sorts of problems — the greenhouse is usually filled with pots and growing bags which contain suitable growing media

Container Types

RAISED BED
Unlike ordinary containers the raised bed is truly part of the patio. A number of walling materials can be used (brick, reconstituted stone, wood etc) — choose one in keeping with the setting. Rockery perennials can be planted in the wall face during construction.

WINDOW BOX
Buy one or make your own — ensure that it is sturdy and that there is adequate drainage.

'SCRAPYARD' CONTAINER
Many scrap items can be used — demolition yards provide some. Chimney pots, old sinks and baths, old car tyres etc.

HANGING BASKET
Buy an open-sided basket for all-over planting or a closed-sided one to prevent dripping.

STONE CONTAINER
Natural stone containers are very heavy and expensive — reconstituted stone ones are much cheaper and are available in a wide assortment of sizes and finishes.

PLANT POT
The basic container where practical considerations outweigh ornamental ones. Fibre pots have a natural look but last only for a couple of years. Plastic pots continue to take over from clay as they are cheap and not fragile.

GROWING BAG
Nearly all greenhouse Tomatoes, Lettuce and Cucumber are grown nowadays in these containers. Cheap, but only use for ornamental display if you intend to cover the plastic surface with trailing plants.

PLASTIC CONTAINER
A variety of heavy-duty plastics (polypropylene, polystyrene etc) is used to make pots and troughs in all sizes. Very popular, light-weight and inexpensive. Wide range of surfaces and colours is available. Drawbacks with ordinary plastic pots and troughs are that sunlight makes them brittle and heat insulation is poor.

WOODEN CONTAINER

Extremely practical and suitable for most situations — thick wood is an excellent heat insulator. Shop-bought or do-it-yourself, make sure that the wood has been properly treated with a preservative. Many types are available — the most popular form is the half-barrel. Check that the boards are not split and the metal bands are secure.

METAL CONTAINER

Many old planters were made of lead, iron or copper — no longer popular. Paint inside with Arbrex.

FIBREGLASS CONTAINER

Pre-cast concrete and fibreglass are often used to create containers where large size and low cost are required.

NOVELTY CONTAINER

The range of unusual containers is enormous — wheelbarrows, coal scuttles, litter baskets etc.

SINK GARDEN

An old glazed kitchen sink makes an excellent container for rockery perennials. Raise up on bricks and use a gritty soil-based compost.

GLAZED POT

Glazed earthenware pots are not often seen in gardens these days, but they are still very useful where a Mediterranean or Oriental look is required. They are breakable and generally expensive.

STRAWBERRY POT

These terracotta pots have sides which are perforated and are used for planting Strawberries or herbs. The strawberry barrel is a larger version and is made of wood instead of clay.

TERRACOTTA CONTAINER

Strictly speaking, any baked clay container is terracotta and that includes the humble clay plant pot. But the term is usually reserved for hand-made high-quality clay pots, tubs and troughs. These items are brittle and lose water more rapidly than other containers. Check that they are frost-proof — some makes are not.

Filling a Tub or Trough

STEP 1:
PREPARE THE CONTAINER
Make sure the inside is thoroughly clean if the container has been used before. Soak if material is porous. New wood must be treated with a water-based preservative. Half-barrels may be charred with a blowlamp for protection against rotting

STEP 4:
ADD THE PEAT LAYER
Add peat to reduce the cost of compost if the container is large — the compost layer above need be no more than 9 in. deep

STEP 6:
PLANT UP THE CONTAINER
Plant firmly. A 1–3 in. watering space should be present after planting. Water in immediately

STEP 3:
ADD THE DRAINAGE LAYER
Cover the drainage holes with crocks or a fine mesh screen. Add a layer of rubble or gravel to help drainage and stability. Omit this stone layer if weight is a problem

STEP 5:
ADD THE COMPOST LAYER
Add moist soil-based or peat-based potting compost or Multicompost. Press this layer down gently with your hands

Always use a wheeled trolley if you have to move a filled and heavy container from one part of the garden to another

STEP 2:
PUT THE CONTAINER IN PLACE
Move the container to the chosen site. This should be firm and level — raise the container above the surface if possible

Filling a Window Box

STEP 5:
PLANT UP THE CONTAINER
Plant firmly — the compost should be level with the soil mark on the stems. Some people prefer to use pot-grown plants and to leave them in their pots — in this case ordinary peat can be used to fill the box. A 1 in. watering space above the surface should be present after planting. Water in immediately

STEP 1:
BUY OR MAKE THE WINDOW BOX
If you decide to make one, use ¾ in. thick hardwood. The minimum depth and width should be 8 in. and the length should be about 2 in. less than the sill length. Use water-resistant glue and brass screws — drill ½–¾ in. wide drainage holes in the base at 4–6 in. intervals

STEP 4:
ADD THE COMPOST LAYER
Add moist peat-based potting compost or Multicompost. Press this layer down gently with your hands

STEP 2:
ATTACH THE BOX TO THE WALL
Attach the empty box to the wall before filling and planting — moving a filled box can be dangerous. Use strong steel brackets — make sure fixings are large enough to support the weight to be carried. An optional extra is a drip tray filled with gravel below the drainage holes

STEP 3:
ADD THE DRAINAGE LAYER
Cover the drainage holes with crocks or a fine mesh screen. Add a 1 in. layer of gravel to help drainage. Omit this step if weight is a problem

The advantages of Container Gardening

- **Ground is not needed** Paved areas, pathways, water-logged soil etc will support containers — you don't even need a garden. Plants can be grown right next to the house and patios can be decorated.
- **Display is improved** Small and dainty plants are easier to see — the various types can be grown at different levels by grouping pots together. Arrangements can be easily altered. Attractive pendant plants can be grown, and so can delicate types requiring the protection of a wall.
- **Some of the work is easier** There is no digging — in addition planting, weeding and dead-heading are easier to do as less stooping is involved. But some jobs are more tedious — watering can be a chore in dry weather.
- **Plants not suited to your soil can be grown** Your soil may be cold, heavy and badly drained, making it unsuitable for many plants. With container growing you use a compost which is known to be suitable.
- **Less chance of pest damage** Plants get some protection against slugs and soil pests.
- **Eyesores can be hidden** Manhole covers can be masked and plain front doors can be transformed with flower-filled containers.
- **Tender plants can be grown outdoors** In the autumn planters containing tender perennials such as Palms and Orange trees can be brought into a conservatory or greenhouse. The plants are brought out again in the spring when the danger of frost is passed.
- **Plants can be moved away once the display is over** A potted Rose bush in full bloom obviously deserves a prime spot, but once the flowering season is over you can move the container to a less prominent site.
- **Plants can be taken with you when you move** Portable containers and the plants they hold are not fixtures and can be taken with you if you decide to move.

Choosing a Container

- **Is it large enough?** Large containers do not have to be watered as frequently as small ones, and you will need considerable planting space if you propose to grow a large shrub or a bedding scheme containing tall-growing dot plants. Containers with vertical sides will need less frequent watering than those with sharply sloping sides.
- **Is it small enough?** The container, the plant and the site should all be balanced. The pot or trough may be too large for the display and site.
- **Is it attractive enough?** Remember that the pot or trough may be devoid of flowers for part of the year. Make sure the material is in keeping with the house and style of garden. Ornate pots may be out of place in a small modern garden and plain plastic is certainly out of place in a large old-world one. Bright plastic colours are undesirable almost everywhere.
- **Is it strong and durable enough?** Not generally a problem with shop-bought pots and troughs, but it can be with odd objects pressed into service. Will it hold the weight of compost required and is the surface truly weatherproof?
- **Is it free-draining enough?** There should be at least one hole (½ in. or more across) every 4–6 in.

Plants

Most tubs and troughs are used for spring-flowering bulbs and summer bedding plants to provide a colourful and often very effective display. But there are several other groups of plants which are suitable for containers and it is worthwhile being more adventurous.

BEDDING PLANTS

Your container garden should never be empty even if you rely solely on bedding plants. The summer bedding display should be followed in autumn with a planting of spring-flowering bedders (Polyanthus, Bellis, Myosotis etc) in some containers and winter-flowering types (Universal Pansy, Polyanthus 'Crescendo' etc) in others.

As a general rule it is wise to pick more compact varieties than are used in outdoor bedding and set them more closely together than you would do in a garden bed. The standard pattern is to have tall plants at the centre of free-standing containers or at the back of pots or troughs placed against a wall. Favourite summer types include Petunia, Geranium, Marigold, Lobelia, Nasturtium, Impatiens and Begonia.

BULBS

Tulips (species, double early and single early), Narcissus (triandrus, cyclamineus and jonquilla), Muscari, Hyacinth and Crocus of course, but you can try a few less usual types — Galanthus, Fritillaria, Tigridia, Erythronium and Ornithogalum are examples.

CONIFERS

A good choice for a year-round focal point. Container conifers include weeping types (Cedrus deodara 'Nana Aurea'), narrow columns (Juniperus virginiana 'Skyrocket'), spreading plants (Juniperus media 'Gold Coast') and round balls (Chamaecyparis lawsoniana 'Green Globe').

TREES & SHRUBS

A tree or shrub can form the permanent centrepiece in a large container or it may be used as the sole occupant. Trimmed Box and Bay have been used for generations to frame doorways and line pathways, and more and more people these days are discovering that containers are for shrubs and not just for bedding plants. Types which have proved their worth include Acer palmatum, Azalea, Phormium, Hydrangea, Camellia, Cordyline, Bamboo, Yucca and Fatsia. Roses, Weeping Cherry, Holly and Clematis — all do well in pots and troughs.

HERBS

Pots of herbs grown close to the back door are welcome in winter, when a trip to the vegetable garden may be a cold and muddy trek. All the popular types will grow quite happily in pots — Chives, Sage, Parsley, Rosemary, Mint, Thyme and so on.

FRUIT & VEGETABLES

Here the range is more limited. Pot-grown fruit include Fig, Strawberry and dwarf varieties of Apple, Plum and Gooseberry — vegetables for containers include Tomato, Cucumber, Runner Bean and Aubergine.

PLAY AREAS

If you have small children then for both their sake and yours it makes sense to create a child-friendly garden. This does not mean turning your plot into an amusement park nor does it mean having a single play feature with which you hope to keep a youngster amused for hours. A child-friendly garden must make you both happy — an attractive yet child-safe place for you and a fun-filled place for them.

The benefit for you is that you can get children outside the house and out from under your feet. The benefits for them are fresh air and more space in which to play. It all sounds such a good idea, but all too often both minor and major problems arise.

The minor problems first. Top of the list is boredom. Pushing a child outdoors should not mean exclusion from all their toys indoors to an expanse outdoors with nothing to do but kick a ball. There should be things to do, and here you have to think like a child rather than like an adult. An expensive see-saw or a solidly-built playhouse may seem a splendid idea to you, but children often prefer a range of simple objects

for their make-believe games — tea-sets, sheets and boxes to construct their castle or pirate ship, buckets and spades and so on. A second minor problem is damage to the garden — pots knocked over, broken flower stems etc. Annoying but only rarely serious, and you can reduce the risk by giving the children part of the garden for themselves. This need not be a permanent arrangement — in later years the sand pit can be transformed into a flower bed or pond and the swing can become an arch for climbing plants.

The serious problem is the risk of accidents. About 100,000 children are treated in hospital each year as a result of mishaps in the garden. The danger time is the toddler to nursery school stage — children are active between the ages of 2 and 5 but with little sense of danger. You must never trust to the good sense of a small child. So many tragedies, and yet nearly all are avoidable if you follow the simple safety rules on page 77.

Illustrated below are the various features you can find in the child-friendly garden. Of course not all are necessary at the same time as they cater for different ages, but do consider them all if both the garden and the family are large.

Anatomy of a Child-friendly Garden

Wild area
Older children want an area where they can play and not be seen from the house. Ideally there should be trees, logs etc for make-believe games

Nature area
A bird table and bird bath give children the chance to study nature close at hand

Paddling pool
An inflatable one is best — empty after use and put away. Great fun on hot days, but never leave a toddler unattended

Cycle track
Some designers advise a path around the garden along which children can ride their bicycles or tricycles

Low fence
A low fence around the border or beds will give protection against rolling balls and some protection against trampling feet

Lawn
An essential feature for ball- and chasing-games. Place goalposts away from windows

Sand pit
A ground-level sand pit or raised sand box is a great delight for toddlers. Make one (see page 77) or buy one — site it close to the house so you can keep a watchful eye

Playground
An equipment area for older children — a strong arch which can hold swing or climbing rope. Other alternatives are slide, see-saw or climbing frame. Base should be soft grass or bark chippings

Children's garden
A very useful feature if the whole garden is not enclosed by a fence. A simple picket fence with a gate keeps children from wandering away and provides an area which they can feel belongs to them. Provide a soft base (grass or bark chippings) and include items such as a playhouse, miniature furniture, flower bed for seeds, etc

Safety Rules

WATER A toddler can drown in a few inches of water — never allow a child under 3 to go near an unguarded pond or to play in a paddling pool without supervision. Protect a pond with a fence or wire mesh cover if children play nearby — consider turning it into a sand pit if protection is not practical. Empty paddling pools when not in use — cover water butts.

GATES & FENCES Make sure that small children can't wander into the road. The best answer is secure fencing with a child-proof gate around the whole garden or else a small section earmarked as a child's garden. Slatted fencing should be vertical rather than horizontal to deter climbing. Where fencing is not practical, constant supervision is the only answer.

GLASS Glass and children definitely don't mix — both can harm each other. Balls can break glass — glass can cause horrific injuries to a colliding child. Keep the play areas far away from the greenhouse and cold frame and do consider using safety glass or a shatterproof glass substitute. Remove objects next to greenhouses, patio windows etc on which children can trip.

PETS Parasites occur in about a quarter of cat and dog droppings. Humans are rarely affected, but the result is serious when it does occur and children are admitted to hospital every year. Dispose of droppings promptly without handling them. It is especially important to cover a sand pit or box when not in use — pets regard an uncovered area of sand as a most desirable toilet.

EQUIPMENT Buy play equipment to BSI standard — don't make your own if you are unskilled. Secure firmly and maintain regularly. Make sure that all wood is sanded down and coated with exterior varnish. Sink nails and screws below the surface. Swings are a major problem — give young children a harness seat and make sure waiting children do not stand too close.

SITING Play areas for small children should be in sight of the kitchen window if possible, and close enough for you to hear their cries if a tumble occurs. Older children usually want some privacy — a trellis screen is useful here. Never put a swing, slide or climbing frame on stone or concrete — provide a base of grass, bark chippings or proprietary play matting.

PLANTS Some seeds and berries (Yew, Hellebore, Lords & Ladies, Juniper, Laburnum, Daphne, Foxglove etc) may be harmful. Teach young children not to eat *any* berries, flowers or leaves — later on you can show them the dangerous ones. Do not set a bad example by picking and eating fruit or vegetables when in the garden with small children.

MISCELLANEOUS Keep tools, machinery and chemicals well away from children, especially when in use. Do not leave rakes, shears, spades and forks lying about — hang them up. Paths are for walking — lawns are for running. Keep paths free from moss, algae and lichen. Do not allow the use of old kitchen equipment such as ovens or fridges as playthings.

Making a Sand Pit

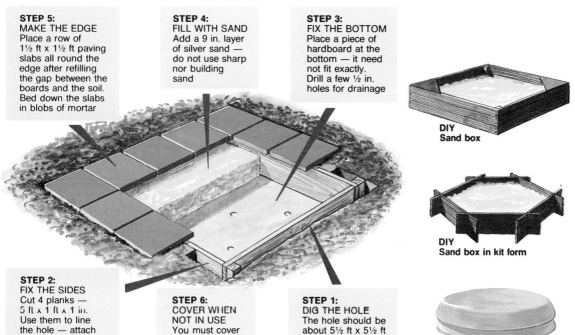

STEP 5:
MAKE THE EDGE
Place a row of 1½ ft x 1½ ft paving slabs all round the edge after refilling the gap between the boards and the soil. Bed down the slabs in blobs of mortar

STEP 4:
FILL WITH SAND
Add a 9 in. layer of silver sand — do not use sharp nor building sand

STEP 3:
FIX THE BOTTOM
Place a piece of hardboard at the bottom — it need not fit exactly. Drill a few ½ in. holes for drainage

**DIY
Sand box**

**DIY
Sand box in kit form**

STEP 2:
FIX THE SIDES
Cut 4 planks — 5 ft x 1 ft x 1 in. Use them to line the hole — attach to 1½ ft x 2 in. x 2 in. pointed stakes driven into the ground as shown

STEP 6:
COVER WHEN NOT IN USE
You must cover the pit after play in order to keep out rain, cats and dogs

STEP 1:
DIG THE HOLE
The hole should be about 5½ ft x 5½ ft and 14 in. deep. Spread a 2 in. layer of sand on the surface

**Ready-made
Plastic sand box
with cover**

Play Areas Illustrated

A toddler strolls into his own garden — once the gate is shut he is out of harm's way. No great outlay is involved — both the fencing and plastic playhouse are inexpensive. ▷

◁ *For many children the sand pit is the favourite play area feature — the wooden surrounds of this one serve as bench seating. When no longer required the site can return to lawn or patio.*

△ *Sunken sand pits, wooden playhouses and timber-framed swings require bases and careful erection — these plastic, metal and cloth units are much more easily erected and dismantled.*

FURNITURE

Making the Right Choice

In the early years of the 1980s an idea took hold — small gardens as well as large ones are for living in and are not merely places for working in and admiring. As a result the sales of outdoor tables and chairs increased dramatically, and now two-thirds of all gardens have outdoor furniture.

There are basically two types of garden furniture — permanent and foldaway. Permanent types stay outdoors throughout the summer, although cushions may have to be brought in at night. In winter most of these tables and chairs are left in the garden, but the lighter ones in plastic or resin may be stacked and stored in the garage or shed. All fitted furniture such as brick-and-wood patio benches and tree seats (see page 82) belong here, of course, and so do all heavy items such as cast iron chairs.

Where outdoor space is very limited or when seating is required for only a short time then foldaway furniture is the obvious choice. The deck chair is the traditional example, but folding metal chairs and recliners are now the best sellers.

The usual plan in furnishing the garden is to begin with enough foldaway chairs and recliners for the family to use on the patio or lawn, and then a patio set (table, chairs and a sunshade as an optional extra) is bought. The standard routine is to buy ready-made furniture — kit-made tables and chairs are much less popular and DIY furniture is quite rare.

No longer need you settle for a group of deck chairs and a folding table. Nowadays there is furniture for all tastes and all pockets, so you can relax in a deeply-cushioned recliner with a built-in sunshade, adjustable foot stool and detachable table with drinks holder.

The big problem with buying garden furniture these days is trying to make up your mind which items to buy. There is such a wide and bewildering range available in garden centres, DIY stores and mail order catalogues, and each year a new influx of styles arrives to make the chairs you bought a few years ago seem positively old-fashioned. So before buying anything answer the following questions — you will find that there is only quite a small range which suits your particular requirements.

WHAT IS THE MOST IMPORTANT NEED — APPEARANCE, COMFORT OR CONVENIENCE? Some chairs and benches are used as focal points — in the larger traditional garden a Victorian-style cast iron seat or wooden bench can indeed be an eye-catching feature, and so **appearance** is all-important here. At the other end of the scale you may want a recliner or sun lounger on which to spend many blissful hours — a pleasant appearance, yes, but here it is **comfort** which is all-important. By all means try it out first. Are the cushions really comfortable? Does the back recline as far as you wish? Can it be easily moved to keep you in full sun? Is there a foot rest? Your quest may be for a table and chairs to allow you to dine outside — here **convenience** considerations are the most important ones. Is the table really steady and sturdy? Are the chairs at the right height? If the site is uneven, are the table legs adjustable? For regular dining buy permanent furniture. With all types of foldaway furniture, convenience is of prime importance — is it easy to fold up and carry to the garage or shed?

WHAT SORT OF STYLE & SIZE ARE RIGHT FOR THE GARDEN? The style should be in keeping with the garden — an ultra-modern Continental chair has no place in a cottage garden. But size is even more important — the furniture may fit the catalogue beautifully but it can be far too overpowering on your small patio. Where space is very limited, look for chairs which are stackable or can be pushed under the table and consider foldaway rather than permanent items.

DO I WANT THE FURNITURE OUT ALL YEAR ROUND? There are several reasons why you may want a permanent rather than a foldaway item. You may require it to serve as a focal point or to be built into the patio, storage space indoors may not be available or you may want the patio to look like an outdoor room all year round. The usual reason is to avoid the chore of bringing out the chairs every time you want to relax. Not all materials are suitable — iron screws and bare steel will rust and non-waterproof cushions will rot. Choose cast iron, cast aluminium, hardwood or moulded resin.

HOW MUCH CAN I AFFORD? Bargain furniture is sometimes a good buy, but much of it lasts for only a year or two. The golden rule is to pick the type of construction material you can afford, and then buy a good quality make in that material.

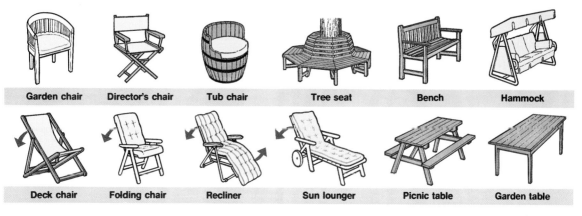

| Garden chair | Director's chair | Tub chair | Tree seat | Bench | Hammock |

| Deck chair | Folding chair | Recliner | Sun lounger | Picnic table | Garden table |

STONE

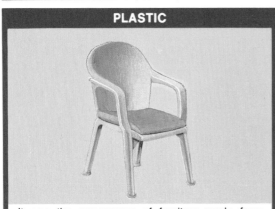

The straight or curved bench in real stone is part of many of our Grand Gardens, but for the ordinary garden such an item is hideously expensive and often quite out of place. However, in a large plot a seat made from reconstituted stone can make an excellent focal point at the end of a path or border. An air of solidity and permanence is provided, and the cost is remarkably reasonable — the price is appreciably less than that of a hardwood bench of similar length. A modern use of reconstituted stone is to build a combined seat/planter using blocks and slabs. An example is shown on page 83 and is not a difficult DIY job — an alternative is to build a combined seat/barbecue on the patio. The drawback is lack of comfort, but stone seats are not meant for long-term lounging. The usual way of dealing with the problem is to make cushions to fit the top of the seat and to remove them when not in use.

WOOD

Hardwood has long been a favourite construction material for permanent furniture, the wood being used alone or in combination with cast iron. Chairs, benches and tables are available in teak and iroko — look for a label stating that the wood has been obtained from a managed forest. This furniture is available in both ready-made and kit form, and is always expensive. Softwood tables and chairs are much cheaper, but rotting is a danger here. The answer is to make sure that the wood has been pressure-treated and to retreat or repaint regularly. When buying wood furniture make sure that the surface is smooth and free from cracks. Check that rust-proof screws have been used. Wooden furniture comes in a remarkably wide range of styles — there are tables, chairs, recliners and sun loungers in sawn timber and rustic poles. In addition there are converted barrels and hollowed-out logs.

PLASTIC

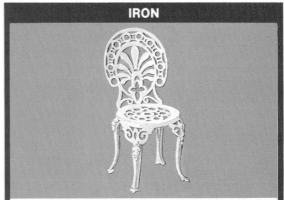

It was the appearance of furniture made from injection-moulded plastic which heralded in the popular 'living outdoors' revolution. Here at last was a way of buying robust tables and chairs for garden dining which could be left on the patio throughout the summer, and yet was a fraction of the price of the traditional permanent furniture materials such as hardwood and cast iron. The range of styles and colours is large, and the units are tough and lightweight. This lack of weight is a mixed blessing — good when moving the chairs but bad when they topple over in high winds or under over-active children. Maintenance is very easy — simply wipe or hose down with water. Quality is variable, so be wary of unusually cheap offers. Plastic furniture becomes brittle and colours tend to fade after prolonged exposure to sunlight, and this can happen very quickly with low-grade plastic.

IRON

Cast iron was the material loved by the Victorians — in parks and Grand Gardens around the country you will still see examples of the ornate flowery styles in chairs and benches made a hundred or more years ago. A heavy and uncomfortable material, but obviously long-lasting. Genuine 19th century benches in cast iron are prohibitively expensive for most gardeners, but you can buy reproductions which look as good (but not as old) as the real thing. Maintain properly — see page 108. The seat part of the bench may be in iron or hardwood — in either case you will need cushions if you intend to sit for long on cast iron furniture. Wrought iron furniture is less robust, but this can be an advantage in a modern setting. Many attractive designs of tables and chairs are available — you can find curved, round or square iron rods supporting glass or other types of table top.

ALUMINIUM

A lightweight and rust-proof material which is used in two distinctly different ways in the production of garden furniture. The better known use is with the alloy form for the construction of inexpensive and lightweight folding chairs and tables. You will find these putaway chairs and recliners with their canvas or cushioned seats everywhere — garden centres, garages, DIY stores, mail order catalogues etc. Try them before buying — they should be easy to open and free from dangerous catches. Store away when not in use — aluminium is not affected by rain but the iron and steel parts will quickly rust if left outdoors. The second use of this metal is in cast form to produce lightweight and inexpensive reproductions of cast iron furniture. Cast aluminium furniture is also produced in modern designs and is available in ready-made or kit form with a white or black gloss finish.

TUBULAR STEEL

A strong material which is widely used for constructing hammocks, tables and some forms of garden seating. The prices vary widely depending on style and quality, but tubular steel furniture is generally less expensive than resin. It is especially important not to be tempted by bargain offers when buying this type of furniture. The reason is that naked tubular steel would quickly rust, and the price of the item is often a reflection of the quality of the protective weatherproof coating. Wherever possible, tubular steel furniture should be stored indoors during the winter. The problem is that although the frame is rust-proof if properly coated, scratched areas and the steel springs and fittings soon become rusty. No problem with storing chairs perhaps, but hammocks and tables usually have to stay outdoors. Resin is a better (but dearer) choice.

RESIN

Magazine articles on garden furniture written during the early years of the 1980s do not mention resin as a construction material — looking through many of the catalogues in the early years of the 1990s gives the impression that resin (also known as GRP) is the *only* material available. This blend of plastics and fillers is rapidly becoming the No.1 material for chairs, recliners and tables — it is more solid than ordinary plastics, it doesn't scratch and the colours do not fade. Styles are usually (but not always) distinctly modern and it is the favourite material for Continental furniture. Resin is in the medium-price range, and is certainly an excellent choice if you can afford it. The usual colours are white and grey. Fittings are generally rust-proof, so resin items can be used as permanent furniture. Lightweight, durable even when stood outdoors all year round, and with easy maintenance — just wash or hose down.

OTHER MATERIALS

The seven basic construction materials used in the manufacture of outdoor furniture have been described in this section. Over the years some like cast iron have declined in popularity and others such as resin have quickly established themselves as new favourites. Outside this group of seven there are several materials which are occasionally used. The most important of these are the bamboo, rattan and willow used for chairs and tables. Often comfortable, sometimes attractive in a traditional way, these cane items have an important drawback. They are damaged by rain, and should therefore be kept indoors and brought out for the day. Other miscellaneous materials include glass for table tops, natural or man-made rope for true hammocks slung between trees and finally fibreglass in the manufacture of tables and chairs. In ancient times grass- and herb-covered seats were popular.

Making a Tree Seat

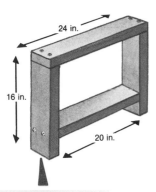

24 in.

16 in.

20 in.

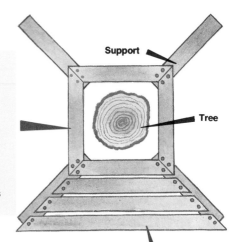

Support

Tree

STEP 2:
SECURE THE SUPPORTS
Firm the soil around the tree —
lay paving slabs to form a firm
and level base. Decide on the
size of the hole around the tree
which will be enclosed by the
seat — make sure this hole will
be large enough to allow the
tree to increase in girth.
Now cut a 4 in. x 1 in. board to
the desired length, using 45° end
cuts and attach to 2 supports, as
shown. Attach remaining supports
around the tree in similar fashion

STEP 1:
PREPARE THE
SUPPORTS
Make 4 sets of
supports using
4 in. x 2 in. boards
of cedar or
pressure-treated
softwood.
Use brass screws
to support the
cross pieces

STEP 3:
SECURE THE
SEATING
Attach the next
row of boards
around the tree,
once again
screwing into
the supports
and leaving
a ½ in. gap
between the
boards.
Continue until
there are 4 rows
of seating
boards around
the tree

Making a Patio Bench

STEP 2:
SECURE THE SEATING
Use 2 planks of durable wood such as teak or cedar — pressure-treated softwood
is a cheaper but less satisfactory alternative. Use rust-proof screws to secure
the planks to the tops of the piers — butt the pieces of wood together

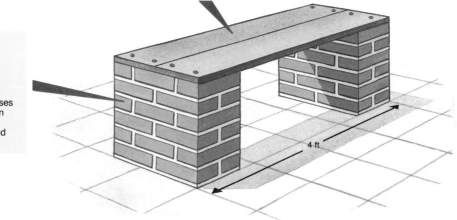

STEP 1:
ERECT THE
PIERS
Make sure the
base is firm and
level. Build each
pier using 6 courses
of brick, as shown
in the diagram.
The 2 piers should
be 4 ft apart

4 ft

Making a Border Seat

STEP 1:
FIX THE FIRST SUPPORT
For each support cut 2 posts — 2½ ft long x 4 in. x 4 in. Set them 2 in. apart in concrete at the edge of the bed or border, anchoring each post 9 in. deep. Make sure the tops are level. About a week later attach the 2 cross pieces (1½ ft x 4 in. x 2 in.) as shown using brass screws

STEP 3:
SECURE THE SEATING
Cut the required number of hardwood strips — 4 ft x 2 in. x 1 in. You will need 9 to cover the space between a pair of supports — butt these strips closely together and secure each one with brass screws driven into the cross pieces at each end

STEP 2:
FIX THE OTHER SUPPORTS
Set the next support 4 ft away — install the remaining supports until the desired seat length is reached

Making a Seat/Planter

STEP 2:
ADD THE FINAL TOUCHES
When the final course of blocks has been laid, add the line of paving slabs to serve as seating and complete the planter with coping blocks — cut to fit. Leave to dry for a couple of days before using the seat — add cushions for comfort. Fill the planter with compost — see page 74 for details

STEP 1:
BUILDING THE STONE FRAMEWORK
Draw a plan to fit your patio. The seat should be about 1½ ft high and 1½ ft square. Paving slabs can be used as seating material. The planter should be 2½–3 ft high. The base must be firm and level. Use reconstituted stone blocks and thin layers of mortar, leaving weep-holes at the base of the planter — see page 5

Furniture Illustrated

This Chiswick Seat made by Chatsworth Carpenters represents the top end of the range. Hand-crafted, hardwood-based — an investment for one's grandchildren. Excellent in the right setting. ▷

◁ *From luxury in the picture above to do-it-yourself utility here. A simple patio bench made with brick piers and wooden planks. A seat for people at a barbecue meal, perhaps, but definitely not for lounging or snoozing.*

△ *The long dominance of the simple chair and the slatted wooden table on the lawn has gone. Now we can buy resin furniture with a degree of comfort and an air of luxury which may surpass the dining room suite indoors!*

ROCKERIES

The rockery or rock garden has never regained the popularity it enjoyed in Victorian times, but this garden feature is making a comeback. The sight of alpine plants tumbling over well-laid stones is indeed an attractive one, but do think twice before deciding to make a rockery. The simple truth is that no other aspect of the garden combines the need for such a high degree of design sense with an equally high level of sheer hard work.

Considering the design side first, most of the rockeries we see in home gardens miss the point. A rock garden should have a natural feel to it, as if it could be an actual outcrop even though we are not fooled for a moment. Instead we so often see overgrown and wholly unnatural rocks sticking out of the ground. The problem here is that we cannot just look up a rockery plan in a book and then go out and order the bits as we can for a fence or patio. With a rockery the final result is governed by the shapes and sizes of the stones you use, and no two loads of stones are alike. The answer is to read the general principles of construction in this section, go and see one or more examples of good design in a botanical garden and then draw up a rough plan once the stone is delivered. There are a few basic rules — use stones of different sizes but all of the same type, do not use too many and keep the slopes fairly gentle.

Now for the hard work. Moving a ton or two of stone and then setting out the rocks at different levels are strenuous tasks — read the 'Moving Stones' section on the next page before you begin. The hard work story doesn't end there — the rock garden is labour intensive as hand weeding, dead-heading and trimming have to be carried out regularly.

There is, of course, a credit side to creating a rock garden, and that is what makes the feature worthwhile for so many gardeners. A bank with a pond at the base makes a rockery almost obligatory, and a flat uninteresting site can be enlivened by this feature. There are two basic types. The **Sloping Rockery** is the more satisfactory — a series of tiers rising backwards gently until the highest point is reached on an artificial or natural bank. The **Island Bed Rockery** is more difficult to create and usually appears less natural — earth and stones are laid on a flat bed to create an outcrop — aim for a series of irregular and broken tiers leading up to a flat plateau at the top.

Anatomy of a Rockery

Key stone
A large and attractive stone. This is the first rock to be laid

Site
Pick an unshaded spot — rockery perennials are sun lovers. Keep well away from overhanging trees — the drips from wet foliage in summer and fallen leaves in winter can be fatal. Clear away all perennial weeds before construction begins

Grain (Strata)
These lines should all run the same way — never have a mixture of horizontal and vertical

Small stones
Wedge together into a group — plant alpines in the crevices

Joints
These should run vertically — do not stagger the joints as if you were building a wall

Grouping
Place rocks in groups rather than in a continuous line one stone high

Grit mulch
Place a layer of small stones around the plants. This mulch will conserve moisture, suppress weeds and keep roots cool

Planting pocket
This area should slope slightly backwards. Consolidate the planting mixture firmly

First tier
The starting point of the rockery. Each stone should tilt slightly backwards and ⅓–½ should be buried. Firm the soil at the base and back of the stone — do not leave air pockets

Planting mixture
2 parts soil
1 part peat or bark
1 part grit or coarse sand

Drainage layer
Good drainage is essential. In free-draining land this layer is not needed — in heavy soil remove the topsoil and add rubble topped with gravel

A 10 ft x 5 ft rockery requires 1–2 tons of stone

Stone Types

There is no single 'right' way to obtain stones for your rockery. There is, however, a distinctly wrong way — it is illegal to go out into the countryside and collect your own.

The usual advice is to find a local quarry, see the sort of rocks they supply and order enough to meet your requirements. It is certainly wise to find a source as near to home as possible, since transport is a high proportion of the cost, but in some areas of the country there is no local quarry. The best general approach is to look up 'Stone Merchants' in Yellow Pages and ask for samples and quotes from some of the listed companies.

There are numerous types of stone used in rock gardens — the best choice depends on locality and personal taste.

LIMESTONE

The great advantage of this type of stone is that it weathers quickly, so that the surface loses its sharp edges and lichens soon appear. The drawback is that the grain may be less pronounced than on sandstone rocks. The colour is often (but not always) grey. The most popular limestone is weathered Westmorland Stone — white or grey and seen in gardens everywhere. Other grey-coloured limestones include Derby and Forest of Dean Limestone — the creamy ones are Cotswold and Purbeck Stone.

SANDSTONE

The advantage here is that the grain is usually bold and attractive but the rock is usually slower to weather than limestone. The exception is Sussex Sandstone which loses its angular bits quite quickly and is a popular type for rockeries in the South of England — Kentish Ragstone is another type which is often seen. Yorkstone is very hard and is better for paving than rockeries — Millstone Grit is a good choice if you want a sand-coloured rockery and Gloucester Red will give you a brick-coloured one.

OTHER TYPES

Granite is not usually a good idea. It is very heavy and the rocks remain sharply angular for a long time. **Slate** has its uses, but the blue, purple or green pieces are usually quite flat. **Tufa** is an excellent choice — this stone is a porous form of limestone plus fossilised organic matter. It is only half the weight of ordinary stone and it is penetrated by the plants' roots. **Artificial Stone** (hollow rocks made of concrete) is also lighter than traditional stone, but is less satisfactory.

Moving Stones

You will be able to move small stones by simply carrying them, either alone or with assistance from a helper. Remember the golden rules — knees bent, back straight, hold the load evenly and then straighten knees with elbows close to your thighs. Never stoop over to grasp the rock and never jerk suddenly to raise it above ground.

You will be able to tackle rocks weighing ½–1 cwt in this way, but in a large rockery you will need some stones which weigh appreciably more. One of the best aids for medium-sized rocks is a sack trolley — you will have to lay down a trackway of boards on soft ground. Do not use a single-wheeled garden wheelbarrow as the load can easily tip over.

Some stones are too large for a sack trolley and these pose a problem. You can make a track of wooden planks and roll the rock along by turning it over with a crowbar, but it is often easier to use the method employed by the Ancient Egyptians when building the pyramids. Support 2 or 3 planks on about 4 logs set at right angles to serve as rollers. Lever the large rock on to the planks and then slowly push the structure along, moving the back roller to the front as you progress.

For the largest rockeries a winch may be necessary, but this is rarely needed when building a rock garden at home.

Plants

Rockery perennials ('alpines') are the most important plants in the average rock garden, but you should add other types as described below. The general rule is to use some bold plants such as dwarf conifers and shrubs as single specimen plants and to grow smaller plants in groups. Do aim to have colour and interest all year round.

ROCKERY PERENNIALS

Be careful if you use the most popular types — Cerastium, Alyssum saxatile, Aubrietia, Arabis and Saponaria. They are easy to grow but they are also invasive and will quickly overrun more delicate types if not kept in check. Fill cracks with rock-hugging plants such as Saxifraga, Sempervivum, Draba, Thymus etc. Bolder plants such as Hypericum, Primula and Pulsatilla can be used to produce colourful drifts.

CONIFERS

Make sure that the varieties are classed as 'dwarf' or 'slow-growing medium' and are not merely young specimens of tall-growing types. Aim for variety — for example blue upright (Juniperus virginiana 'Skyrocket'), golden upright (Chamaecyparis lawsoniana 'Ellwood's Gold') and green upright (Juniperus communis 'Compressa'). There are also blue prostrate (Juniperus horizontalis 'Glauca') and green globular (Pinus mugo 'Gnom'). See The Tree & Shrub Expert for a detailed list.

SHRUBS

Popular ones include Acer (Japanese Maple), Hebe, Pieris, Miniature Rose, Deutzia, Daphne, Rosemary, Azalea, Skimmia, Erica and Calluna.

BEDDING PLANTS

Don't sneer at these in the rockery — when used in moderation they can provide a bright splash of colour throughout the summer in an uninteresting area.

OTHER PLANTS

Dwarf bulbs, ferns and grasses should be included.

Rockery Rejects

For nearly 100 years fanciful names have been given to poorly-designed rockeries. Despite changes in taste the two examples shown below have always been criticised by designers and yet are still found in gardens today.

The Currant Bun

The Dog's Grave

Rockeries Illustrated

Stones rather than plants dominated ▷
the first rock gardens built in Britain —
this modern version of 'rockwork'
represents a limestone outcrop
studded with conifers, Rhododendrons
and rockery perennials.

◁ *Alyssum saxatile, Aubretia deltoidea and*
a pocket of Tulip 'Oriental Splendour'
clothe the weathered stones in this
example of a Sloping Rockery. No choice
alpines, but the effect is still satisfactory.

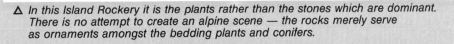

△ *In this Island Rockery it is the plants rather than the stones which are dominant.*
There is no attempt to create an alpine scene — the rocks merely serve
as ornaments amongst the bedding plants and conifers.

GREENHOUSES

In millions of gardens throughout the country the greenhouse is a much-loved and well-used feature. Here Tomatoes are grown, garden plants are overwintered and pot plants are raised. Seeds are sown, cuttings are taken and there is something very comforting about working in a well-run greenhouse. You are warm and dry when the wind is blowing or the rain is falling outside, and the results depend entirely on your skill rather than on the vagaries of soil type and weather.

All very appealing, of course, but before rushing out and buying your first greenhouse do consider three points. Firstly, greenhouse growing is not a matter of common sense — you will have to learn a lot of new skills. Secondly, quite a lot of work is involved. Constant attention is needed when the plants are growing, and this means every day in summer unless you install an automatic ventilator and an automatic watering system. Finally, take the money-saving claims with a pinch of salt. An average-sized heated house will cost you about £300 and the fuel bill will be about £100 per year to keep the temperature at a minimum of 42°F in winter — it certainly won't pay for itself.

So greenhouse growing is not a simple pastime for occasional action nor is it a money-making proposition. It is instead an absorbing hobby which enables you to produce plants earlier than outdoors or which cannot be grown in our climate. All sorts of shapes and a wide range of sizes of greenhouses are available, but the fundamental difference between one house and another is the minimum temperature at which it is kept. The **Cold House** is the simplest — no artificial source of heat is provided and so in winter the temperature will almost certainly fall below freezing point. Despite this, the cold house extends the growing season by trapping the sun's heat during the day. Tomatoes are the favourite crop — during the rest of the year there are cuttings to take, seeds to sow and early vegetables to grow.

The cold house is rather limited as you cannot grow frost-sensitive plants in winter and early spring. The usual practice is to turn it into a **Cool House** in which winter temperatures do not fall below 42°–45°F. You can now grow 'greenhouse plants' — Azalea, Cineraria, Cyclamen, Freesia, Streptocarpus and many more. Half-hardy bedding plants can be raised and a succession of flowering plants can be grown for the living room. Try to buy the next size larger than you have planned as most people who purchase a greenhouse soon run out of space. Keep it as a cool house by installing a simple heater — see page 91.

The attraction of having a **Warm House** (minimum temperature 55°F) is the ability to grow exotic semi-tropical plants but such conditions are undesirable for some plants and you will have a fuel bill of about £300 a year. The **Stove House** with a minimum temperature of 65°F is for the tropical plant specialist and not for you.

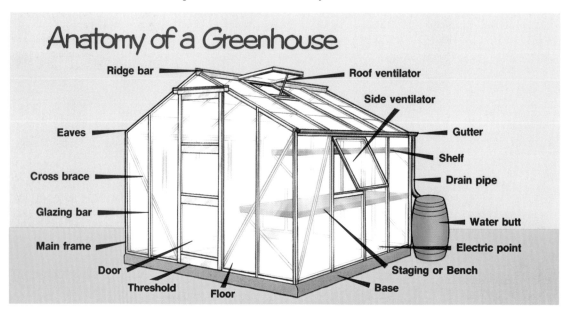

Anatomy of a Greenhouse

Ridge bar
Roof ventilator
Side ventilator
Eaves
Gutter
Shelf
Cross brace
Drain pipe
Glazing bar
Main frame
Water butt
Electric point
Door
Staging or Bench
Threshold
Floor
Base

Greenhouse Types

SPAN ROOF

The traditional style has vertical sides. Use of space and heat is efficient, and enclosed lower part cuts down winter heat loss. Choose an all-glass version for growing-bag and border crops.

THREE-QUARTER SPAN

Lighter and more airy than a lean-to — useful for growing wall plants such as Grapes and Figs. Expensive, however, so the choice should be between a span roof house or a lean-to.

LEAN-TO

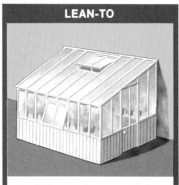

Useful for a south- or west-facing wall. House wall stores heat so the fuel bill is reduced. This is the usual conservatory pattern — an interconnecting door makes it part of the home.

DUTCH LIGHT

Sloping sides and an even span roof — angled glass makes it warmer and brighter than a traditional span roof house. Also more stable, but supporting upright plants from floor to roof is more difficult.

CURVED HOUSE

There is floor to roof glass with glazed panels. These form a smooth curve up to the ridge without the distinct angle at the eaves as occurs in the span roof and Dutch light. Supporting upright plants is difficult.

POLYGONAL

Many sides — six, seven or nine. Basically ornamental — attractive when filled with pot plants and sited close to the house. Expensive, however, and not a good buy if you want maximum space for your money.

DOME

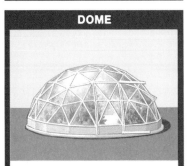

Three advantages — attractive appearance when filled with flowers, maximum stability and maximum light absorption. The major drawback is its unsuitability for growing tall crops effectively. Ornamental rather than practical.

MINI-HOUSE

Very useful where space is strictly limited — a lean-to which will accommodate the plants but not you. Treat as a cold house, but small size can mean a very rapid rise in temperature in summer. Keep an eye on the thermometer and open vents as necessary.

POLYTUNNEL

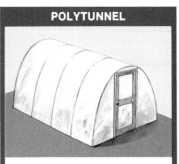

Plastic sheeting is stretched across a series of metal hoops — this is the cheapest form of greenhouse. Good for low-growing crops such as Lettuce and Strawberries, but not really suitable for Tomatoes and Cucumbers.

Greenhouse Features

SIZE

The standard sizes are from 6 to 20 ft long and widths of 6, 8 or 10 ft. The one you choose will depend largely on the money and space available — remember the annual cost of fuel as well as the initial outlay. The most popular sizes are 8 ft x 6 ft and 10 ft x 8 ft — choose the larger one if you plan to have staging on both sides. If you intend to grow Tomatoes the height to the eaves should be at least 5 ft and the ridge height about 7 ft. It is more difficult to control the environment in a small house than in a large one where the greater size reduces the problem of draughts and sudden fluctuations in temperature.

Length	Width	Height to eaves	Height to ridge	Eaves to ridge	Volume	Surface area	Approximate glass area
6½ ft	4½ ft	5 ft	7 ft	3 ft	175 cu. ft	158 sq. ft	150 sq. ft
8 ft	6 ft	5 ft	7 ft	3½ ft	288 cu. ft	208 sq. ft	195 sq. ft
8 ft	8 ft	5 ft	7 ft	4½ ft	384 cu. ft	248 sq. ft	235 sq. ft
10 ft	8 ft	5 ft	7 ft	4½ ft	480 cu. ft	286 sq. ft	270 sq. ft
12 ft	8 ft	5 ft	7 ft	4½ ft	576 cu. ft	324 sq. ft	305 sq. ft

FRAME

Aluminium alloy has taken over from wood as the most popular material. It is cheaper than wood, requires no maintenance and the thin glazing bars mean more light within the house. Warping of the ridge does not occur and re-glazing is a simple matter. There are several minor drawbacks. Aluminium greenhouses lose slightly more heat at night than wooden ones and condensation drips are more likely to occur. The metal frame is received in bits and so construction is usually more difficult than with a timber model. A white bloom occasionally appears on aluminium frames — this is normal and nothing to worry about.

Wood is considered by many to be more attractive than metal, especially in an old-world setting. There is no need to bore holes to attach staging, support wires etc — nailing or fixing hooks is a simple matter. Buy western red cedar, teak or oak. Treat every few years with a water-based preservative or linseed oil. Pressure-treated softwood is cheaper — treat occasionally with Bio Woody. Untreated softwood is a poor buy — regular painting is necessary.

Galvanized steel greenhouses are no longer popular. They are heavy, hard to erect and rust can be a problem when the surface is scratched.

uPVC is the latest material. It is generally quite expensive, but maintenance requires nothing more than an occasional washing down.

PROPAGATOR

Cuttings need a moist and reasonably warm atmosphere in order to root satisfactorily. Seeds of some important plants, including Cucumber and Tomato, require a temperature of 60°-75°F in order to germinate properly. Obviously it would be ridiculous to create these conditions throughout the greenhouse — a heated propagator is the answer. A propagator is a plastic or aluminium container with a glass or transparent plastic cover. Choose one heated by electricity rather than by paraffin, and look for thermostatic control and one or more ventilators at the top of the cover. There are mini-greenhouses in which you can keep tropical plants in stove house conditions, but you will need something much simpler. There should be enough floor area for at least 2 seed trays and enough headroom to hold pots containing 6 in. high plants.

STAGING & SHELVING

Benches or staging are essential if you grow pot plants — constant stooping to ground level would add backache to greenhouse gardening. The two terms are interchangeable in popular use, but strictly speaking staging is a permanent structure whereas a bench can be removed. The basic choice is between a perforated and a solid surface. Slatted wooden staging about 2½ ft above the ground is the traditional form. Air can circulate in winter, cutting down the risk of disease. Solid staging lacks this advantage, but it can conserve heat in winter. Shelving is a miniature form of bench which is secured at head height to house small pots or trays when space or sunlight is restricted. Nowadays you can buy metal benches and shelves as an optional extra. Collapsible types enable you to grow bedding plants and bulbs at a convenient height in spring and then you can dismantle the benches in summer to grow Tomatoes in growing bags. A portable potting bench is a good idea — use a wooden or metal tray with solid sides to hold compost, trays and pots when taking cuttings, filling seed trays etc.

GUTTERING

Guttering is a useful extra as rainwater dripping from the roof can undermine the foundations. Some models have built-in guttering as a standard fitting — check before you buy. The water from the gutters should be channelled to a soakaway or into a plastic water butt. The butt should have a tight-fitting lid to keep out leaves and other debris. Experts do not agree whether such water is safe to use for watering greenhouse plants — never use it if the water is obviously polluted.

FLOOR

The traditional pattern for the floor of the greenhouse was to have one or both sides as border soil for growing plants and a central pathway covered with pea shingle, concrete, concrete slabs or wooden slats (duckboarding). The pathway remains as important as ever (rammed soil is not satisfactory) but most experts no longer recommend using border soil for growing annual plants such as Tomatoes. The reason is a build-up of diseases and other problems in the soil. Growing bags and pots are preferred these days. If you plan to use the border soil, dig in 4 oz per sq. yard of Growmore plus a liberal amount of garden compost well before planting time. Do not plant the same crop in the border year after year. If you don't intend to have borders then concrete the whole area or cover the ground on either side of the pathway with shingle.

DOOR

Hinged or sliding — both types have their disciples. Sliding doors can be used as an extra ventilator and they don't slam shut. But hinged doors generally fit better and so are less likely to be a source of draughts.

HEATING

The unheated or cold greenhouse is a place for Tomatoes and Cucumbers in summer, Chrysanthemums in autumn and alpines, bulbs and cacti in winter. Some form of heat is needed if you wish to extend this range — the usual plan is to maintain a minimum temperature of 42°–45°F (cool greenhouse) during the depths of winter. The ordinary gardener can forget about higher temperatures — the fuel costs are prohibitive.

A wide choice of fuels is available — coke, coal, wood, natural gas, bottled gas, oil and electricity. Gone are the days when everyone had to rely on hot water pipes heated by a coal- or coke-fed boiler. Nowadays the popular choices are paraffin, bottled gas and electricity. The appeal of paraffin is obvious — heaters are inexpensive and you don't need an electric cable. Still, the problems outweigh the advantages — thermostatic control is not practical and regular attention is essential. Bottled gas heaters are more satisfactory, but the large cylinders are heavy and the heaters are cumbersome. Electricity is generally considered the best source of heat — clean, easily controlled and disease-promoting humidity is not produced. A word of caution — installing electricity outdoors is a job for a professional electrician.

Make sure the heater you choose is sufficiently large to heat the greenhouse to 45°F when the temperature outside is only 20°F.

There are several formulae to calculate the size of heater required to ensure this capacity. Use the simple one below:

	Size of heater required
Surface area x 33	BTUs per hour
Surface area x 10	Watts

As an example, an 8 ft x 6 ft house (surface area 208 sq. ft) requires 6864 BTUs per hour (paraffin, oil or gas) or 2080 watts (electricity) when the temperature is 20°F outside.

GLAZING
Glass is heavy and not as safe as plastic, but the advantages outweigh the drawbacks. More light enters and it is both easier to clean and to shade with paint-on materials. Even more important is its ability to retain heat compared with other glazing materials such as polycarbonate and acrylic. See page 104 for further details.

ELECTRIC POINT
A power point is essential if you are going to take greenhouse growing seriously. Even if you do not heat your house by means of electricity you may still need a 3-pin point for the propagator, winter lighting, extractor fan etc.

THERMOMETER
A maximum/minimum thermometer is vital. Suspend it close to the plants but make sure that air can circulate freely around the thermometer. It should be close to eye-level at the north side of the house. There are 2 types — the traditional mercury thermometer with internal tiny iron bars which you set with a magnet and the new digital type which you reset by pressing a button. Make a note of the readings at frequent intervals.

VENTILATORS

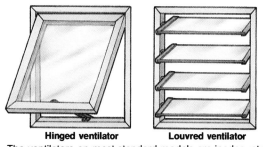

Hinged ventilator   **Louvred ventilator**

The ventilators on most standard models are inadequate. There should be at least one roof ventilator and one side ventilator — a single ventilator at the top of the house is not enough. The total ventilator area should be at least 20 per cent of the floor area — this usually calls for one roof ventilator and one side ventilator for each 8 ft of length. Louvred ventilators are better than the traditional hinged type, but make sure that they close properly. Extra ventilators can be bought as optional extras — make sure that side ones are set low down to ensure proper air circulation. An automatic ventilator may be described as an 'optional extra' in the catalogue, but it is an essential if you take your greenhouse seriously and cannot spare the time to go out daily to open or close the ventilators.

INSULATION
The general principle is to put up an inner skin of transparent plastic close to the glass — this reduces illumination slightly but even a simple arrangement will cut fuel bills by 20–30 per cent. The time for installing insulation is between December and April (Southern counties) or May (Northern counties). Tailor-made panels are offered by some greenhouse manufacturers, but the usual practice is to attach polythene sheeting to the sides of the house with drawing pins, staples or adhesive strip so that a ½–1 in. layer of air is trapped between glass and plastic. Alternatively you can use bubble polythene which has air trapped within it. Whichever method you use it is necessary to avoid blocking the ventilators.

WATERING EQUIPMENT
A can with a long spout is essential for watering individual plants. Watering is a time-consuming job which must be undertaken every day in summer. An automatic or semi-automatic system is essential if you cannot spare the time. There are 3 basic systems — capillary matting, capillary bench and trickle irrigation.

BLINDS

Plants must be protected from the sun's rays in summer. Blinds are one of the answers available — these are roller types with wooden slats, plastic slats or plastic-coated sheeting. These blinds are fitted either inside or outside the greenhouse. Automated blinds are a useful luxury — these slatted blinds go up and down according to the temperature within the greenhouse.

Choosing a Greenhouse

Greenhouses come in all sorts of shapes, sizes ... and prices. Choosing the right one is difficult, and if you make a mistake you will have to live with it for a long time. Take time before deciding. Read the advertisements and study the catalogues by all means, but the best plan is always to look at a range of actual greenhouses. Go to your garden centre, DIY store or to a large horticultural show such as Chelsea, Hampton Court or Southport.

- **Is it the right size?** Too big or too small — both pose a problem. The greenhouse should not dominate the garden nor should it provide much more space than you can fill. On the other hand it must be large enough for your needs — a popular rule is to buy the next larger size than the one you originally planned to buy. It is not just a matter of length and width. If you are above average height, is it tall enough to allow you to work without stooping? Is the door wide enough for your width, and for your wheelbarrow if you plan to work in the border soil?

- **Do I like the look of it?** Wood has a more traditional appeal than aluminium and a domed house is much trendier than a standard span roof one. Above all, the question you must ask is — does it appeal to you and the family? Remember that you will have to live with it as part of the permanent garden display.

- **Can I afford it?** Making your own house from scratch is not an economical option these days — the wood and glass will cost you more than a home-assembly greenhouse. In general you will get what you pay for — so do not regard 'bargain offers' as great value. When money is no object you can think of a double-glazed hardwood greenhouse, but that can cost up to 10 times more than the same size house in the cheapest materials. If funds are limited the best choice is an aluminium house with glass cladding from a reputable supplier. Transparent polythene instead of glass will reduce the price, but this is false economy as heating will cost you so much more. Don't forget these fuel costs — there is not much difference between the various types, although electricity is usually the dearest.

- **Is it right for the uses I have in mind?** If you plan to concentrate on tall plants like Tomatoes and Cucumbers, choose a greenhouse with vertical sides and floor to roof glass. Half-timbered sides are suitable if you want to reduce fuel costs and you propose to grow only pot plants.

- **Is it soundly made?** You cannot expect top-quality craftsmanship if you have bought a low-priced model, but it should still be soundly constructed. Do the ventilators and door fit properly? Is the ridge bar rigid and firmly held? Press the glazing bars — are they unyielding?

- **Are essentials included in the price?** Make sure that essentials are not classed as 'optional extras' unless you can afford the additional cost. Check exactly what is included in the price. Glazing material, benches and an adequate number of ventilators are essentials, but are not always included in the basic price. A foundation may be offered as an optional extra, but treat it as an essential feature. Make sure that you are told about any delivery or erection charges.

Siting & Erecting a Greenhouse

Planning permission is not usually necessary for an average-sized house in a standard location. It is still best to check — there may be rules about the distance from the boundary, and a lean-to attached to a house may need permission.

Most experts recommend that the house should be set so that the ridge runs from East to West. A few believe that the house should run North to South, but all agree that orientation is not a key factor for an average-sized house.

Do not site a glass greenhouse close to the road or a play area — replacing broken panes is always annoying. Other sites to avoid are waterlogged soils and frost pockets — never try to erect a greenhouse on recently-dug soil.

Site the greenhouse well away from trees — 30 ft is the recommended minimum distance. An overhanging branch casts shade, drops dirt on the glass below and may break off in high wind. Choose a sunny site, away from buildings which could shade out winter sun.

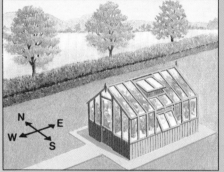

Larger houses are generally set on concrete foundations, but this should not be required if the house is 8 ft x 6 ft or less. You will need a firm and level base — see page 95 for advice. Buy the recommended foundation if offered by the manufacturer — follow the instructions exactly.

A windbreak such as a hedge is useful on the North and East sides, as strong winds can damage the structure and even ordinary winds increase the heating bill. The greenhouse should be sited at least 10–15 ft away from the hedge.

Site the greenhouse as close as practical to the house — electric wiring is costly and carrying other forms of fuel to the far end of the garden is a chore in winter. If possible run both water and electricity to the greenhouse.

Read the instructions carefully before you start to erect the structure. Lay out the parts and number them if necessary. Wait for a still and dry day before glazing. Make sure the frames are square — never use the glass to straighten aluminium glazing bars.

Greenhouses Illustrated

*You will still see some around but they are steadily disappearing.
An old Victorian span-roof greenhouse — wooden glazing bars, high brick sides and a boiler at the rear.
Quite impractical these days.* ▷

◁ *A modern span-roof house.
This Robinson model is the most popular size — approximately 8½ ft x 6½ ft.
Good features include aluminium bars with uPVC cladding, a stout sliding door and kick-panels at the base.*

△ *An hexagonal greenhouse such as this Hall's one may be a good idea where floral display is more important than practical considerations such as low cost and maximum use of space. Note the louvred side vent.*

BUILDINGS

Buildings have been a feature of British gardens right from the beginning. Some of these early garden buildings were impressive creations in brick and stone, but here we are concerned with more modest structures.

Greenhouses are primarily designed for the cultivation of plants and have the entrance sited in the garden — see pages 88–93 for details. Conservatories are also primarily designed for the cultivation and enjoyment of plants, but they are usually more ornate than greenhouses and there is an entrance within the house — they are not within the scope of this book. The remaining garden structures which you can enter are classed as 'buildings'.

There are four basic types. The most popular one is the **Shed** — a building which is primarily used for storage. It may also serve as a place for a variety of gardening and non-gardening jobs and it can provide shelter from rain, but it is a practical rather than an ornamental structure. The **Summerhouse** differs in two respects — it is an ornamental building to be admired from the outside, and it also should have an aspect which allows the garden to be admired from the inside. This means that proper siting, attractive appearance and the presence of an adequate number of windows is all-important. The **Gazebo** and **Arbour** are rather similar in purpose to the summerhouse, but the sides are open or latticed. And finally there is the **Playhouse** for children, which can be as grand as a miniature chalet with veranda to a simple bedsheet stretched between two chairs on the lawn.

Choice is very difficult these days as so many types are available. Wood is no longer the only material and all sorts of clever variations are to be found, but the basic rules remain. Firstly, study catalogues if you wish, but you should inspect the actual buildings before buying — go through the basic checklist on page 95. Secondly, clarify what is included in the price before deciding between one supplier and another. The quote may or may not include floor, glass, lining, delivery and erection.

Do apply for planning permission — some older books say this is not necessary but the Building Regulations were tightened up in 1985. As a result larger buildings and those to be erected close to the boundary do need permission. In addition, look at your insurance policy and include your new shed or summerhouse if such a structure is not covered.

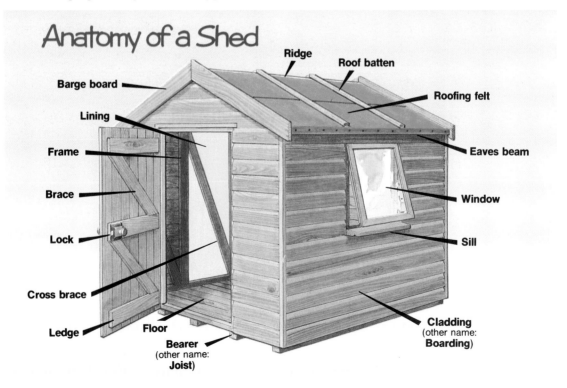

Anatomy of a Shed

- Barge board
- Lining
- Frame
- Brace
- Lock
- Cross brace
- Ledge
- Floor
- Bearer (other name: **Joist**)
- Ridge
- Roof batten
- Roofing felt
- Eaves beam
- Window
- Sill
- Cladding (other name: **Boarding**)

Choosing a Building

- **Floor** Sound construction is essential. Both sides should be treated with a preservative — tongued-and-grooved boards are much better than plywood or hardboard.

- **Bearers** These should be heavy-duty timbers, pressure-treated and at least 2 in. x 1½ in. across.

- **Framework** The upright frames should be no more than 2 ft apart and there should be stout cross braces between them.

- **Door** Make sure it is wide enough for your needs. With a shed it must allow ready access for the mower, wheelbarrow etc. It should be soundly constructed with at least 3 ledges and 2 braces. A strong lock with key is essential. Hinges and all other metal parts should be rust-proof.

- **Windows** At least one window is essential if you intend to work or sit in the building. A single window will do in a small shed, but you will need more windows if you intend to use it for potting. In a summerhouse for garden viewing you will need extensive windows which are both well-fitting and attractive. A top-hung window can be left open when it is raining. A sloping sill with a drip groove on the underside is necessary.

- **Eaves** There should be sufficient overhang to make sure that rainwater from the roof is kept well away from the walls.

- **Roof** Choose one made of tongued-and-grooved boards rather than plywood if you can afford it. Roofing felt should be thick and it should cover the eaves beams completely. Make sure that the headroom is high enough for the tallest member of the family.

- **Cladding** The boards must be weatherproof and rot-proof — softwood should have been pressure-treated with a preservative. Feather-edged and waney-edged weatherboarding is the cheapest, but it is the least weatherproof. It is better to choose tongued-and-grooved or shiplap cladding — see page 96. Whichever type you choose, make sure that it is free from cracks or numerous knot holes.

Erecting a Building

The usual routine is to buy the building in prefabricated sections and then to screw or bolt them together using your own labour or the people sent by the supplier. If you can afford the small extra charge it is a good idea to let the supplier do the work — instructions can be a little puzzling and the men they send have done it before.

If you do it yourself then you will certainly need an able-bodied helper. Read the instructions carefully and follow them exactly. If possible lay out all the pieces beforehand. The standard order of erection is 1. Base 2. Floor 3. Walls 4. Roof 5. Roof covering 6. Door 7. Glazing. Remember that all fittings must be rust-proof.

Making a Base

A firm base is essential. A solid concrete foundation is sometimes recommended for a large summerhouse, but this involves a lot of work and is not usually necessary for an average-sized building unless your ground is particularly soft or boggy. In many cases you can lay a wooden floor with bearers directly on to firm and levelled ground, but it is usually better to lay a base of paving slabs.

STEP 3:
LAY THE SLABS
Place a line of slabs along one of the lengths of string. Check that the slabs are level and insert two wooden spacers (¼ in. thick) between each pair of slabs. It is a good idea to secure the outside slabs by lifting each one and placing 5 blobs of mortar below, as shown, during the laying process. Continue until all slabs are laid

STEP 4:
FINISH THE JOB
Remove the spacers and brush a dry mortar mix (1 part cement : 3 parts sand) into the cracks

STEP 2:
MARK OUT THE BASE AREA
Use pegs and string to mark the area to be covered with concrete paving slabs. This area is usually slightly smaller than the floor of the building. It should extend beyond the walls to serve as a mowing edge if the shed or summerhouse is to be surrounded by turf

STEP 1:
PREPARE THE SOIL BASE
Remove earth and consolidate firmly to produce a level surface. Add a 1 in. layer of sharp (not building) sand. Level and press down with a board

Cladding

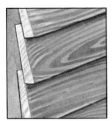
Feather-edged

Waney-edged

Shiplap

Tongued-and-grooved

Barrelled (Log cabin)

Sheds

Apex Roof shed

Pent Roof shed

Dual Purpose shed

Not every garden has a shed. Some tiny plots are just too small to accommodate one, and some people with larger gardens make do with the garage. This is generally not a good idea — the car has to be taken out in order to get to the lawn mower, overcrowding is almost inevitable and bodywork can be scratched as tools are moved.

So do buy a shed if you have the space and the money. It will give you a place to store all that gardening equipment, a place to potter and carry out repairs and for some gardeners a place to be on your own. The usual advice is to choose one which is bigger than you think you will need — 8 ft x 6 ft is the most popular size.

Size is often determined by the area available at the chosen site. Where space is limited it is a good idea to pick a spot where nothing seems to grow. Most people site a shed as far away from the house as possible as the building is regarded as an eyesore, but this need not be so. Attractive sheds are available, and a trellis covered with climbing plants can be used to hide a plain-looking building. Ideally it should be situated quite close to the house and have a path leading to it. Make sure the doorway is at ground level to allow easy access for the lawn mower.

There are 2 basic types from which to make your choice. The **Apex Roof** shed has a pitched roof with a central ridge. This is considered by most people to be the more attractive style and it is the preferred choice. The **Pent Roof** shed has a flat roof which slopes gently backwards, and you should check that it has the necessary headroom before buying. Before rejecting this style do remember that these models cost less than Apex Roof ones, and a Pent Roof shed with one side bearing windows right across makes an excellent potting shed. A third type of shed has recently arrived on the scene and is worth considering. The **Dual Purpose** or combo-shed is a greenhouse on one side and a shed on the other — ideal for people who do not have room for separate buildings. For those who do not have room for even one building there is the mini-shed (page 100) which is a store rather than a shed.

The final thing you will have to consider before you buy your shed is the construction material. Wood remains the traditional and most popular choice. These sheds fit in with most surroundings, have good heat-retention properties and can be easily fitted with hooks and shelves. For economy pick one of the many softwood ('deal') types — do make sure that the wood has been pressure-treated with a preservative and not merely painted with one. Modular softwood sheds are available which can be extended as your needs or finances grow. Western red cedar is more attractive but it is also more expensive. Routine treatment with a preservative is not needed but a cedar stain should be applied occasionally to retain the richness of the colour.

Sheds made from rigid PVC on a galvanized steel frame are strong and need no maintenance, but some people find them positively unattractive. Metal sheds have the same problem, but at least they are rust-proof these days. You can buy a hot-dipped galvanized steel shed with a baked-on coloured finish which is guaranteed for 10 years. Concrete sheds are not widely available and are not cheap — they cost about the same as a cedar one. But they are the longest lasting of all types and can be obtained with a stucco or pebbledash finish.

Summerhouses

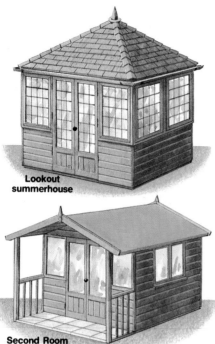

Lookout summerhouse

Second Room summerhouse

Summerhouses are sometimes cluttered with a variety of tools, pots and various unwanted household items, but storage is not the basic purpose of these buildings. A summerhouse should be reasonably or strikingly attractive in its own right and it should be a place of refuge, a viewing point for the garden or an extension of living space for the family.

Brick is the standard material used in the construction of summerhouses in our Grand Gardens, but wood is the most popular basis of the ordinary garden model. There is a wide range of ordinary softwood types which can be stained or painted, but as with sheds it is essential that the wood should be pressure-impregnated with a wood preservative. With a shed it may seem extravagant to buy a cedar or a hardwood model, but for a decorative summerhouse the extra expense is certainly worthwhile.

The range of shapes and sizes is much more extensive than that of garden sheds, and it is not easy to make up your mind. The most popular style is the Apex Roof (see page 96) and there should be more glass than you would find in the average shed. Looking around the yard of a large supplier or leafing through a comprehensive catalogue you will find summerhouses that are square, round, hexagonal and ranging from the humble to the highly elaborate. There are 2 basic types. The **Lookout** type is a summerhouse in which you can sit and admire the garden, protected from wind and rain. The walls are extensively glazed which means you will have to open doors and windows in high summer, and you must site it in a reasonably sunny spot in an attractive part of the garden. The **Second Room** type is basically an extension of the house to give more hobby, work or leisure area. Here there are fewer windows and there is often a veranda to protect the windows from the midday sun. The chalet-type is popular and you can build a patio in front of it if the space is available.

Gazebos & Arbours

Hundreds of years ago both these features were extremely popular, but the 20th century garden had little time for them until recently. Now they are making something of a comeback in the larger garden.

The original gazebos were two-storey buildings from which the owner or visitor could gaze about (hence the name). The modern gazebo is quite different — it is an open-sided structure which is placed as a focal point in the garden. The supports are often trellised and the roof may be solid to provide protection from rain. Wood is the usual construction material, but attractive cast aluminium and even plastic ones are also available. Arbours are basically similar to gazebos, but the lattice work on the sides and uprights is usually more extensive and it is used to support climbing plants such as Roses, Honeysuckle or Clematis.

Playhouses

The Wendy House has been a godsend for both parents and children over the years. Built in either chalet or shop style, this softwood building has plastic windows and a range of optional extras such as verandas, stable doors and window boxes. A basic problem with the Wendy House is that children do grow up and it then has no purpose — some parents prefer to buy a standard summerhouse and fit it with acrylic or PVC windows. Whatever type of wooden playhouse you choose, make sure that the wood is smooth and all protruding nails are hammered down.

For toddlers a small rigid plastic playhouse sited close to the house is the preferred choice. Highly coloured and fitted with tables, play telephone etc, these models are bought in kit form. Unfortunately they soon outlive their usefulness and older children require a more adventurous building. The tree house is an old favourite, but don't attempt to build one if you are a DIY novice. A modern alternative is the two-storey playhouse.

Buildings Illustrated

The traditional apex-roof shed. ▷
*It is made from smooth Deal cladding
and has a triple-hinged door.
The tongue-and-grooved floor is
supported on joists and a
top-hung window is present.*

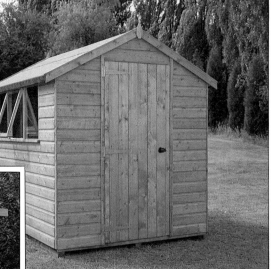

◁ *This Regal pent-roof shed has
western red cedar cladding, so regular
treatment with a preservative is not needed.
The door is soundly constructed and
the 3 windows ensure good illumination
for the potting bench within.*

△ *The combined greenhouse/shed is useful where space is limited and the
under glass needs are small. Certainly worth considering if you want an area
for potting and raising seeds and cuttings, but not for growing Tomatoes etc.*

A neat and compact summerhouse. ▷
The hexagonal shape ensures
maximum light and the leaded panes
remove the greenhouse/garden shed
look. Brass fittings and window stays
add a touch of luxury.

◁ An elegant wooden gazebo with seats and
attractive trellis-work — a fine focal point in
a large garden but completely out of place
on a small plot. A wide range of simpler
types is available for modest gardens.

△ Going up and down stairs in a double-storey Wendy House
certainly trebles the fun for children, but there are problems for
the parent. The cost is high, the structure can be too dominant in a
small garden and there is no use for it when the children grow up.

STORAGE & ENCLOSURES

The purpose of garden enclosures is to provide protection for the plants within — things may be kept out (insects, animals, frost, rain etc) or kept in (heat, moisture and so on). The **Fruit Cage** is an obvious example of an enclosure — the buds of soft fruit are attacked by birds in winter and spring, and the flowers which survive produce fruits which are attacked when ripe. Up to three-quarters of the Raspberry or Strawberry crop can be lost in this way, and the only satisfactory answer is to erect a temporary or walk-in fruit cage.

The role of the glass or plastic **Cloche** is different. Small plants are protected from bird damage, but the main function is to raise the air and soil temperature at the start of the season. Cloches are used to provide weather protection for plants grown in rows — for plants grown in pots a **Cold Frame** is a better idea. Basically this is a low unheated structure which bears a sloping roof made of glazed sections (lights) which can be raised or slid apart. Brick or wooden frames with wooden lights were once universal, but nowadays you can buy wooden, aluminium, steel or plastic framed models with solid or glazed sides. Glass is the traditional material for the lights, but twin wall clear polycarbonate is a good substitute.

Storage units protect non-living material (tools, compost, rubbish etc) from rain, wind etc, but unlike sheds they are too small to permit entry. There is a **Dust Bin** in every garden, and there should also be a **Compost Bin**. This structure needs a rainproof cover and the walls should be thick enough to provide good insulation.

Finally there is the **Mini-shed** — large enough to store the lawn mower, hose pipe etc but not large enough to enter. There are 2 basic types — the squat storage box shown below and the tall hexagonal garden store.

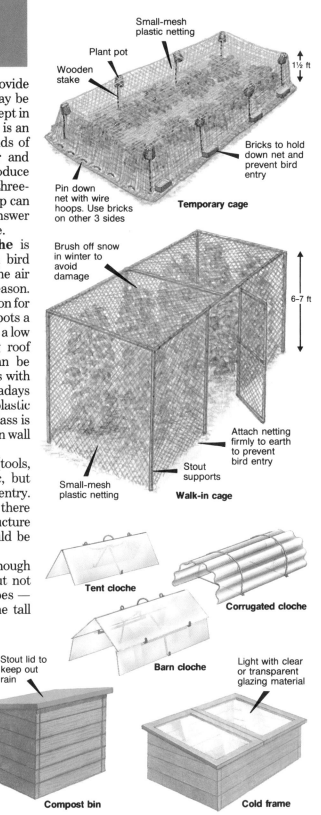

Temporary cage

Small-mesh plastic netting

Plant pot

Wooden stake

1½ ft

Bricks to hold down net and prevent bird entry

Pin down net with wire hoops. Use bricks on other 3 sides

Brush off snow in winter to avoid damage

6-7 ft

Attach netting firmly to earth to prevent bird entry

Stout supports

Small-mesh plastic netting

Walk-in cage

Tent cloche

Corrugated cloche

Barn cloche

Light with clear or transparent glazing material

Hinged lid

Stout lid to keep out rain

Sliding door

Mini-shed

Compost bin

Cold frame

CHAPTER 3

MATERIALS

Wood

Wood plays an important part in the garden for creating fences, gates, buildings, furniture and so on. It is therefore important to know something about its properties — you may never pay a trip to a timber merchant but you will still be involved at some time or other in buying fixtures or fittings made of wood. To purchase the wrong type or to maintain it in the wrong way will lead to disappointment.

As a rough and ready guide, one of the softwoods known as 'Deal' is used where we want to buy a thoroughly practical but inexpensive item. The problem here is that such wood soon rots outdoors, especially if it is in contact with the soil. For this reason you should use Deal which has been treated with a preservative — see below for details.

Some softwoods like western red cedar and larch have good rot resistance — a property shared with the hardwoods such as teak and iroko. These naturally-protected woods are more expensive than the ordinary softwoods, but are always the preferred choice if you want your building or item of furniture to exhibit the natural beauty of wood.

Where large sheets of wood are required the choice is between tongued-and-grooved boarding (see page 96) or a manufactured board. In both cases you must make sure that you obtain exterior grade for outdoor use.

SOFTWOODS

Softwood is cut from a conifer such as pine, larch, fir or spruce. The wood is usually lighter and softer than hardwood, but not always — yew is heavier and denser than some hardwoods.

A typical softwood comes from a cool or cold climate. It is pale in colour and there are resin-bearing streaks and a number of knots. It is cheaper than hardwood and is easier to saw, plane, nail etc. This is the wood which is used for nearly all general joinery and house construction work. When the home handyman wants to buy natural (not manufactured) boards or planks for a DIY job the usual choice is between Redwood and Whitewood — both commonly called 'Deal'. These two woods are widely available in both rough or planed form and in a series of standard widths and thicknesses. For outdoor use you will need either a rot-resistant type or Redwood which has been pre-treated with a preservative. This should not have been merely brushed on — buy 'tanalised' wood if you can. This will have been pressure impregnated to carry the preservative below the surface. If the Redwood has not been treated see page 103 for details of what to do.

TYPE	DETAILS
CEDAR, WESTERN RED	Reddish-brown with a silky surface. Resists both rot and insects and so is popular for cladding, fences and greenhouse frames. It has its problems — colour fades with time, nails work loose and the surface is easily dented
LARCH	A British wood, tough and difficult to work. There are 2 important characteristics — it has good rot resistance and holds nails well. As a result it is used for supports and fences in the garden
REDWOOD	Commercial names: Scots Pine, Baltic Pine and Red Deal. Popular for outdoor use — reliable, easy to work and good for staining and painting. Colours range from cream to reddish-brown. Rots easily — treatment with a wood preservative is necessary
WHITEWOOD	Commercial names: Spruce, White Deal. Softer and with a finer texture than Redwood — cream colour does not fade with age. Popular for indoor use but does not absorb preservatives. **Not for outdoor use**

HARDWOODS

Hardwood is cut from a deciduous broad-leaved tree, such as oak, mahogany or teak. The wood is usually denser and harder than softwood. A typical hardwood is heavy, rot-proof and close-grained, which means that it is more attractive than softwood. It is also more expensive and more difficult to saw, drill etc.

There are basically 2 types. The temperate hardwoods grow in Europe and other places with cool or cold winters, which result in a clearly distinct patterning due to the difference between winter and summer growth. They are usually pale-coloured and notoriously difficult to work. The tropical hardwoods are nearly always darker and the patterning is less distinct, but they are generally easier to work. Look for a label stating that the wood has come from a managed forest.

TYPE	DETAILS
IROKO	A popular teak substitute from W. Africa for garden furniture — just as hard wearing but much cheaper. The colour is rich brown but the texture is rather coarse
MAHOGANY	One of the great woods — but generally too expensive for outdoor furniture. African is rich orange-brown — American is even more lustrous and expensive
MERANTI	A mahogany substitute from Malaysia — cheaper, redder and easier to work than real mahogany. Used for making garden furniture
OAK	British oak is the strongest and most durable, but it is expensive, difficult to work and splits easily when nailed. European oak is a little softer
TEAK	The traditional hardwood for garden furniture — it resists rot, water and fire. The rich brown colour is marbled with darker streaks

MANUFACTURED BOARDS

Manufactured board is made from wood in sheet, strip, shredded or pulped form with resins or glues bonding the pieces or pulp together. There are various types and you must choose carefully if the board is to be exposed to wind, rain, frost and sun. Some like Chipboard are not suitable for outdoors — with the ones listed below you must make sure that you buy the grade recommended for outdoor use.

TYPE	DETAILS
PLYWOOD	Thin layers ('plies') of wood are glued together to form a board which has neither the warping nor splitting tendency of natural wood. Number of plies 3–15, thickness ⅛–1 in. Look for WBP (weather- and boil-proof) or EXT (outdoor) Grade
BLOCKBOARD	The inner core of glued strips of softwood is sandwiched between two thin layers of wood — usually birch. Thickness ½–1 in. Worked in the same way as ordinary timber — look for Outdoor Grade
HARDBOARD	Pulped wood is mixed with adhesives and rolled into sheets. Thickness ⅛–¼ in. — very little inherent strength. Sometimes used to cover floors or walls inside sheds and summerhouses — specify Tempered Grade for water resistance

Looking for faults

LIVE KNOT
No surrounding black ring. Small knots do not weaken the wood, but oozing resin may make working and finishing difficult

FELLING SHAKE
Split across the grain — generally occurs in bands. Wood is weak — discard affected area

WANEY EDGE
The outer edge of the tree — often left on hardwood boards. This area of bark and sapwood (paler than the inner heartwood) should be removed

WARPING
The straightness of a board can be lost during the drying (or seasoning) process. Cupped and bowed wood can often be used as long as the pressure in the construction is against the curve. Twisted wood is a serious problem — the warp generally gets worse with time

BLUE STAINING
Caused by mould growth in softwood. Disfiguring, but not weakening — apply a preservative

SURFACE SHAKE
Shallow split along the grain — formed during the drying process. Disfiguring, but not seriously weakening unless the split is deep

DEAD KNOT
Black bark ring around edge. Wood is weakened — knot may fall out. Discard affected area

CUP SHAKE
Split along an annual ring — formed during the drying process. Discard affected area

NON-VERTICAL END GRAIN
For maximum warp resistance annual rings should run vertically across the thickness of the board

END SHAKE
Split at the end of the board usually along the grain. Very common — caused by drying out of the exposed surface. Discard affected area

Twisted   Cupped   Bowed

Buying Timber

Most of the timber you will buy for your garden will be in the form of ready-to-erect fences, gates, furniture etc or in a kit which calls for simple joinery to produce the finished article. Here the wood has been chosen and cut for you, but there are times when you may have to buy unworked timber for supports, posts or a more lavish feature if you are a DIY enthusiast. When buying timber there are a number of considerations — the basic ones are size, quality and dryness of the wood you have chosen.

SIZE

Softwood is usually sold in confusing units known as metric feet — a metric foot is 300 mm. Standard lengths are in 1 metric ft increments up to 21 metric ft (20 ft 8 in.). The width and thickness are equally confusing. Standard thicknesses range from ½ to 3 in. and standard widths from 1 to 9 in. But you do not always get the exact size stated on the label. The cheapest form of softwood is **rough sawn**, which means that the surfaces are in the state left by the power saw. Shrinkage may have taken place, so that the *actual* width and thickness may be very slightly less than the *nominal* width and thickness by which it is sold. Where appearance is important it is better to buy planed timber — **PAR** (planed all round) or just **PBS** (planed on two large faces only). Do remember that planing removes about ⅛ in. from the nominal size.

Hardwood is expensive, hard to work and is not as readily available as softwood. The width of boards is usually ½–1 metric ft and the thickness ¼–¾ in. It is usually sold as PAR. The timber is stored by the merchant as rough sawn boards and these are then cut and planed to your specification. Buying manufactured board is much more straightforward. The standard sheet size is 8 ft x 4 ft — cutting the sheet increases the cost but makes transport much easier.

QUALITY

As a general rule you will find that the softwood stored by the merchant is offered in 3 grades. The cheapest is **carcassing** used for joists, posts etc. Here you must expect some knots and a moisture content of about 20 per cent, which means that warping may occur as the wood dries out. **Standard joinery** is drier (15 per cent moisture content) and is the usual grade purchased for DIY jobs. The top grade (**best joinery**) is only for inside work where the surface is to be polished.

There are no standard hardwood grades — it is up to you to inspect the wood and judge quality for yourself. The experts looking for high-quality timber avoid wood from the outside or the inner core of the tree, buy only old boards and select them from undisturbed stacks.

DRYNESS

Timber has to be dried before use — this increases strength, rot resistance and the prevention of warping. Wood can be dried naturally by stacking it under cover in the open air — hardwood can take 3–4 years to dry in this way. Air-dried wood is used for nearly all garden work — indoor furniture is made from kiln-dried wood with a moisture content of less than 13 per cent.

RUSTIC POLES

Poles of chestnut, larch, hazel and birch are used for arches, fences etc and are available from large hardware stores and garden centres. Use larger ones (3–5 in. diameter) for uprights and narrow ones (2–3 in.) for cross beams.

Treating Timber

Most softwoods are susceptible to rot when used outdoors, and so it is essential to use some form of protective treatment prior to exposure to the elements. Some people choose white paint for fences and gates, but the usual choice is a preservative which contains a stain. Whichever material you choose, read the section below before you begin the treatment.

PRESERVATIVES

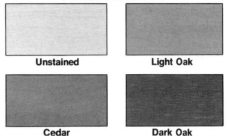

| Unstained | Light Oak |
| Cedar | Dark Oak |

The rule is worth repeating — make sure that softwood items for the garden have been pressure-treated before you buy them. If they have not or if you have made your own then you will have to apply a suitable product. Most products are oil- or solvent-based and should be kept away from naked flames — wear gloves when applying such preservatives and keep well away from foliage. The water-based products are harmless to plants, but may be less effective. Brushing-on is the usual application method, and is satisfactory for top-up treatment, but for fresh wood the immersion method is much better. Stand posts in a bucket or place boards in a shallow bath containing preservative for at least an hour. This is essential if the wood will be in contact with the ground. Colourless preservatives are available, but the usual choice is a product which contains an oak or cedar stain.

PAINTS

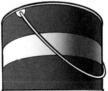

Gloss paint on top of a primer/sealer is sometimes used, but is not really a good idea. Blisters are a frequent sight on wooden surfaces covered with old gloss paint. The cause is a build up of water vapour under the airtight skin. Think instead of a microporous (breathing) paint. Basically it is a water-based paint containing acrylic resin and is for application to bare (that is, unpainted) wood. The great advantage claimed by the manufacturers is the ability of any moisture trapped in the wood to escape, and the film is flexible. This means that the cracking and bubbling associated with traditional gloss paint when used on outdoor surfaces can be avoided. A second advantage is that brushes can be simply cleaned under a running tap. These microporous paints are widely used in the U.S and Scandinavia but have not taken off in the same way in Britain. Microporous stains are available with the same advantages as microporous paints.

Glass & Glass Substitutes

Glazing material such as glass or a glass substitute is required for greenhouses, cold frames, cloches, summerhouses and sheds. The traditional material is glass, but there are two instances (cloches and playhouses for children) where plastic is the preferred choice. Plastics have the highly desirable property of being shatterproof, which is so necessary if the greenhouse or shed is near a children's play area or close to the road. They are also lightweight, which means that stout window lights or frames are not required. But until recently their drawbacks outweighed their advantages. Insulation properties were not good, clarity was often quite poor and the early PVC types deteriorated with exposure to sunlight. Things have improved in recent years as indicated in the description below of the rigid plastics now available.

Glazing has also improved in recent years. In the modern aluminium greenhouse the introduction of glazing clips means that replacing glass has become a simple job. Wooden frames call for use of the traditional method of a sealant compound plus glazing sprigs. Putty is now largely a thing of the past — these days it is much more common to use a non-hardening mastic.

GLASS

Glass is the usual choice for greenhouses and buildings and there are a number of reasons. First of all comes clarity — good quality glass allows about 90 per cent of the sun's radiation to enter. Next comes heat retention — even in frosty weather the temperature in a glass-covered greenhouse will be about 8°F higher than outside. It does not deteriorate with prolonged exposure to ultra violet rays and it is easy to shade with paint-on materials. But it does have its drawbacks. It is heavy and both the window-glass and horticultural grades readily shatter when hit, and so a good plastic is preferable in a high-risk area.

For greenhouses and cold frames buy horticultural grade glass which is described as 3 mm (its thickness) or 24 oz (the weight of 1 sq. ft). This is good quality glass which should be free from air bubbles — these bubbles can act as small lenses in sunlight and so cause leaf scorch. For sheds and summerhouses 4 mm (32 oz) float glass is a better choice. If you want to glaze summerhouse doors down to ground level and you wish to avoid plastic then you will have to choose either toughened or wired glass.

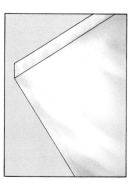

ACRYLIC

Perhaps the best of all glass substitutes if you want full transparency. The 2.5 mm sheet has light transmission properties which are similar to glass and it is very strong. Acrylic sheet is one of the less expensive glass substitutes but it should still last for 12 years or more outdoors. Mark cutting lines and drilling holes on the protective paper or polythene cover — use a tenon saw for cutting and a hand drill (not a power one) for making holes. Sawn edges should be smoothed with glasspaper after which the protective covers should be removed.

PVC

Here you have a choice. Clear rigid PVC is guaranteed for 10 years — the 3 mm sheet does not have quite the same clarity as acrylic and it is also more expensive. A more popular form of PVC is the corrugated sheet used for cloches and rooflights — one of the first clear sheeting materials on the market. In the most popular form the corrugations are 3 in. apart and there are both lightweight and heavyweight grades. Some manufacturers offer a 10 year guarantee. The box profile type with square instead of rounded corrugations is more attractive, but it is also more expensive.

TWIN WALL POLYCARBONATE

The rising star in the glass substitute world. This is a double-skinned material made from polycarbonate, the toughest of all the plastics listed on this page. Because of its cellular structure the light is diffused, but the makers claim that actual light transmission is not much less than that of clear glass. Its outstanding property is heat retention — the double glazing structure means that it is superior to glass in keeping heat from escaping. Choose the 4 mm grade for greenhouses, cold frames and sheds, and the 10 mm grade for roofing.

TWIN WALL POLYPROPYLENE

A substitute for twin wall polycarbonate for cold frames — good insulating properties at a much lower price. Easy to handle — it can be cut with scissors and attached with drawing pins, but it is translucent and not transparent.

Glazing an Aluminium Greenhouse

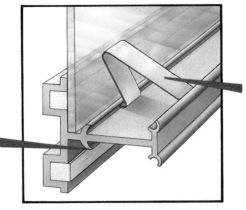

STEP 1:
REMOVE BROKEN PANE
Put on a pair of strong gloves. Unhook the glazing clip and remove the broken pane. In some greenhouses the panes overlap — in this case the upper pane will also have to be removed

STEP 2:
SECURE THE NEW PANE
Place the new pane in position and replace the clip. A simple and straightforward job

Glazing a Wooden Greenhouse

STEP 1:
REMOVE BROKEN PANE
Wear gloves to remove broken glass. Use a screwdriver or chisel to get rid of all old putty. Remove any glazing sprigs, metal clips or beading and then brush away dirt and dust

STEP 2:
PLACE PUTTY OR MASTIC IN REBATE
Buy the right grade of putty, mastic or caulking compound. Mould the putty in your hands until it is soft — squeeze a ¼ in. thick strip into the rebate

STEP 5:
INSERT GLAZING SPRIGS
Place new glazing sprigs in position. Knock the sprigs into the rebate with the side of an old chisel — slide the blade along the surface of the glass — do not use a hammer

STEP 6:
ADD MORE PUTTY OR MASTIC
Run another strip of putty in the angle between the new pane and the wooden frame. Only a small amount of putty will be needed if a wooden strip (beading) is to be fitted around the pane

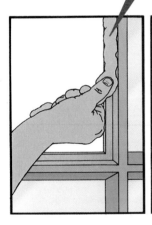 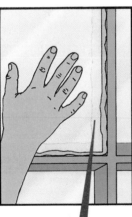 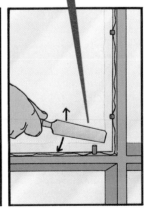 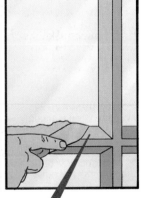

STEP 3:
PUT NEW PANE INTO OPENING
The new pane should be ⅛ in. smaller than the width and height of the opening. Make sure you buy the right grade and thickness — see page 104

STEP 4:
PRESS GLASS INTO PUTTY OR MASTIC
Press the glass into the putty until it is firmly bedded in place. Put the bottom of the pane into position first and then press forward — always press the edges and never the middle of the glass

STEP 7:
SMOOTH PUTTY OR MASTIC
Use a putty knife to smooth the putty as a neat bevel. Mitre the corners and then remove all excess putty from glass surface and glazing bars

STEP 8:
CLEAN GLASS
Wipe off remaining traces of putty and fingerprints with a cloth soaked in methylated spirits. Run a moist brush along the putty surface and leave for 2 weeks to harden

Concrete & Mortar

Concrete and mortar are literally the foundations of your house. Concrete is used to form the footings on which the bricks are laid and mortar is employed to hold these bricks together. In the garden these two materials may seem to play a less vital role, but concrete is widely used as the foundation for walls, fences, paths, greenhouses and so on, and mortar is used to secure paving slabs and to hold bricks and stone blocks in place. There are obvious similarities between concrete and mortar — both begin as a mixture of solid materials which turn into a rock-like product following the addition of water. Cement and sand are generally key ingredients, but it is surprising that there is not one single ingredient that is found in all concretes and mortars.

There are several steps to success. First you must choose the right mixture for the job in hand and you must then decide whether to buy the ingredients separately (cheaper for a large job) or already pre-mixed in a bag (more convenient for a small job). With concrete you can have ready-to-lay concrete delivered to your door. When mixing on site you must blend the ingredients thoroughly.

Ingredients

BASICS

CEMENT

The basic binding agent for all types of concrete and most types of mortar. The standard bag size is 50 kg (110 lb) but smaller sizes are available in DIY shops. Careful storage is necessary if you do not intend to use the bag immediately. Store the bag flat off the ground in a dry place — cover with polythene or tarpaulin if left outdoors. An unopened bag can be stored for up to 6 weeks.

There are 2 basic types. The most popular one is **Ordinary Portland Cement** — a fine grey powder used for making concrete. The other one is **Masonry Cement** used for making mortar. Other types include **White Portland Cement** where white jointing between blocks is required and **Rapid Hardening Cement** for making paths and drives.

LIME

Hydrated lime is added to mortar made from Portland cement and building sand in order to slow down the drying process. This means that the mortar remains workable for a longer period and is less likely to crack when set than a cement/sand mix. Careful storage is necessary if you do not intend to use the lime immediately. Keep bags in a dry place — if you store outdoors then cover the heap with polythene or tarpaulin. As an alternative to using lime you can add a plasticiser.

ADDITIVES

PLASTICISER

Plasticiser is used to produce aerated mortar — tiny air bubbles are formed which increase the workability of the product and increase resistance to frost. The risk of cracking is reduced. Masonry cement is a mixture of Portland cement and plasticiser.

COLOURING AGENT

A range of pigments is available to produce coloured concrete or mortar, but it is difficult to ensure that each batch you produce will be the same colour. Do think carefully before deciding to add one of these colouring agents to your mix.

AGGREGATES

An aggregate is a material derived from rock which is mixed with cement or lime to form concrete or mortar.

Fine Aggregates less than 5 mm

BUILDING SAND

(Other names: Soft Sand, Builders' Sand)
Small range of particle sizes — various colours (white, yellow, orange). Used for making mortar, **not** concrete.

SHARP SAND

(Other name: Concreting Sand)
Wide range of particle sizes — feels coarse and gritty to the touch. Used for making concrete, **not** mortar.

SILVER SAND

Variable range of particle sizes.
Used for making white concrete or white mortar.

Coarse Aggregates more than 5 mm

GRAVEL

Used as the Coarse Aggregate fraction with cement and sand when making concrete. Graded according to size — 10 mm or 20 mm.

BALLAST

(Other names: All-in Ballast, All-in Aggregate, Combined Aggregate)
Mixture of small stones down to dust — replaces 'sand plus coarse aggregate' in concrete mixes. Standard grade is 20 mm down to dust. Clay and silt should not be present. Ballast can be bought in bags from DIY stores.

SUB-BASES

A sub-base is a firm and rigid layer on which concrete is laid to form either a path or a foundation for other building work. 'Hardcore' is used in this book as a general term for a sub-base, but good quality hardcore (see below) is hard to find. Three types of material are used to produce sub-bases.

HARDCORE

(Other name: Builders' Rubble)
Broken-up building material — brick, concrete, stone etc. Best avoided as it is difficult to pack down and may contain harmful items such as plaster and wood.

HOGGIN

A blend of fine stone and clay. A cheap material which packs down well but is hard to find these days.

SCALPINGS

A wide-ranging term for a blend of broken-up stone — sometimes broken-up concrete ranging from 25 mm down to dust. This broken stone beds down well and is the best material to use.

CONCRETE

Concrete is a mixture of cement, aggregates and water.
Additives such as rapid hardeners are sometimes included.

● MIXES	Proportion by Volume			
	PORTLAND CEMENT	SHARP SAND	20 mm AGGREGATE	BALLAST
CONCRETE for foundations	1	2½	3½	—
	or			
	1	—	—	5
CONCRETE for paths & drives	1	1½	2½	—
	or			
	1	—	—	3½

● **MIXING ON SITE** is the traditional method of making concrete. You can buy the ingredients separately or as bags of ready-packed dry mix. Obviously mixing on site calls for more work than having ready-mix concrete delivered to your garden, but there are advantages. Relatively small batches can be mixed at one time, and this is important if you are inexperienced or have limited assistance. But mixing on site can be a real chore if you have a large amount to make — it is a good idea to hire a concrete mixer.

Mixing by hand

Measure the required amounts of sand and coarse aggregate (or all-in ballast) using a bucket. Mix into a heap on a flat, level surface. Flatten the top and make a central crater using a shovel. Pour the cement into this crater. Mix and turn the dry materials until the heap is uniform in colour. Begin at this stage with ready-packed dry mix. Once the heap is an even colour flatten the top once more and make a crater. Add some water to the hole and slowly bring the outer wall into the centre. Mix and turn — add sprinklings of water until the concrete is well mixed and thoroughly moist.

Mixing by machine

Set the machine on a firm and level surface — place the drum upright and switch on the motor. Add half the required coarse aggregate and some water — when these two have blended add half the sand and cement and then gradually add the rest of the materials one at a time. Add water little by little — after a few minutes pour out a small amount of concrete and test. Add more water or more ingredients until consistency is right.

> **THE CONCRETE TEST**
> Press the top of the pile with the back of the shovel and then slide the blade across. The surface should be firm, closely-knit and moist without a surface layer of liquid.

● **READY-MIX CONCRETE** is delivered ready to lay. It will save mixing time, but remember that you will have to use the whole delivery within a couple of hours. The first job is to order your requirement well in advance — tell the supplier what the concrete is for and how much you will need. Ask for a retardant agent if you want to delay the setting time. Arrange for discharge as close to the site as possible — make sure that all the formwork is in place. Do have several willing (and able) helpers standing by — 1 cu. metre will mean that 25–30 barrowloads will have to be moved.

After 2 hours ▷	Concrete without additives: Workable — no strength at all	
After 4 hours ▷	Concrete with setting retardant: Workable — no strength at all	
After 3 days ▷	Concrete no longer workable — little strength	● **THE STRENGTH OF CONCRETE**
After 7 days ▷	Solid concrete — half strength	
After 30 days ▷	Solid concrete — full strength	

MORTAR

Modern-day mortar is a mixture of cement and sand plus lime or a plasticiser.

● MIXES	Proportion by Volume			
	CEMENT	BUILDING SAND	HYDRATED LIME	PLASTICISER
MORTAR for bedding slabs and laying bricks and blocks	1 (Portland cement)	6	1	—
	or			
	1 (Portland cement)	6	—	Maker's instructions
	or			
	1 (Masonry cement)	5	—	—

Mortar has to be mixed on site — the best plan is to use the masonry cement/building sand mix if you have a large job to do or buy a bag of ready-mixed Bricklaying Mortar if you need only a small amount. A 25 kg bag will be needed for 50 bricks or 150 reconstituted stone blocks. It is important to add the right amount of water — it should hold the impression of the trowel, but it should not be watery nor should it be crumbly.

Prepare mortar on an old board. Dampen and then make a pile of half the sand. Add the other ingredients and then the rest of the sand. Mix these ingredients thoroughly. Build a heap, flatten the top and make a crater. Add some water to the crater and slowly bring the outer wall into the centre. Mix and turn — add sprinklings of water until the mortar is well mixed and properly moist.

Metal

Iron once formed the outer skeleton of millions of gardens in Britain. From tiny terrace houses along inner city streets to the grand estates of the aristocracy there were iron railings and gates, and within larger gardens the seats, tables and ornaments were often made partly or entirely of iron.

Much of this ironwork was taken away for recycling into munitions during World War II, and the vogue for iron has never come back. These days the most popular materials for surrounding gardens are wood, brick and stone, and within the garden aluminium, plastic, resin, wood and coated steel have taken the place of wrought and cast iron.

This does not mean that iron is despised. Ornate garden seats and ornaments now command high prices in antique shops — but iron may need protection against rust, so manufacturers have turned to other materials.

Aluminium is a metal which has greatly increased in popularity since the War, but not much is used in the pure metal state. Its alloys are much more popular — an alloy is a metal blended with another metal or non-metal to produce a material with improved properties.

CAST IRON

Iron with about 4 per cent carbon and tiny amounts of other elements. Objects are moulded (cast) from this material and it has the advantages of being inexpensive and tough. But it is also brittle — a sharp blow can fracture it. Cast iron rusts slowly when exposed to air — protect with undercoat and paint.

WROUGHT IRON

Iron with some carbon and at least 5 per cent slag. It can be worked in many ways — twisted, bent etc and is hammered and welded into gates, furniture and railings. Wrought iron rusts only very slowly when exposed to air. It is expensive these days — so-called 'wrought iron' objects are generally made of mild steel.

MILD STEEL

Despite the name it is almost pure iron — the carbon content is less than 0.1 per cent. It is easily worked — mild steel can be cut, bent, soldered or welded and is used for the whole range of fixings — screws, hinges, brackets and so on. The problem is that it rusts quickly — protect with undercoat and paint.

STEEL ALLOY

Iron with other metals added — chromium, nickel, manganese, tungsten and molybdenum are examples. The product is much harder than mild steel, but it is more difficult to work. Steel alloys are widely used for tools such as saws, spades etc. Rusts quickly — protect steel alloy tools with oil.

STAINLESS STEEL

Steel alloy in which both nickel and chromium have been added to the iron. It is easily soldered but it is a very difficult material to work. The outstanding property of stainless steel is that it neither tarnishes nor rusts — an excellent choice for forks, spades, trowels etc if you can afford the extra price.

GALVANIZED STEEL

Zinc is a corrosion-resistant metal which is soft and easily worked. A thin layer of this metal is coated on to iron to produce galvanized steel — a material widely used for wheelbarrows, wire netting, nails etc. Rust-proof, but this property is lost if the surface is scratched.

JAPANNED STEEL

Iron or steel protected from rust by having an oven-baked coating on the surface. In the old days this was an asphalt-based material known as Black Japan, but this has been replaced by modern baking enamels which are extremely tough and are available in many colours.

ALUMINIUM ALLOY

Cast aluminium is lightweight and is the modern substitute for cast iron in the production of ornate garden furniture. The problem is that the pure metal lacks strength. Aluminium alloy produced by adding small amounts of copper, manganese and magnesium is almost as hard as steel — used for chairs, tables, greenhouses, etc.

Corrosion & Rust

The surface of a bare metal in contact with air forms a metallic salt which is different from the metal itself. Some of the metal is lost in the process — the metal has corroded. This corrosion layer may be very thin as with the tarnish of silver, the patina of bronze and the thin white layer seen on aluminium greenhouses and furniture. Unfortunately on some metals it may be unsightly and thick enough to weaken the metal — this is the case with rust on iron and steel.

The trouble with rust is that it can develop very quickly and the process continues as long as moisture and air are present— this situation often arises under a broken film of gloss paint on gates, railings etc. To prevent rust on new iron and steel fixtures and fittings you should apply a rust-preventing primer and then an undercoat and topcoat. If rust is present on old ironwork you will need a tannate-based rust converter. Brush away loose rust and rub down the surface until smooth. Paint on the rust converter — this compound changes the remaining rust into harmless magnetite which forms a rust-preventing undercoat.

You will need one coat (two coats if the surface is pitted) and then a topcoat of outdoor-quality paint.

CHAPTER 4

MAINTENANCE & REPAIRS

One of the basic themes in this book is that a surprisingly large amount of the garden is covered by neither soil nor living plants — there is a basic skeleton of walls, paths, steps, fences, gates, garden buildings, ornaments, paving slabs and so on. Occasionally we add something new to this non-living part of the garden — in recent years the idea of outdoor living has resulted in the purchase of both barbecues and patio sets by millions of householders, and there does come a time when a path or a fence has to be replaced. But once the garden has been established we generally live with what we have got, and that means that both regular maintenance and timely repairs should be matters of prime importance.

Unfortunately this is not usually so. When we want something new a lot of time is spent considering the options. We study the catalogues, shop around, look at the item from all angles, ensure it is soundly made and then, and only then, do we introduce the new ornament, building, tool etc into the garden by bringing it home or having someone else deliver or construct it for us. But after that we so often let it look after itself.

As a result paving slabs sink, concrete crumbles, ponds become unpleasant, hinges rust and an air of neglect settles over the garden. The answer is to remember that the list of essential gardening jobs includes more than just planting, pruning, weeding, mowing and so on — you must add two other vital tasks. There is maintenance of the non-living sector, which means keeping it in good order. And there are also repairs to the non-living sector, which means restoring items to good order when something has gone wrong.

Quite simply, you must have a regular maintenance and repair programme. This involves keeping your eyes open during your working hours in the garden — make a mental note if rust or rot is appearing, if paint is flaking and so on. At the end of the working day in the garden clear things away properly and make sure tools are cleaned. Once a year you should carry out a detailed inspection of walls, fences, buildings etc which will involve some cleaning and perhaps some repairs. This is the equivalent of spring cleaning indoors, but out in the garden this would be quite the wrong season for annual maintenance work. Spring is far too busy a time outdoors — choose instead a dry day in late autumn when there are not many pressing jobs to be done. And two final points — try to carry out repairs as promptly as possible, and don't attempt tasks which are beyond your skill and/or fitness.

An obvious benefit from carrying out a regular maintenance and repair programme is that the non-living part of the garden will be in good condition and not an eyesore. But there are three less obvious benefits which are equally important. First of all, if you neglect proper maintenance your work in the garden can be made much more difficult and less efficient. Examples here include heat loss from a greenhouse with badly-fitting ventilators, extra effort needed when using a spade caked with dried mud and the damage done to a lawn by a mower in need of proper setting or sharpening. The second problem if you neglect proper maintenance is that some simple repair jobs can rapidly become major headaches if they are delayed. A few spots of rust can turn into ruined furniture, an unrepaired loose or rotten fence post can result in the whole fence being blown down by strong winds, and a small area of rot in timber can lead to the destruction of a whole window frame if not tackled promptly. The third problem arising from a failure to carry out proper and timely maintenance is the most serious of all — the risk of accidents. Every casualty ward doctor has heard the cry "If only I had fixed that loose step", "If only I had put the secateurs away" or "If only I had got rid of the slime on the path".

As you can see, there are several reasons for making sure that the non-living part of the garden is properly looked after and repaired when necessary. The purpose of this chapter is to show you how.

MAINTENANCE & REPAIRS

WALLS

Look at garden walls during your routine maintenance inspection — brick walls are more likely to have problems than reconstituted stone ones and earth-retaining walls are more at risk than free-standing ones. Moss, algae and efflorescence are unsightly but do not pose a serious problem. Gaps in the mortar can be repointed and frost damage (spalling) to a brick will call for its replacement. Unfortunately much more serious problems can occur. Poor foundations, poor quality bricks or mortar, disturbance by plant roots or rising damp in an earth-retaining brick wall can lead to serious vertical cracking or the development of a dangerous tilt. In these cases it will be necessary to demolish the affected area and rebuild the wall.

Cleaning dirty walls

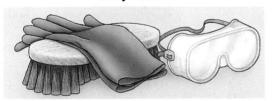

There are several steps involved in cleaning brick and stone walls. Where a covering of white powder is the problem, follow the instructions in the Efflorescence section on page 111. The usual trouble is a combination of dirt, moss and green slime (algae). Begin by using a stiff brush to remove the dirt and surface growths. Next, scrub with plain water — never use soap or detergent. Where moss, algae and mould are present you should use a proprietary moss killer and fungicide. Alternatively you can apply household bleach (1 part bleach : 4 parts water) — leave for about a couple of days and then wash off with plain water. A word of warning — wear goggles when using an anti-slime solution. This chemical treatment will clean the wall but will not solve the basic problem — moss and algae usually indicate excessive dampness, and this must be tackled or the trouble will return.

To renovate brickwork, rub the surface with a piece of similar brick. Stone should be treated with a stone 'sanding block' in the same way — keep the block wet at all times. Mortar as well as masonry may be discoloured — use a proprietary acid-based stone cleaner.

Waterproofing walls

Stone walls are resistant to damp, but brick walls absorb moisture and can become saturated for long periods when located in areas of high rainfall and shaded from the sun. The result is that both bricks and mortar are weakened and the surface can be seriously damaged by frost.

In order to make brickwork impervious to moisture you will have to treat the wall with a water repellent. This colourless fluid will stop water entering the brick but will allow water vapour to escape. Before use clean the surface thoroughly and repair any cracks. When dry apply the water repellent with a brush, pushing the liquid into the brick surface and mortar joints to make sure the surface is completely covered. Apply a second coat a few days later.

Repairing cracks

Non-serious cracking is illustrated above. The crack follows a zig-zag path through the mortar and may extend for several courses. Apart from the crack the wall remains firm and vertical, and in this case remedial action is fairly simple. All you have to do is to rake out the damaged mortar in the affected area and then repoint as described on page 111. You should soak the bricks thoroughly before repointing and take care to push the mortar deeply into the space between the courses. If the cracking occurs at the top of the wall it is generally more satisfactory to remove the bricks involved and relay them as illustrated on page 8. The problem of matching the surrounding mortar colour is the only difficult feature of repairing non-serious cracks — see the Repointing section on page 111 for advice.

A key feature of serious cracking is that bricks as well as the mortar are split and the crack generally runs vertically. It may be that the wall has received a heavy blow or that the mortar used was far too wet, but the usual cause is subsidence. This occurs when the foundations move downwards — upwards movement is called heave. The reason may be that the base was improperly laid — but even a properly-laid foundation can move on heavy clay which has been subjected to very wet winters and very dry summers.

If the serious cracking has caused the wall to lean or become unstable then the only course of action is to pull the wall down and rebuild. Do this immediately or rope off the area if the damaged wall is a danger to passers-by. Provided the wall is vertical and firm, the next step is to determine whether the crack is widening. This calls for the glass slide test illustrated above. Glue a thin glass slide over the crack. If the glass breaks within a few weeks then the problem is progressively getting worse — the only course of action is to demolish the wall and start again. Only if the wall is vertical, firm and with cracks which are not widening should you attempt to repair the damage by simple repointing.

Repointing

Sooner or later the combined effects of wind, rain and frost will loosen some of the mortar between the bricks or blocks. The effect is unsightly and the weather resistance of the wall is reduced. Repointing of the affected area is the answer. Remove the loose mortar to a depth of about ½ in. with a screwdriver, a club hammer and cold chisel or an electric drill fitted with a chasing bit. Make up mortar from basic ingredients (page 107) or buy a bag of ready-mix — do not add too much water and incorporate some PVA bonding agent to increase its sticking properties. Never mix up more than you can use in an hour. Clear away all bits and dust with a stiff brush and then thoroughly soak the bricks and underlying mortar with water.

FLUSH JOINT

RUBBED JOINT

WEATHER STRUCK JOINT

RECESSED JOINT

Use a pointing trowel to force the mortar into the gaps — start with the upright joints and then fill the horizontal ones. Now smooth the mortar — cut away the excess and follow the joint style which has been used on the wall. For a rubbed joint use a small length of garden hose or a jointing tool. The final step is to brush off any traces of mortar when the repointed area is almost dry. These instructions are the standard ones you will find in any DIY manual, but they can lead to an unsightly patch if the whole wall is not repointed. It is a wise precaution to make up a small amount of mortar and repoint the gap between a brick or two before starting on the whole area. You may find that the new mortar when dry has quite a different colour to the rest of the jointing. You can buy colourants for mortar mixes — experiment until you find the right colour before repointing the whole area which requires treatment.

Reconstituted stone blocks are repointed in the same way as bricks. In recent years Mix 'n Point has appeared — this is a mortar mix which is applied directly from the bag to the space between the blocks — the strip of mortar is then smoothed with either a piece of cloth or a pointing trowel. Five colours are available, ranging from buff to charcoal. Another pointing aid is the Pointmaster which can be used to produce a professional-looking finish in a variety of joint types.

Dealing with efflorescence

A white deposit frequently appears on the surface of new brickwork. This is due to the water-soluble salts within the bricks being drawn to the outside as the walling materials dry out. Once at the outer face of the brickwork these salts crystallise and appear as a white fluffy film.

This efflorescence is quite normal and all you have to do is to remove the deposit with a wire brush until it ceases to appear. Never try to scrub it away with water — you will only make matters worse by bringing fresh salts to the surface. This efflorescence should not persist for more than a year or two on a free-standing wall, but it can go on for much longer on an earth-retaining one.

Repairing spalling

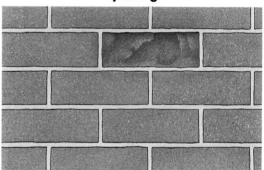

Isolated bricks may be unusually soft and this allows moisture to penetrate. On freezing this moisture expands and the outer surface of the brick breaks away. This is known as spalling and it must be treated, as it looks unsightly and the affected area becomes even more prone to damage by moisture. Use a club hammer and cold chisel to remove the mortar around the spalled brick and then take out the brick itself. If this proves difficult use an electric drill with a masonry bit to bore numerous holes into the surface of the brick, which will then readily break into pieces.

Clean and dampen the opening, and then mortar in place the replacement brick with a cement-rich mix (1 part cement : 3 parts building sand). Match the jointing style of the wall and then paint the whole surface with a water repellent — see page 110.

This technique will not do if numerous bricks have spalled. All you can do here is to treat the whole wall with a stabilising solution to hold the loose surface together and then cover the wall with a textured masonry paint.

MAINTENANCE & REPAIRS

FENCES & GATES

Fences and gates are often neglected until a serious problem occurs — a length of wooden fencing blows over in a storm or the front gate sags so that it will no longer close. Regular inspection and maintenance is the key — serious faults can usually be prevented by taking timely action.

With wooden fences and gates the main danger is rot. Treat with a good preservative every couple of years — if plants are growing on or near the fence you should use a water-based product. Do this job when the wood is fully dry — this aids penetration. Pay special attention to areas in contact with the soil and to the top of posts. Look carefully at metal fittings — if they are corroded then either replace or treat with a tannate-based rust converter —see page 108. Rot is not the only problem — shrinkage can result in loose joints.

With metal fences and gates the problem is rust rather than rot. Regular repainting is essential — use a tannate-based product to destroy rust if corrosion is present.

Repairing an arris rail

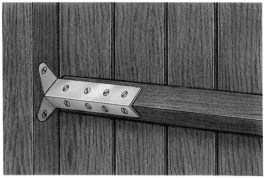

Arris rails are vital as they support the pales in a closeboard fence. If much or all of the rail is rotten then part of the fence will have to be dismantled and a new rail fitted, but the trouble is usually less serious. A common problem is that the rail becomes loose due to one end snapping where it fits into the slot in the fence post. Secure it to the post by screwing on a metal arris rail bracket, as shown above.

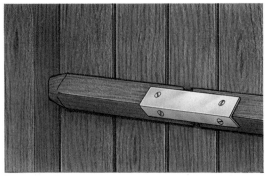

Occasionally an arris rail splits at a point along its length. The technique here is to screw on a bracket to one side of the broken rail, and then insert the other two screws as the pieces are pushed together by an assistant.

Repairing a loose wooden fence post

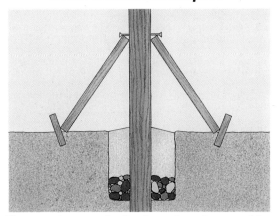

The correct course of action depends on the state of the post. If the base is free from rot but the post is leaning over because it has worked loose, dig a hole around the post, about 8 in. deep and 8 in. wide. Using a spirit level bring back the post to the vertical position and hold with temporary wooden struts, as shown above. Now ram hardcore around the base of the post and then set in concrete as shown on page 14. Remove struts after 3-4 days.

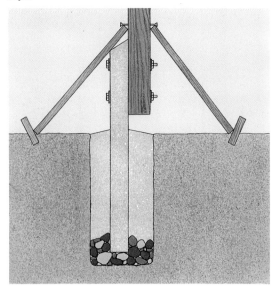

Unfortunately the usual cause of a leaning fence and a loose post is the presence of rot at the base. The easiest way to tackle this problem is to dig a hole and cut away the rotten part of the post — the hole should be about 1½ ft deep. Now insert a concrete spur so that it rests against the fence post. Push galvanized bolts through the holes to leave a mark on the post — drill the 2 holes and paint the base with a preservative. Bolt the post to the spur and secure with temporary wooden struts. Check that it is vertical. Ram hardcore around the base of the spur and then set in concrete as described on page 14. Remove struts after 3-4 days.

Replacing a gravel board

The purpose of the gravel board at the bottom of the fence is to protect the pales from contact with the soil. In order to prolong the life of the gravel boards check during your maintenance inspection programme that earth is not piled against them. However, it is generally inevitable that rotting will occur after a few years. Replacing a gravel board is usually a simple matter. Cut a piece of pressure-impregnated wood to the same dimensions, unscrew the rotten board from the 2 holding battens on the fence posts and then screw on the new gravel board. Leave a ½ in. gap between the bottom of the pales and the top of the gravel board.

Routine gate maintenance

Metal gates are usually trouble-free — all they need are anti-rust treatment if corrosion spots are seen, oiling of hinges and the latch, and painting every few years.

Wooden gates tend to be more of a problem. Winter rains can lead to rot, hot summer sun can cause shrinkage and regular use can loosen the latch, hinges and joints. Begin your maintenance with the hinges — oil them and carry out the anti-corrosion procedure (page 108) if they are rusty. Loose hinges should be unscrewed, the holes plugged with dowels and then rescrewed. Broken hinges should be replaced with galvanized or japanned steel ones — a gate 5 ft or more high will require 3 and not 2 hinges.

Small areas of rot should be treated promptly. Cut out the affected portion of wood and use the 2-part treatment available from DIY stores. The first treatment consists of painting the cavity and surrounding area with a wood hardener. When dry the hole is filled with a fibre glass wood filler.

The most serious problem with a wooden gate is binding — the catch stile (see page 18) grips either the path or the catch post. The cause may be nothing more than worn hinges — replace as noted above. But the reason may be more serious — a displaced gate post or a sagging gate. Check the gate posts first with a spirit level. If one is leaning, bring it back to vertical with the technique set out in the next column. If the gate posts are vertical and the hinges are satisfactory then the cause of binding is a sagging gate — follow the procedure on the right.

Repairing a leaning gate post

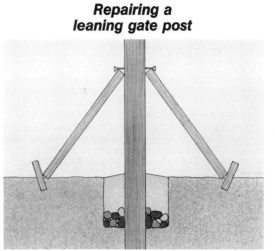

If a gate post works loose and begins to lean over then the gate will no longer open properly. Provided the wood is sound it is relatively easy to correct this problem. Dig a hole around the post, about 6 in. deep and 8 in. wide. Using a spirit level bring back the post to the vertical position and hold with temporary wooden struts, as shown above. Now ram hardcore around the base of the post and then set in concrete as shown on page 18. Remove struts after 3–4 days.

Repairing a sagging gate

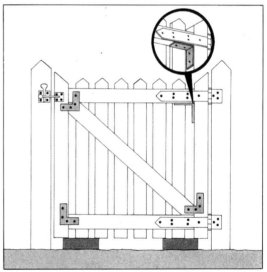

With a sagging gate the side next to the catch post drops so that the catch stile binds against the post or the path. The usual cause is poor construction — loose joints, lack of a brace or the use of inadequate timber. If the wood is basically sound it is often possible to cure this problem without too much trouble. The first step is to place wedges or blocks under the gate so that the top is perfectly horizontal and the stiles vertical. Now tighten all the screws and repair any rotten patches (see Routine gate maintenance section). Finally attach heavy-weight galvanized steel braces, as shown above, and remove the supporting blocks from the base of the gate.

MAINTENANCE & REPAIRS | PAVING & STEPS

Paths, patio and steps require regular maintenance to keep them clean, safe and free from damage. For hard surfaces such as concrete, slabs, bricks and asphalt the basic equipment is a broom and a hose pipe. Use a stiff-bristled broom and a high-pressure sprayer for maximum efficiency. It is a wise precaution to wear goggles when washing down with a high-pressure hose.

This broom and water treatment is sometimes not enough. Weeds may be present in the cracks between stones — use a dab-on weedkiller or a specific path herbicide. Moss and green slime may be encrusted on the surface. This should be tackled straight away with a product made for the job — pbi Path & Patio Cleaner is an example. Brush the area thoroughly with the diluted chemical and leave for at least 10 minutes before rinsing well with water. Concrete with a dusty surface can be cured with a proprietary sealer. Gravel is cleaned by raking and then topping-up if necessary.

Sometimes the problem needs to be repaired. There are a few simple rules here. Defects which raise a safety problem (loose steps, raised slabs etc) should be dealt with immediately, but cracks in concrete should be left until there is no further movement. Mortar and concrete mixes used for repairs should be on the dry side, and a PVA adhesive should always be incorporated to improve the bond.

Removing oil stains

Oil stains from vehicles standing on a driveway can be unsightly. With a gravel surface this does not pose a great problem — just remove the oil-stained stones, add fresh material and rake over the surface. On some other surfaces you can use a proprietary Oil Patch Cleaner — use undiluted on old patches and diluted with hot water on new ones. Useful for surface stains, but this treatment cannot be used on newly-laid drives and is only partially effective where the oil has soaked into porous material such as concrete.

Repairing hollows in gravel

Do not rake gravel from the surrounding area to fill the hollow — this will merely create a depression elsewhere. The proper technique is to scrape back the gravel covering the hollow until a firm base is reached. Consolidate further if necessary, then add new gravel to restore the level. Finally, rake over the whole area to blend the new surfacing material with the old.

Repairing cracked concrete

There are several reasons why cracks appear in concrete paths and drives. The base may be too weak, the concrete mix may have been defective, expansion joints (see page 28) may be missing or subsidence may have occurred. If cracks are numerous and their number is increasing then the only answer is to break up the damaged concrete and relay the path or drive. If there is just a single crack then mark a spot along its length and measure the width. Remeasure after a month or two.

When the crack is stable and no longer widening you should undercut it using a club hammer and cold chisel — the prepared crack should be an inverted V as shown above. Remove all dust and make up a mortar mix of 1 part cement : 3 parts building sand. Add a little PVA adhesive to this mixture. Brush the crack with a dilute solution of PVA adhesive — make sure you get into all the crevices. When the surface is tacky use a trowel to fill the crack with the mortar — pack in thoroughly. Finally, use a trowel or float to smooth off the surface.

Repairing hollows in concrete

The hollow must be at least ½ in. deep for filling. Cut round the edge with a club hammer and cold chisel. Remove some of the concrete within the hollow if the depression is less than the ½ in. minimum — remember to wear goggles. Clean the area, paint with dilute PVA adhesive and fill with a fairly dry concrete mix plus a little PVA adhesive, but wherever possible try to make up the same mixture used for making the path — getting a good colour match is a prime objective when filling concrete hollows. Smooth the surface with a float.

Repairing crumbling concrete edges

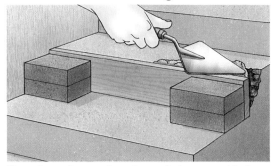

The edges of concrete paths and steps crumble for a number of reasons. Poor construction points include using the wrong mix, failure to push the concrete firmly into the edges of the formwork or removing this formwork before the concrete has properly set. The main poor use point is taking a heavy wheelbarrow or mower over the edge.

The first job is to break up the crumbling surface until you get to sound concrete — wear goggles and use a cold chisel and club hammer. Brush away all loose material. Cut a board to match the height of the concrete surface — secure against the edge with bricks as shown above. Paint the damaged concrete with dilute PVA adhesive and when the surface is tacky fill with a fairly dry concrete mix. The usual formula is 1 part cement : 5 parts all-in ballast plus a little PVA adhesive, but wherever possible use the same mixture from which the path or steps were made. Press the concrete well down into the formwork so no hollows are left. Smooth the surface with a trowel or float and wait about 4 weeks before removing the board and bricks.

Repairing hollows in macadam

After some time hollows tend to appear in asphalt driveways, especially if the car is left out overnight. Mark out the area of the depression (use a spirit level) and cut out the damaged section with a club hammer and bolster chisel to a depth of 2 in. Brush away all loose material and then paint the base and sides of the hole with bitumen emulsion. When this has turned black add a ½ in. layer of ready-mixed cold asphalt and ram down with a home-made tamper (see above). Add further layers until the surface is reached — smooth the path with a lawn roller which is kept wet. Unfortunately the patch may be unsightly and it may be necessary to resurface the drive — see page 24 for instructions.

Replacing broken and sunken bricks

If the blocks and bricks have been laid on mortar, follow the slab repair instructions below. Bricks and blocks laid on sand as flexible paving call for different treatment. Prise out the offending brick or bricks with a trowel. Add more sharp sand and level with a trowel so that the new brick or bricks stand about ½ in. above the undisturbed ones. Use a block of wood and hammer to tamp the new bricks down gently until they are level with the others — finish the job by brushing fine silver sand over the surface to fill the cracks between the bricks.

Replacing broken and sunken slabs

Paving slabs may sink, crack or become loose if the foundation was faulty at the time of laying. In the case of sunken paving slabs it will be necessary to lift out all the affected ones — use a board and spirit level to determine the extent of the hollow. Prise out one of the slabs once you have broken through the mortar at the edges and base with a trowel. Carefully remove all of the affected slabs in the same way. Add a dry mortar mix (1 part cement : 6 parts building sand) to bring the foundation level to the height of the surrounding area. When set relay the cleaned slabs as directed on page 30.

Slabs crack when subjected to a heavy weight on the surface and the base is inadequate. The affected area is usually much smaller than a sunken patch as described above, but the remedial treatment is quite similar. Break up the slab with a club hammer and cold chisel into small removable pieces. If at all possible, obtain your replacement slab or slabs from another part of the paved area where the absence can be disguised in some way. Failing this you will have to buy replacement slabs, and some colour variation is almost inevitable. Lay the new slabs as directed on page 30.

MAINTENANCE & REPAIRS PONDS

Page 53 sets out a year-round pond maintenance programme. This should enable you to have attractive plants, clear water and healthy fish. Things do go wrong, however, because it is not always possible to create an ideal environment — the pond may be too small. To stay clear you need a surface area of at least 40 sq. ft, and this is not possible in a small garden. The result is that the fight against green water is a perpetual struggle — and one has to rely on chemicals and not on plants alone to keep down algal growth. Cracks may or may not be your fault, but whatever the cause it is necessary to re-seal the damaged area or plants and fish will suffer.

Getting rid of algae

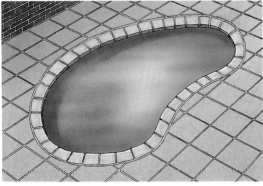

There are 2 distinct types of algae which affect garden ponds. The first type are microscopic forms which float on or below the surface turning the water cloudy or the colour of pea soup, depending on the conditions. The other type of algae are the blanketweeds — long and silky green threads which are attached to the bottom and sides of the pond.

The cause is simple to understand. When the surface is unprotected from sunlight and the water contains mineral salts and organic matter, the growth of algae is greatly stimulated. The ideal answer is set out in the Pond section of this book (pages 46–56). Make sure the surface area is large enough (at least 40 sq. ft) and have various types of plants present to shade the surface and to absorb the minerals from the water. Other maintenance points to prevent algal growth include removing fallen leaves, avoiding using too much fish food, raking out or netting blanketweed and avoiding the use of plant fertilizers.

Unfortunately it is not always possible to follow this advice. Many pools are much smaller than 40 sq. ft so securing a proper balance with plants (see page 53) cannot be achieved. The answer here is not to empty the pond and fill with fresh water — it is to use a chemical treatment. The growth of algae is worst in the spring as the weather warms up — buy an algicide and add it to the water. If fish and plants are present it is vital to follow the instructions. These proprietary brands work in various ways. Most of them are toxic to algae but are much less so to plants and fish. Acurel E on the other hand works by flocculating suspended material (algae, sediment etc) and depositing it on the bottom. Aquaclear is a harmless dye which filters out the light which algae need for growth. None of these treatments can control the trouble permanently — repeat applications are necessary.

Repairing cracks

Don't assume your pool is cracked if the water level falls in summer — a drop of ½ in. per week is quite normal during a warm and dry spell. However if the level is going down more than this under ordinary weather conditions then you do have a leak. There is no point in trying to live with the problem by filling up regularly with a garden hose — the water will be constantly green and the surrounding area will become boggy.

Concrete ponds crack because the mix was wrong for the purpose, foundations were insufficient or subsidence has disturbed the foundations. The first thing is to take out the plants and the fish. For a small pool a series of large plastic (not metal) buckets filled with pond water is the best solution — for a large pond with many fish and numerous plants it is better to make a temporary pool. Do this by digging a hole in an out-of-the-way spot in the garden and lining it with butyl sheeting. Again use water from the pond. If possible keep plants and fish in separate containers. Now empty and clean the pond. Any cracks wider than ½ in. in a concrete or rigid liner pond should be filled with a waterproof mastic cement and the whole surface should be painted with a proprietary sealing plastic. This technique is satisfactory if just a few cracks are present, but if the surface is badly damaged it is better to fill the cracks with mortar and then install a flexible butyl liner — see page 49. Whichever method is used, restock the pond as described on page 50.

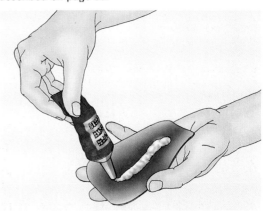

Flexible liners have a limited life span, but this varies from just a few years for cheap polythene to 50 years for top quality butyl sheeting. It is not worth trying to repair a cracked polythene-lined pool — remove it and replace with PVC or butyl sheet. If one of these better quality materials becomes torn or cracked, buy a repair kit from your garden centre or other supplier. Empty the pond to a level below the damaged area. Cut a piece of the repair sheet from the kit — it should be at least twice as long and wide as the tear or hole. Clean this patch and the area of the damage with methylated spirits and apply the waterproof adhesive to both the patch and the area around the tear. When the adhesive feels dry to the touch, press the patch over the damaged area and smooth it to drive out any air bubbles. Place a weight on the repair, as described in the kit instructions, and do not refill before the specified time. Follow the instructions on page 50 if restocking is necessary.

MAINTENANCE & REPAIRS   FURNITURE

Outdoor furniture is subject to rain, frost, pollution, the heat and ultra-violet rays of the sun, knocks and stains as well as the ordinary wear and tear of normal use. Not surprisingly some maintenance is required, but it is impossible to generalise about the way to do it. Non-folding resin chairs need virtually no maintenance — metal hammocks with ordinary fabric seats require regular maintenance if they are to last more than a few years. There are perhaps only 3 rules which apply to all types of garden furniture. Carry out a cleaning programme at least twice a year (spring and late autumn), store indoors if instructed to do so, and repair tears or breaks as soon as possible.

Cleaning & treating outdoor furniture

Hardwood In autumn dust teak or iroko furniture and then scrub with water. Rinse the surface and allow to dry before treating with teak oil. The purpose of this treatment is to maintain the rich colour and texture of the wood.

Softwood Western red cedar is naturally durable so treat as for hardwood, using teak or cedar oil. The other softwoods are susceptible to rot, so the furniture should be treated every couple of years with a preservative containing a fungicide. Wash the furniture and allow the wood to dry before treatment — choose a fine day.

Plastic, **Resin** and **Aluminium** Very easy — just wipe or scrub down when the surface is dirty. Treat with a proprietary cleaner if the furniture is badly stained.

Painted furniture Wipe or scrub down when the surface is dirty. If the base is wood, repaint immediately when the surface is cracked or flaking. If the material is iron or steel, treat with a tannate-based rust destroyer and repaint at the first signs of corrosion.

Plastic-coated furniture Wipe or scrub down when the surface is dirty. If the surface is scratched and the metal below is rusty, treat immediately with an anti-rust compound.

Waterproof cushions and **Seat covers** Wash down to remove surface dirt and grime. Use a detergent if the material is stained.

Fabric cushions and **Seat covers** If they are removable there is no problem — simply wash them indoors and replace. If they are not removable and require cleaning, you will have to use an upholstery shampoo. Do follow the instructions — it is important not to soak the cushion filling.

Storing outdoor furniture

Most folding furniture made of metal or wood is put away at night after use, together with cushions and covers. The reason is that damp-susceptible parts must be protected from dew, and wherever possible the furniture and furnishings should be allowed to dry before storage, especially if the material is ordinary fabric. With most folding chairs the proper way to fold them is obvious, but with director chairs it must be remembered that both the seat and fabric back should be lifted forward so that the cloth is not trapped by the wooden parts.

At the end of the summer most furniture is put away in the garage or shed — the only items which can be considered truly sun, frost and rainproof are non-folding items made of moulded resin, hardwood or cast aluminium. In addition genuine cast iron has good weather-resisting properties. Before items are put away in a dry place, some treatment and oiling (see below) may be necessary. Make sure all screws are tight — treat a loose rivet by placing the base on a solid surface and hitting the head of the rivet with a hammer.

It is not always possible to move weather-susceptible items under cover in winter, and that means that chairs and hammocks with metal springs and rivets can rust badly. The answer is to buy waterproof woven polythene covers, as illustrated above.

Oiling furniture

Oil performs 2 functions. Choose an aerosol product with a label which makes it quite clear that it inhibits rust when sprayed on to metal, and that it also has an extension tube which allows it to be used as a lubricant for springs, rivets and hinges. Before winter storage, all exposed iron and steel parts should be lightly coated with oil, and all moving parts should be treated. Aluminium alloy chairs should be treated in the same way — wipe off the oil before use next summer.

MAINTENANCE & REPAIRS

GREENHOUSES

Virtually all of the maintenance and repair techniques set out in this chapter are designed to keep the appropriate features sound, attractive and safe for you and your family. With the greenhouse there is an additional factor — much of the maintenance is designed to keep plants in peak condition and to inhibit pests and diseases. The routine is to carry out an annual overhaul in autumn and to take immediate action at any time of the year if there is an emergency.

Autumn cleaning indoors

For a thorough annual cleaning, it is necessary to move out as many plants as possible — the recommended procedure is to choose a settled and reasonable day in autumn when the Tomatoes have finished cropping. Move the plants to a convenient spot outdoors — the more delicate types may have to be placed indoors.

Remove rubbish, old pots etc and then use a stiff brush to remove the dirt from the path. The next stage is washing down — for this you will need a stiff brush, scraper, sponge and a dilute warm-water solution of a disinfectant recommended for horticultural use. Scrub staging, walls and the framework — it is important to get into the crevices where insects breed. With aluminium houses the T-section bars are a hiding place for pests — these insects can be removed by rubbing down with wire wool. Use a sprayer to get into cracks and pay special attention to the glass panes (see the next page). When you have finished all surfaces should be clean and there should be no caked-on dirt — the path should have been brushed with the disinfectant solution.

Leave several hours for the disinfectant to do its work and then hose down the inside of the house. Use a long-handled brush and plain water to reach into corners so that all the disinfectant is removed. Leave the door and vents open so that the glass and framework can dry as quickly as possible — put the heater on if necessary. One safety point — it is a good idea to cover up electric points when washing down.

Make sure that all pots and trays are cleaned at this stage. When the greenhouse is dry the plants can be returned — clean the pots and remove dead and diseased leaves before they are put back in the greenhouse.

Autumn cleaning outdoors

Begin with the glass and framework, using water and detergent or a dilute solution of a horticultural detergent. This job is much more difficult outdoors than inside the house — you will need a long-handled mop to reach the roof sections. After washing down the glass and glazing bars it is the turn of the walls (if present) and base. Scrub brick and block walls with water and a specific cleaner — for wooden sides remove algae and moss with a proprietary moss killer.

General maintenance

There may be more to do than just cleaning the glass, framework, shelves, staging etc. Check all iron and steel fittings, hinges and screws for rust — if sound apply a thin film of oil. If corrosion is present, treat with a tannate-based rust destroyer before painting. Replace badly-rusted hinges.

Draughts are a special problem, as they are not only uncomfortable for you but they can be deadly for the plants. Check that vents and doors fit tightly — fit self-adhesive draught-proofing strips if they don't. Louvres are a common cause of draughts, so check them carefully.

Inspect the sides of the glasshouse if it is not glazed to the ground. Repoint brick walls as necessary and replace any boards which may be missing from a wooden base.

The wooden framework of the house should be inspected and the gutters will need cleaning and repairing if necessary — see the sections on the next page. Check the wires used for supporting tall plants inside the house — these generally need replacing every few years. Replace broken or cracked panes and renew damaged or missing putty.

Looking after glass

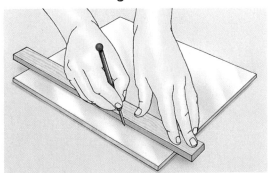

It is not the unsightly nature of dirty glass which poses the real problem — it is the reduction in light intensity within the house and this can be serious during the winter and early spring months. Routine cleaning was described on the previous page, but the development of algae and the presence of encrusted dirt between overlapping panes call for special action. Use a proprietary greenhouse glass cleaner, a forceful jet of water and a thin sheet of cardboard or plastic to push between the sheets of glass if necessary.

In greenhouses containing plants, broken panes during the colder months are generally replaced without delay. They should, of course, be reglazed immediately at any time of the year as the draught can cause a great deal of harm. It is the cracked pane of glass which usually gets neglected, and this is regrettable as it can so easily blow in during a storm. See page 105 for notes on reglazing aluminium and wooden houses. Metal-framed greenhouses are reglazed in a similar way to wooden ones, but clips are used instead of glazing sprigs and you will need to buy special metal window putty.

Looking after wood

If you have a greenhouse made of teak or cedar then rot should not be a worry, but a softwood house should have its framework painted with a plant-safe preservative every 2 years. Open all vents and the door after treatment to speed up drying. Rot can be a serious complaint and you should check carefully every year. Look for the tell-tale signs — spongy wood which a steel point penetrates easily, an unusually dark colour and cracks along the grain. The trouble spots are generally around the boards at the base of the house, the lower glazing bars and the bottom of doors and vents. It is possible to repair small areas of rot with hardener and filler (see page 120 for details) but it is usually more satisfactory to replace the damaged wood.

Looking after the door

The door is a basic part of the greenhouse and is often one of the first areas to go wrong. With conventionally hung doors make sure they open easily, which calls for keeping the hinges oiled, the screws driven in tightly and a free-turning lock. Note that the lock should never be oiled if it is stiff — use instead a graphite lubricant. This smooth opening is vital because going into the greenhouse is often a one-handed job, the other one being used to carry pots, watering can or sprayer. This need for free-running is equally vital with sliding doors, and these seem to go wrong more often than ordinary ones. Clean the upper and lower tracks — dirt and small pieces of grit are common causes of jammed doors. Another cause is the presence of worn nylon wheels — replace if necessary.

Looking after guttering

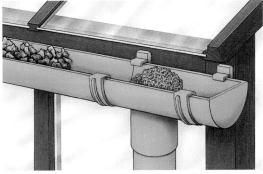

Sound guttering is essential — any overflow or leakage will pour down the glazed area and framework, leading to algal growth on the glass or transparent plastic and rot in the glazing bars. The first job is to clear leaves and other rubbish out of the gutters at least twice a year. If a filter is absent at the top of the downpipe, you should put a ball of wire netting into this spot.

Follow the directions on page 121 to cure sagging and leaking gutters. The fault, however, may be the downpipe and not the guttering. If there is a leak in this pipe (look for a damp patch or green slime at the back) it is quite a simple job to fix a fibreglass bandage or self-adhesive flashing strip round the affected area. If the downpipe is blocked, put a bowl at the base and poke a stiff wire upwards through the shoe at the bottom to remove any lower blockage. Now work from the top of the pipe — remove any rubbish from the opening and then use a piece of hooked stout wire to lift up any debris. Finally, push a long bamboo cane down through the pipe.

MAINTENANCE & REPAIRS   BUILDINGS

Garden buildings are made of many materials — brick, stone, wood, metal, concrete, uPVC. All may need some maintenance from time to time, but the amount of work required varies widely.

Metal sheds do not pose the rust problem of former days. The modern metal buildings are made of galvanized steel and the surface finish is baked on. They come with a 10 year guarantee and all you have to do is wash or scrub down if the surface is dirty. Treat uPVC buildings in the same way, and concrete sheds require even less maintenance as a weathered look is usually acceptable.

Wood, however, remains the favourite material and here there can be problems. Hardwoods such as teak and the softwood western red cedar are by far the easier ones to maintain as they are naturally resistant to rot. All that is required is to rub down the walls occasionally with teak or cedar oil.

The 'Deal' type of softwood is a different story and does pose a problem. Pre-treatment with a preservative will have bestowed a few years protection against fungal attack — remember always to check that a new softwood building has been made with pressure-impregnated ('tanalised') wood. This protection will have to be topped-up by routine applications of a suitable preservative liquid — see the section alongside on Dealing with rot. The building may have been painted for protection — here you must repaint at regular intervals. If you are dealing with a new building it is well worth considering a microporous (breathing) type of paint or stain which allows water vapour to escape from the wood without allowing rainwater to enter.

Rot of side walls and window frames can be a problem, but it is usually the roof which goes first if it is made of felt. Read the Repairing the roof section on the next page carefully.

Curing draughts

It is annoying to have a draught blowing on your face or ankles when you are trying to work in the garden shed — it is even more annoying when you are trying to relax in the summerhouse. The most likely cause is a badly-fitting door or window. Look for a gap between the door or window and its frame — if one is present, tighten the screws on the hinges and fit self-adhesive draught-excluding tape inside the frame. If the crack is in the frame itself then use ordinary waterproof sealing tape.

The door or windows may not be the culprit — there may be a gap between the cladding boards due to shrinkage or the presence of a knot-hole. Repair may be possible, but an easy way to draught-proof the walls is to line the inside with building (lining) paper. In a summerhouse it is better to fit a proper insulation system — see the next page.

Dealing with rot

The fungus which causes softwood to rot requires both air and a high moisture content. The high risk areas are the parts of the building which are the last to dry out — the bottom of the window frames, the bearers below the floor and the lowest planks of the side walls.

The cardinal rule is that prevention is much easier than trying to cure the problem. New wood should be either naturally resistant to the fungus or it should be protected against rot by having had preservative forced inside the grain and not merely painted on the surface. With softwoods you have two choices — you can either treat the surface with a preservative every couple of years or you can paint it at intervals to maintain a waterproof coating.

Preservative rules first. Choose with care — creosote has its followers but tends to be messy and smelly. Best of all are the modern water-based preservatives which form a waterproof but breathing film over the surface — check that a fungicide is present. Scrub down the walls, doors etc and allow to dry thoroughly before treatment. Choose a dry day and apply the preservative liberally with a brush. Pay particular attention to cut ends of timber and begin work at the bottom and progress steadily up to the roof.

With paint you should carry out all necessary repairs before you begin — replacing rotten wood, reglazing broken windows etc. Choose a settled spell and rub down the surface with glass paper after filling cracks and holes. Work from the top downwards.

Unfortunately, rot may already be present. Test with a small screwdriver or steel point — rotten wood is soft. If only a small area is affected, use a wood repair kit. Cut away the rotten area and paint with hardener to strengthen the timber. After about 6 hours restore the original level with the wood filler. Insert the preservative tablets into the surrounding sound wood.

This technique is obviously better suited to painted than stained surfaces. With stained wood it may be better to cut out rotten areas and replace with sound timber —this course of action has to be taken in any case if the area of rot is extensive.

Repairing the roof

The standard pattern for the roofs of sheds is a base of plywood or wooden planks covered with felt. This should stay sound for a number of years — its life span will depend on the thickness and quality of the felt. However, no type of felt can be considered truly long-lasting, and without routine maintenance it will deteriorate in 3–8 years.

The first problem is that the felt becomes porous. The answer here is to apply a coat of a bitumen paint every 3 years — do it immediately on a dry day if the roof has already started to leak. A leak may be due to a tear or hole rather than an increase in porosity. Tackle this by cutting a piece of felt and bedding it on to the surface with mastic — hold it in place by hammering in a few galvanized nails. There are 2 points to remember. Always clear off algae, moss and surface rubbish by scrubbing with water and applying a moss killer before painting or patching, and always kneel on a board spanning the roof to protect the felt surface.

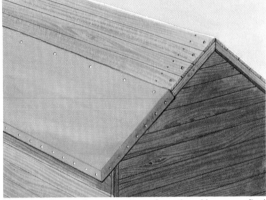

Examine the roof as a matter of routine. You may find that there is general deterioration and the only answer is to replace the felt. This is not a particularly difficult job, but do get someone else to do it if you have no DIY experience. Buy heavy grade felt — a 10 m roll will do for a standard-sized shed. Cold felt can crack — keep the roll indoors for about 2 days and plan the work during a warm spell of weather. Now cut your lengths, bearing in mind that you will need an extra 1 in. at each end to turn over the edges and there will be a 3–6 in. overlap between the sheets.

Remove the old felt and pull out the old nails ('clouts') with a claw hammer or pincers. Lay the first length of new felt along the bottom of one side of the roof leaving a 1 in. overlap at the sides and eaves. Nail as shown above at 6 in. intervals with ½ in. galvanized clouts. When secure, nail down the ends and eave strips using clouts at 2 in. intervals — make sure that the corners are neatly folded. Repeat the procedure on the other side of the shed.

Lay a second strip above this first one if the felt is more than 3 in. away from the ridge (apex roof) or side (pent roof). Nail down the top of the strip as described above, seal the overlap with roofing adhesive and nail down the ends. Continue to lay strips of felt until no more than 3 in. of bare wood remains on either side of the ridge. Now cut a 1 ft-wide capping strip of felt — bend over the ridge and secure with roofing adhesive. Nail down at 2 in. intervals and then fold down the excess felt at each end of the ridge — secure by nailing this corner surplus on to the wood. Replace roof battens (see page 94) if these were present on the old roof.

Repairing guttering

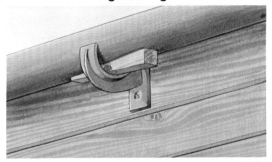

It is sometimes possible to repair a sagging gutter by inserting a small wooden wedge between the gutter and bracket. This should be regarded as a temporary answer — for a permanent solution attach a new bracket with new screws close to the faulty one. A leaking gutter can often be fixed quite easily. If the joint in metal guttering is faulty paint it with a sealing compound or seal it with self-adhesive flashing strip. With plastic guttering unclip the section and replace the defective seal. A small hole or crack in an iron gutter can be repaired with self-adhesive flashing strip. With iron gutters and pipes you should try to prevent rust rather than trying to repair its effects. At the first signs of corrosion scrape the area clean, paint with a tannate-based rust converter and then apply a topcoat of gloss paint.

Insulating buildings

Much work has to be done in spring in the garden shed and it is pleasant to sit in the summerhouse on cloudy and rainy days at the start of the year or at the end of summer. It can be too cold for comfort, however, and insulation is the best answer. This will also help to reduce draughts, reduce the risk of frost damage to susceptible plants kept in the shed and will reduce the risk of rust on tools and equipment. Nail rigid expanded polystyrene slabs between the wall and roof frames and cover these with sheets of Tempered Grade hardboard or EXT Grade plywood.

MAINTENANCE & REPAIRS | TOOLS

The proper maintenance of garden tools is not merely a way of making them look good and last longer — it will also make garden work easier. A spade caked with clay is heavier and less effective than a soil-free one, and dull secateurs are harder to use and give a ragged rather than a clean cut. The basic rules are to remove dirt and debris after use, keep metal parts oiled and cutting edges sharpened. All hand tools should be hung on the walls or placed on shelves rather than being stood on the floor, and all sharp tools should be kept well away from children.

DIGGING & CULTIVATING TOOLS
After use

If the soil is sticky you should clean the blade regularly during the digging operation and not wait until the end of the day — scrape off clods of earth with a putty knife or dip the blade in a bucket of water.

At the end of the day remove all the soil from the blades or tines of spades, trowels, hoes and forks. Wash if necessary and leave to dry. If the edge of the blade has become blunt or burred use a flat file to restore sharpness. Wipe or spray metal parts with oil if you do not intend to use the tool again in the near future.

The sand bucket is a good maintenance method used by professional gardeners. Fill a large bucket with oily sharp sand and plunge spades, hoes and forks into it several times before storage.

End of season maintenance

Scrub blades and tines with warm water and a wire brush. Allow to dry and then file edges if necessary. Grip the blade of the spade or hoe in a vice and sharpen both sides with a flat file. Work evenly and slowly, and do not try to produce a knife-like edge. Remove all earth from shafts and handles — wooden ones should be smoothed with sandpaper and rubbed with a rag soaked with linseed oil. Finally, spray all metal surfaces with a water repellant anti-rust aerosol.

POWER TOOLS

With electric models check over cables to see if there are signs of wear or if it leads to the plug are loose. With petrol-driven machines empty the fuel tank, drain off oil if recommended in the instruction manual and look at the spark plugs. Clean all parts and spray all exposed metal with a water repellant anti-rust spray. If servicing is required send the machine away in autumn if it is not needed for winter use.

CUTTING TOOLS
After use

Clean the blades thoroughly and wipe down with an oily rag. If cutting has been difficult then it may be necessary to sharpen the tool — whether you do the job yourself or send it away depends on your skill, sharpening equipment and the type of tool. Sharpening garden knives is a DIY job — you will need a fine grade oilstone for a razor-sharp edge or a medium grade oilstone for an ordinary (and safer) edge. Use methylated spirits to clear plant residues from the blade and apply a little oil to the stone. Hold the blade at a constant angle of about 30° and press down slightly with your finger. Move the blade in a circular motion. Most blades will need sharpening on both sides but some expensive ones are designed to be sharpened on one side only.

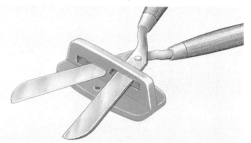

Experienced gardeners occasionally rub the blades of shears or secateurs with a slipstone when using them. This just holds the edge — it does not sharpen the blade. Sharpening shears and secateurs on an oilstone is less straightforward than sharpening a knife. It is usually a good idea to send shears and secateurs away to be set and sharpened if they are really blunt. However, you can buy 2 inexpensive sharpeners which make the job quite easy by controlling the correct honing angle. There is the Multi-sharp Shear & Scissor Sharpener for shears and the Secateur & Lopper Sharpener for secateurs.

The blades of shears which work badly may be too loose or too tight rather than dull. When you hold a pair of shears downwards by gripping one handle, the other blade should slowly open. Adjust the screw if this does not happen.

End of season maintenance

Clean blades thoroughly, carry out DIY sharpening as described above and wipe with an oily rag. Store the tools in a dry place.

Some tools should be sent away for sharpening or setting rather than doing the job yourself, unless DIY is your hobby. These tools include saws and chainsaws and also include shears and secateurs which have blades which are damaged or do not meet properly at the tips.

SPRAYERS

Wash out immediately afer use — spray with clean water to make sure that chemicals have been removed from all parts of the equipment. If the sprayer works poorly or not at all, check the nozzle and filter. Do not blow through the nozzle or use a piece of wire if it is blocked — wash thoroughly under running water. Another common fault is a worn or cracked washer — replacements are usually available.

LAWNMOWERS

After use

A quick wipe of the blades and then back into the garage or shed to await the next visit to the lawn is *not* the way to look after your mower. Proper cleaning and a careful check for faults should take place either just after mowing or in good time before the next cut. There is nothing more annoying in gardening than to have to spend an hour or two repairing or cleaning the machine before mowing, only to find that rain has started to fall just when you are ready to go on the lawn.

The first thing is to move the machine on to concrete or other hard surface. Disconnect the power supply — switch off and pull out the plug for an electric mower; with a petrol mower shut off the fuel supply and then allow the engine to cut out with the drive disconnected.

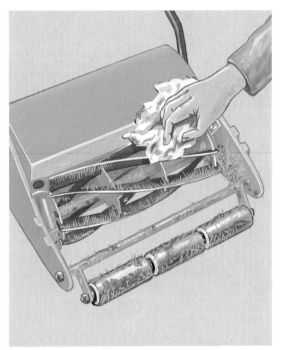

With a rag and stiff brush remove all clippings and caked earth. The areas to be cleaned are the grass box, blades, rollers, cylinders and under the canopy of a rotary or hover mower. Dry the various parts and then wipe over with an oily rag.

A battery mower should be recharged immediately after use. Every fortnight examine the water levels in the cells — top up with distilled water as necessary. Wire brush the battery terminals occasionally and coat them with petroleum jelly.

Check the blades. If a blade or cutter assembly has been damaged or is loose, the mower could be inefficient or positively dangerous if used again before it is repaired. With a rotary mower, check that the bolt holding the cutter bar is tight. If this cutter bar is blunt it can be sharpened quite easily with a reaper file, but if it is badly worn or damaged you should take the machine to your dealer to have a new blade fitted and balanced.

Correct storage is essential. The mower must be kept under cover, of course, and there should be no chance of rain or dripping water reaching it. A hover mower can be conveniently hung on the wall.

Routine maintenance & repairs

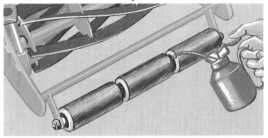

Carry out regular routine maintenance. Oil the front rollers and cutting cylinder bearings. Apply grease (not oil) to the chains and clean the air filters.

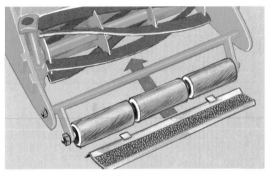

Re-sharpening damaged blades on a cylinder mower is not easy, but you can buy a simple tool (the Multi-sharp Cylinder Mower Sharpener) to give a keener edge to blades which are in good condition. This metal strip bearing an abrasive surface is clipped on to the bottom fixed blade and the cylinder rotated for a few minutes.

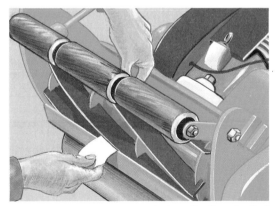

A cylinder mower with sharp blades will still cut badly if the distance between the moving blades and the fixed blade is not correct. Check the cutting action by placing a piece of paper between one of the moving blades and the bottom fixed blade. Revolve the cylinder — watch your fingers! The paper should be cut cleanly, and the same thing should happen at all points along the cutting surface. Adjust the cutting action by turning the end screws until the gap is close enough to shear the paper cleanly.

Routine maintenance & repairs (contd.)

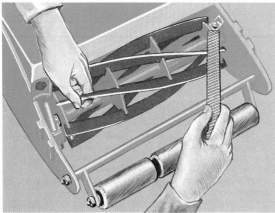

Running over a stone may cause a 'high spot' on the blade. This bump can interfere with the smooth running of the cylinder and should be rubbed down with a file or carborundum stone.

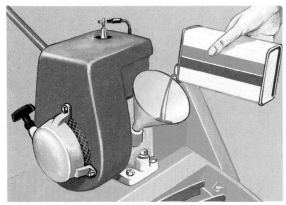

The remaining routine maintenance tasks will depend on the source of power. Petrol mowers should have the oil level checked. Top up if necessary; if the oil in the sump is black then change it. Look for leaks — oil and petrol dripping on to the lawn will cause scorch. An electric mower should be checked carefully to ensure that all wires and plugs are in good condition and firmly held.

Failure to start

In the lifetime of every motor mower there will be an occasion when it refuses to start. Even if you know nothing about machinery there are a number of checks you can carry out.

● Are there oil and petrol in the machine?
● Has the petrol been standing for several months?
● Are all the leads connected?
● Has the fuse blown?
● Is the air filter clean?

Your detailed guide must be the manufacturer's instruction book — make sure you have a copy *before* the machine breaks down. Follow the faults chart and fix it if you can, but *don't* attempt a complex repair unless you have the necessary skills and tools. It is much better to take it to your local machinery dealer.

End of season maintenance

PETROL MOWER

Drain off all oil and petrol. Clean and adjust the gap of each sparking plug.

Carry out general autumn maintenance (see below) and then top up with clean engine oil, as recommended by the manufacturer.

BATTERY MOWER

Remove the battery, top up with distilled water, re-charge and then store in a warm dry place.

Carry out general autumn maintenance (see below).

ELECTRIC MOWER

Check all leads for loose connections. Carefully examine the cable for cracking or physical damage. If a cut is detected, repair with a special waterproof connector — never use insulating tape. Carry out general autumn maintenance (see below).

General autumn maintenance — all models

Clean away all mud and grass — rub off any rust with wire wool or a wire brush. Oil or grease all the bearings, and spray the exposed metal parts with a water repellent anti-rust aerosol. Store the mower on wood or hardboard rather than on concrete or earth.

This end-of-season maintenance programme is designed for a mower which is in good condition. If cutting has been poor then the blades may be damaged, burred or in need of re-grinding. This is a job to leave to a machinery specialist, although rotary blades are much easier to tackle than cylinder ones — the DIY sharpener to buy is the Multi-sharp Rotary Mower Sharpener. If your cylinder mower needs re-grinding, remember that it is much cheaper to take just the cylinder along to the dealer instead of the complete mower.

You will have to take the complete mower to the service agent if there has been a loss of power during the grass-cutting season — book this service in autumn rather than waiting until the grass has started to grow in the spring.

CHAPTER 5

INDEX

A great deal of care has been taken to ensure that the information in this book is as accurate as possible, but the Publishers cannot be held responsible for any errors or omissions that may be found in the text or may occur at a future date as a result of changes in rules, laws or equipment.

Acknowledgements

The author wishes to acknowledge the painstaking work of Gill Jackson, Paul Norris, Linda Fensom, Angelina Gibbs and Constance Barry. Grateful acknowledgement is also made for the help or photographs received from Jane Llewelyn, Attracta Products Ltd, Atlas Stone Products, British Gates & Timber Ltd, Chatsworth Carpenters, J B Corrie & Co Ltd, Forest Fencing Ltd, Grosfillex (UK) Ltd, Haddonstone Ltd, Halls Homes & Gardens, Larch-Lap Ltd, Lotus Water Garden Products Ltd, Marshalls, Regal Garden Buildings, Robinsons of Winchester Ltd, Stapeley Water Gardens Ltd, Tarmac Topmix Ltd, Joan Hessayon, Carleton Photographic, Harry Smith Horticultural Photographic Collection, Michael Warren, Zara McCalmont/The Garden Picture Library, Ron Sutherland/The Garden Picture Library, Brian Carter/The Garden Picture Library, Michelle Lamontagne/The Garden Picture Library, Elizabeth Crowe/The Garden Picture Library, David Askham/The Garden Picture Library, IPC Magazines Ltd/Robert Harding Picture Library, Elizabeth Whiting & Associates, Carl Dietrich-Buhler/Elizabeth Whiting & Associates, Jerry Harpur/Elizabeth Whiting & Associates, Tomlins Ltd and C Porter Ltd.

John Woodbridge provided both artistry and design work. The artists who contributed were Deborah Mansfield, Norman Barber, John Dye, Fred Anderson and Roger Shipp.